TALES FROM THE GOLDEN CITY

Carl-Eric Williams

Copyright © 2025 Carl-Eric Williams

All rights reserved

To Mum

I am so glad you got to read this before you departed our world. Thank you for your love and support throughout my life, especially with this project.

God Bless

CONTENTS

Title Page
Copyright
Dedication
Preface   1
Chapter 1 - New sights   5
Chapter 2 - Burnt pea soup   15
Chapter 3 - Chicken Run   30
Chapter 4 - Golden City Enterprises   49
Chapter 5 - 'The Little Chef'   75
Chapter 6 – Norkem Park High School   93
Chapter 7 - To the Drakensberg mountains...and beyond!   120
Chapter 8 - Veld Skool   138
Chapter 9 - Christopher and the burning bush   156
Chapter 10 - Escape from sports day   207
Chapter 11 - 'Mandela Day' thoughts   243

PREFACE

I went to school with a lot of children who were born into families where both parents were content with their lot. They had lived in the same house, or farm since birth. Their parents had never wanted to move away from the town or village they were born in. They never got itchy feet or had their curiosity raised to a sufficient level to make them want to visit another shore. 'Abroad' was off-limits. England had all they needed and would ever need. Foreign food was nasty, and not nearly as nice as a Cornish pasty. Their children would be brought up having the same mindset. Not so for me and my brother. Our parents had nomadic blood coursing through their veins, moving through, what seemed like, endless counties and towns in the short ten years that I had graced the planet. Little did I know that at age 10 my life was about to get tipped upside down, as the lure of wealth opportunities, and endless sunshine was beckoning my parents to track to foreign shores. In the late seventies a lot of couples of a similar age to my parents were getting bitten by the same bug, and packing up home to settle in, and explore places like Canada, Australia, and New Zealand. My parents, however, (much like a lot of other English families), had been lured towards the land of Goldmines & Diamonds - 'deepest, darkest Africa', as my father would call it, or to be more precise Johannesburg, South Africa. The city of dreams, the city of opportunity, the 'Golden City'.

What happened in June of 1980 changed my and my brother's lives forever. We would end up being moulded by far more than England had to offer. We were going to travel the length and breadth of South Africa seeing exotic places, meeting interesting people of different cultures, and tasting strange foods and drinks. Experiencing weather like we never had before and cheating serious harm or worse on several occasions. In addition, we would be introduced to an alien world of racial segregation that we at first could not understand, but that sadly became the 'norm' for us over time. I learned a lot about certain parts of Africa in my first year of Secondary School in Honiton. Most of the history classes were based around Neanderthal man and in particular Australopithecus man whose remains had been found in caves in Sterkfontein. As far as modern-day South Africa was concerned, neither I nor my schoolmates knew much about it. I had been assured by my parents that we were not going to be living in the jungle but in a city. When my school friends found out they were first to point out that we would have to immediately adopt the native dress. That is loincloth, spear, and of course 'bone through the nose'! Remember, this was 1970's Britain. No Internet for education as yet. The only Africans most children my age had seen were those fighting Michael Caine in 'Zulu', and apparently, according to my school chum 'Simon Potts', I would very soon be joining them, living in a mud hut somewhere, with frequent visits to the local Witchdoctor to sort out my ailments. There were suggestions that after some time exposed to the African sun, I would be adorning the same colour skin as the 'Black and White Minstrels' and talking in a dialect consisting mainly of throat-based clicks. Unfortunately, I was in no position to fend off these absurdities with facts about my intended destination, and the effect it would have on my physical characteristics and ability to talk English. Time will tell. I don't remember being afraid at the thought of leaving my home and travelling all that way. I had never stayed at a school for longer than a year anyway, so this was just the next time to 'up-sticks' and move on. At age ten you follow your parents wherever they go without question. I vaguely remember them sitting my brother and me down to tell us where we were going, but ten year old's had bigger fish to fry, like seeing what contraption you could next purchase to adorn your racing bike, (my paper round money was burning a hole in my pocket yet again!). Little did I know that my little green racer was not coming with me. Not much was going with me. This was going to be a new start, which meant leaving a lot of treasured possessions behind. I may have not understood at the time, but I was going to receive riches far more precious from my parents over the next 7 years. Not material items of value you understand, but some wondrous sights, experiences beyond belief, and exposure to people and cultures that some may never be lucky enough to interact with. The only thing South Africa house wanted in return was that my brother and I had to hold dual nationality and also had to perform National Service when at the required age.

I thank both my parents for having the courage to do something different, and for opening my eyes to a new world that I am sure had a positive effect on my personal growth. What follows is an accurate account of most of the things I can remember from this adventure. The important things that get etched on your memory, for as long as you can put off old age and memory loss. I would like to say it's a 'true story', but I dislike the word 'story', as it seems to conjure up the idea of fabrication. I'll simply say it's a 'true account', as that is exactly what it is. Only the names have been changed, to protect the innocent (no they haven't). Especially 'Simon Potts' that is. He deserves a mention. After all, the guy could memorize and match everyone to their parents' car registration plate, which was quite a feat considering I used to walk to school! One of the first 'Derren Browns' I think. There are a lot of confessions within this book. Things that I have told my parents, and some that I haven't which they will find out whilst reading this. I reserve the right to not be held accountable for my actions during my teenage years and exclude myself from any verbal prosecution that my parents feel the need to dish out at this late stage of my life. It is a book about my life in South Africa over 7 years. A place so different from my country of origin. My experiences with the culture, the people, and the places during a very difficult period of the country's history, coupled with tales of my adventures and daily life.

This is a book whose concept and design have been on my mind for well over 15 years, but I have failed to start it, as I thought to myself 'Nobody will be interested in any of this.'. I have got to the stage in my life where that thought no longer matters to me. It doesn't matter if it never gets published. There are many tools available to self-publish nowadays. If nobody buys it, at least the writing journey has been a wonderful experience of reminiscence, and I have left behind something for my children, grandchildren, and generations after to hopefully be interested in exploring. This book is dedicated to my parents, and especially my dear, departed mother, who have been a lifeline through some tough times in the last ten years or so and have helped to bring me through so many challenges. Also, to my three children Oliver, Stephanie and Jonathan and my Grandson Rhys, and Granddaughters Ava and Ivy. All of whom bring brightness to my life whenever I see them.

CHAPTER 1 - NEW SIGHTS

When you are ten years old things seem to take a hell of a long time to come around. The period between each Christmas seems like forever, summer holidays seem to last a lifetime. The time to wait until we emigrated to South Africa though, seemed to pass very quickly indeed. I remember my parents going to South Africa house in London one day. I remember having to have a smallpox vaccine at the doctor's and having to keep the injection site dry. I remember choosing the items I would take with me and filling half a tea chest with them. I remember my parents having a farewell party with their friends and the staff from the Newsagent they Managed. After that, it seemed like we were off. I don't know how long the process took, but it passed very quickly for me.

I had never been to an airport before, and so going to Heathrow for our departure was a very exciting day. Watching huge planes take off and land through the departure lounge window made me want to be a pilot someday. We were going to fly on a South African Airways 'Jumbo – 747', on a journey that would last just over 19 hours. I had no idea what to expect, what the sensation of flying would feel like, or what I was going to.

It was all uncharted territory and every part of it was going to be a new experience for me. I have little recollection of much of the flight. I remember the take-off. That roar of engines as throttles are engaged as the plane thunders up the runway, and that odd slight bang of the undercarriage as the wheels leave the tarmac. After that the shock of being hurtled through the air at an angle that made me feel very uncomfortable. That feeling has stayed with me throughout my entire life. To this day I do not like take-offs. I can handle the flight, am at ease when the plane is descending, and am even happier when it has touched down. The most exciting thing back then, and the only thing I look forward to when flying these days, is the in-flight meals. I know flying at that altitude, in a pressurized cabin makes your taste buds almost useless, but for some strange reason, I get immense pleasure from finding out what the meal consists of and working my way through all the elements of it. It's a strange thing to enjoy I know, but for some reason I do. Possibly for the same reason, I enjoy food and eating on the ground too. Our family is food lovers and food creators. Most of us have worked professionally in the food industry. Bakers & confectioners, chefs, chief cooks, and bottle washers. We've done it all.

One of the things that have to happen before you emigrate abroad is that you have to find employment. My father trained as a chef in 1966 at the 'Plough Hotel' in Cheltenham, and now he was going to be able to dust off his chef whites, sharpen his knives, and show off his skills at the Carlton Hotel in central Johannesburg, where he had been taken on as chef 'Garde Manger' or (cold buffet chef). The Carlton back then was a prestigious 5-star hotel. Unfortunately, today it is nothing but a derelict building. The last time I saw the building it was being used in an alien film called 'District 9'. The neon sign at the top of the hotel that used to say, 'The Carlton' was replaced with a CGI sign saying 'MNU'. Anyway, enough about that for now, as later on I will introduce you to the 'Carlton' properly, as it was my home for the first month after arriving in South Africa.

I am not sure what time it was exactly but in the early evening, many hours into the flight, and after we had stopped at Las Palmas for refuelling, the stewardess came over to speak to my parents to ask them if I and my brother would like to visit the captain and see the cockpit. Well, you can't imagine how excited I was about this. A bit nervous initially about going there without my parents, but that soon passed. I was about to live a dream, a dream that even nowadays I wish was still possible. It was nearly dark outside, but you could still see the clouds outside the cockpit window as we entered. We were introduced to the captain and co-pilot, and he even let me come right forward so I could view outside the front of the plane, pointing out a flashing red light a fair way below us, that was another plane flying in the same direction but at a different flight level. I'll never forget seeing all those switches, buttons, and lights. So many it was overwhelming. How on earth do they remember what all these do? It was the highlight of the trip to South Africa for me, and one I still talk about to this day, as security restrictions nowadays disallow anything of this sort happening for today's children. It was an experience that stayed with me. I didn't fulfil my dream of becoming a pilot, well not quite, but in my 30s, I enjoyed playing with Microsoft Flight Simulator software on my home computer with a flight joystick and learning how to interpret aviation chatter between pilots and air traffic control.

The next thing I remember is it being morning. We woke up and had some breakfast as we flew inland over South West Africa towards Botswana. The pilot pointed out the visibility of the border between the two countries, it being as straight a line as any. It didn't seem long after that when we were flying over to our new home Country. A man and his wife who had a window seat asked my parents if we would like to have a look out of the window as we descended. It looked so barren; no towns or cities were visible at that time. Just what looked like African bush.

This concerned me a little. Was Simon going to be right after all? Was my mud hut down there in amongst the bush I thought? As we got closer to Johannesburg we had to return to our seats and buckle up, so I was not able to see that we were going to fly over the city. I could look to my right and see out of one of the windows from where I was sitting, and as we landed, all I could see was more of the same. It looked like there was just a desert out there. Nothing else. I was relieved to see a terminal building eventually. We disembarked, collected our luggage, and then sought the pick-up that had been laid on to take us to the Carlton Hotel. We were finally here and had to stay here. It was our new home. A new start for the entire family. I was relieved to see that our pick-up taxi was, in fact, a Toyota mini-bus and not a wheeled cart being pulled by the local tribesmen. Simon was wrong, very wrong. I could see buildings, roads, vehicles, and factories, and not a hint of a loincloth and spear...well at least not yet. Perhaps we were going to be alright after all?

I remember the taxi ride very clearly. A taxi driver was in the front seat, and us sitting in rows behind. I was next to the right-hand side window and had a good view of everything passing by. There were so many new things to take in. Various people were selling their wares at the side of the road. Corner shops in the middle of nowhere, laced with ageing advertisements for Coca-Cola, washing powders, and some brands and items I had never heard of. Animals, many different from the cows and sheep I had seen regularly in Devon. Lorries, cars, and trucks that I was not familiar with. The land was flat, apart from the mounds that seemed to be everywhere around us. Large mounds that turned out to be the deposits from gold mining. Johannesburg was a city of gold mines. Travelling down the carriageway towards Johannesburg you could see the city peeking out between two large hills or mountains in the distance. I could see the tower that was the 'Hillbrow' tower, and some large structures around it that looked like large office blocks. The weather was pleasant on our arrival. It wasn't raining and there was a blue sky and some clouds. It didn't seem to feel particularly hot to me, not as I was expecting anyway. But it was June, and we would not get to witness the hot African sun until November/December. Maybe this was planned by my parents so that we all had the chance to acclimatize slowly. It may well have been planned like that, but what my body wasn't ready for was the difference in altitude. I would very soon be suffering from nose bleeds due to the 1767m the city was above sea level. My last home in Honiton, Devon was only 113m. The journey seemed long but was extended due to the heavy traffic around the blocks in Johannesburg centre. It reminded me of television programs I had seen of New York. Busy, very busy. Taxis are everywhere, hustle and bustle. So many people and huge buildings. We pulled up outside the Carlton Hotel. I stood outside the minivan, as suitcases were being retrieved from the back, and looked up. There was the Carlton with huge white signage at the very top. A strange building in that it had a base like a large foot, that gradually graded inwards on both faces, sort of an upside-down 'Y' shape. Next to that though was something even more impressive. The highest building in Johannesburg, the 'Carlton Centre'. This was an even taller building, 50 stories tall in fact. It was dizzying looking up at it. I felt small, insecure, and insignificant in this city. Inside the hotel was posh. Lots of glass, metal, and stone, all highly polished. You have to remember that at age ten and growing up most of my life in the country, I had never seen anything quite like it. It was all far removed from what I was used to being exposed to. Small towns like Honiton and Launceston, the biggest city being Exeter. Local farming communities, fetes, and carnivals. That was my world up until this day. To suddenly set foot in such a palatial building knowing you were going to stay there, was both daunting and exciting at the same time. After a short while, we were taken to our room. One double and two single beds in the room. On the 26th floor, the view from the window was frightening. Well at least for me anyway. I am not a lover of any sort of height, even to this day. Looking out from that window and seeing the world pass below, made me feel nauseous every time I did it. The curiosity, however, was too much not to do it. I had to survey my new world and find out what made it tick. The hotel had a total of 30 floors with a rooftop pool terrace that could be covered by a tinted retractable roof. We were there in 1980. The same year terrorists locked themselves in a room on the 15th floor, along with 25 pieces of dynamite, electronically hooked up to detonate. A six-hour encounter with police and anti-terrorist units, fortunately, ended without tragedy. Three years previous an individual had tried something similar in the Carlton Centre, which ended up with him blowing off his hand.

As my father was a chef in the hotel, he didn't have far to travel to work each day for the first month or so. He worked long hours, weekends, sometimes early shifts, sometimes late. We didn't see much of him at all in the early days as he was too busy preparing food for distinguished guests, often contributing to the menu in the world-renowned Three Ships restaurant. Many famous people had stayed in the Carlton over the years and dined in its internal restaurants such as Margaret Thatcher, Henry Kissinger, and Mick Jagger. Later Hilary Clinton, Whitney Houston, and Francois Mitterrand would stay there. Days were boring, and it must have been very difficult for our mother to try and keep her two boys entertained on her own for long periods. It was a new city for her too, and it must have been a frightening thought to have to venture out of the hotel to get a change of scenery before we all went stir crazy. Fortunately, we did not have to venture far for something different to look at. Directly underneath the hotel, and sprawling beneath the Carlton Centre too, was several levels of a shopping mall. It was accessible from the lifts that were in the hotel lobby, so no need to walk the streets of the unknown. There were many shops, eateries, and restaurants. It was a welcome break being taken out to lunch there. It was where I had my first experience with a 'toasted sandwich'. I had never heard of them before but tried one with everyone else. Cheese and tomato were my choice, and I instantly fell in love with it. I particularly liked tomatoes in South Africa. Not deep red and soft like those in England. Instead, a combination of light red, orange, and green. Firmer and a liked them especially when cut thinly. At age ten I was already into my gadgets. I still am today. Anything electronic and out of the ordinary always catches my eye. It was whilst looking in the window of one of the toy shops, that something stopped me in my tracks. It was called an 'EK' kit. It was an electronic board made of plastic, that came with a load of electronic components housed in plastic cubes. The cubes could be placed onto the board to complete all different types of circuits, like water detectors, alarms, crystal radios, and lie detectors. You name it and it could do it, or so it claimed. More expensive versions had meters and sensors built into the board that expanded its possibilities. I wanted one bad. Wherever I saw one I had to stop and look at it. Mainly to drool over it and dream of the things, I could make but also make sure that any parent in the vicinity knew that this was top of my Christmas list!

The evenings were as boring as the days. South African television had not taken off yet. They were far behind in that respect. Evenings were taken up by reading books or comics. The 'Cubs Away' book was keeping me entertained at the time. Later on, I would move on to the 'Willard Price' adventure series. One night though things were going to be different. My brother and I were going to meet our long-lost cousins and aunt and uncle who lived in Pretoria. I think my father had bought a car very early on and was storing it in the hotel car park. A green Austin Marina with a strange reddish-brown seat colour. Very brave of my father to attempt the journey, but we did and got there safely. My aunt and uncle and two of my cousins lived in a suburban street in Pretoria. A lovely big house with a huge front garden and an adequately sized rear terrace with a separate gated pool area. I cannot remember what my uncle did for a living, but my aunt was involved in the drinks industry somehow. Sales I believe. Hence there was plenty of booze in the house, and my cousin Timothy's bedroom was adorned with plaques for all the popular booze brands like Grants Whisky and Coco Rico. My other cousin, Sharon also lived at home but was slightly older than Timothy. My third cousin David was in the South African Air Force, I believe doing his yearly, mandatory service at a camp somewhere. We would meet him later, although it would not be for the first time. When I was six, he visited us in Cornwall at age 18. I remember it distinctly as he was the person who taught me how to tie my shoelaces. A bit of encouragement, and showing me the correct technique, soon had me doing it on my own with ease. A valuable life skill that he didn't mind passing on to his six-year-old cousin. The evening was great, a lovely dinner all together and finding out about our family members. It made a nice change and lifted my spirits. We visited my aunt and uncle on several other occasions. Lunches outside by the lemon trees, followed by swims in the pool with our cousins. Finally meeting David again when he finished his current tour of duty. On one occasion Timothy was asked to go to the local shop to get something by his mother. Tim asked David if he could borrow his motorbike, and David agreed. He also convinced my parents and aunt and uncle to let me ride pinion, to which they agreed. This was my first time sitting on a moving motorbike. A Kawasaki GPZ750. A bike that I would one day yearn to have myself. Tim drove sensibly the short distance to the shops, which took around 2 or 3 minutes. Taking care not to frighten or expose his younger passenger to any danger. We disembarked the motorbike and started to walk towards the shop entrance. Then something strange happened that I didn't quite understand at the time, but later on in life realized the importance of. A local black man was wandering away from the shop, probably at a distance of 50 to 100 yards. With a brief warning of 'listen to this', my cousin started to hurl racist abuse at the man, calling him an unrepeatable name that was too often heard in South Africa at the time. This shocked me even at the age of ten. I could not see any reason for it. The guy was minding his own business, and here he was being subjected to verbal abuse. It was the first occurrence of something of this nature I had been subjected to and unfortunately would not be the last. As I grew up in South Africa I soon found out that there was a majority of the country dwellers who believed that this was the way to treat their fellow man. If his skin colour happened to be black that is. I wasn't naive in any way. I had noticed that there were a lot of people of a darker skin colour in this country than in England. Back in Exeter, there was only one black child in my school. I knew the country was laid out differently ethnically but didn't realize there was segregation between the two main groups and such a dislike of the black South African people by the white South Africans. It was my first introduction to life for black South Africans under 'Apartheid', and one I have to admit I struggled with. In defence of my cousin, he had been born in South Africa and almost completed his life of schooling. He had been indoctrinated from the start. Been exposed to this way of living and acting, as if it was supposed to be acceptable. I like to think that had he been born and raised in England, his treatment of other ethnic groups would have been much different. I know it was that way for me.

Over the coming years, my eyes will be opened further. I would witness the ill-treatment of so many black South Africans. Would see first-hand how they were forced to obey laws that forbid them from freely roaming their land. How they had to live in separate areas. Travel on separate buses. Attend separate hospitals. Eat in separate cafes. Use separate toilets. One incident, three years ahead of me would leave me questioning humanity. It would shock me so much that I would feel ashamed of my race and feel the need to apologize on behalf of them to my fellow black co-workers.

Living at the Carlton was nice, but I think we had to move out and free up the room for paying guests. Dad found another hotel, in a less desirable part of the city to which we could move temporarily

Meeting our Uncle, Aunt and Cousins for the first time and enjoying some pool time in Pretoria

CHAPTER 2 - BURNT PEA SOUP

The hotel 'Stephanie', to put it lightly, was completely at the other end of the scale, when compared to the Carlton. I doubt if this place had a single star. It was in Berea, a suburb of Hillbrow, a 20-minute walk from Joubert Gardens or thereabouts. On a road opposite some high-rise flats lay this bright, green-painted hotel. There is a small garden out front with a long veranda behind, with the occasional bench placed for the elderly and retired residents to sit on and watch the world go by. Inside was drab. Old looks with lots of wood panelling and one of those elevators with the door made of wood with a small glass window. Inside that was a concertina-style gate which you had to pull across properly for the lift to work. There was a large dining room where all the meals were served, and various sitting rooms for residents, most of whom were old enough to be my grandparent's parents. There was the odd splash of youth, for instance, two families, with children were using the hotel as the last stop off before getting back to England. They had been here for years and decided to return for some reason. Room 63 was OK, although a little cramped. Once again a double and two single beds, a wardrobe and chest of drawers, bedside cabinets. One bathroom with the throne raised on a platform. You sat there feeling like a king, although your reign was short-lived because four had to share the ablution facilities.

There wasn't much to do at the Stephanie and much of the time we got told off for being a nuisance to residents whilst playing with the other children 'doing time' there. During the day it was better as we could go on walks to the park, but it was lonely until the weekends as the other children were still attending school. We saw them in the morning at breakfast, for a short period after they had finished school, at dinner time, and if we were lucky, a little into the evening. The first evening we arrived we came down to dinner at around 6:00 pm when service started. A menu was on the table which we perused, and at first glance, I thought this would be all right. There was a choice, albeit a small one, for the main course, with an optional starter and dessert. Each set of tables had a waiter assigned to them. A man dressed in a clean blue uniform with black trim, complete with a hat. Sort of like the side caps that American military personnel sometimes wear, or that people working as cooks in takeaways have on. The guy was always well-dressed and well-mannered. We asked what the soup of the day was, to which he replied 'Pea'. It seemed like a good choice and everybody went for that as a starter. Big mistake. I think my father was the first to dip into it, and pass comment. Now you need to know that my father knows a lot about food, how it should look, and how it should taste, and if it doesn't fit his bill for both those categories, it fails and someone is going to hear about it. 'People eat food with their eyes first', he always says. Unfortunately for this soup that is all people should have been advised to do with it. Something had gone drastically wrong in the kitchen that evening. A fire or explosion maybe? Whichever it was, the peas used to make this soup were in very close proximity to it. Either that or the chef had taken his eyes off the ball whilst bringing it to the boil and had caught the soup on the bottom of the pot. You could imagine the state of the bottom of the pot simply by tasting the soup. As soon as your taste buds were subjected to the exotic, burnt, charred, smokey pea flavour, your mind conjured up the image of a large soup pot sitting in the kitchen, with some poor soul having to take a hammer and chisel to the bottom of it to remove the charred remains of what once used to be peas. If this is what is to come over the next few weeks, Stephanie's cooks and my dad are going to be having words. There were words that evening, passed onto our waiter for immediate dissemination to those involved.

The hotel 'Stephanie' was in Hillbrow. A very near suburb of Johannesburg that housed the Hillbrow Tower, a tourist tower. You could go right to the top to the viewing deck, or eat in the revolving restaurant. Something I really wanted to do but never actually did in my time in South Africa. Hillbrow back then was a sort of a rebel area. Anything went. Drugs, prostitution, stabbings, killings, shootings. You name it and it happened. What we were not expecting was a stabbing to happen in the hotel, and involving members of the staff. I can remember word getting out about the incident, and being confined to barracks until the dust settled. The suburb had many shops. Shops that were out of the ordinary. If you needed imported vinyl records, you came to Hillbrow because that is the only place you would find them. I often did in my late teens. Anything else bootleg, or illegal could be found there. If you walked the streets, you walked knowing that danger could be around any corner, or that you could be confronted to be mugged at any minute. When I used to go there in my late teens, you always came in pairs or more. You dressed the part, a part that would not fit in anywhere else. More importantly, you walked around like you belonged there. Then you were left alone. The safest areas were around where the hotel was, as long as it was daylight. It was during these daylight hours that my mother would take me and my brother, as well as some of the other children from the hotel, to either the park or Joubert Gardens. The park was a good place to go as there were swings, climbing frames, and the like, and plenty of room for us to mess about, building human pyramids and other such kids' stuff. Joubert Park was different. It was a showcase for all things plant-like. A bit like walking around a poor man's Chelsea flower show. Even though I was a ten-year-old boy, I could still appreciate the diversity and the strange-looking plants that I had not encountered before. One particular plant stood out to me immediately. 'Strelitzia', A strange looking plant where the vibrant coloured petals of the flower element sprayed out like a fan from the tip of the green stem, escaping the green pod-like shroud that once encased it. It is the only plant that has remained in my memory, and that I can recall the name of with ease today. A few years down the line it would grace the badge on my blazer pocket at Norkem Park Primary School in Kempton Park.

Apart from the park, there wasn't much else to do but make a nuisance of yourself in and around the hotel. Some of the other boys showed us how they had made catapults with what they referred to as 'Scooby-doo' wire. I have no idea where it got its name. Maybe because nobody had a 'Scooby-doo' what it was called. Anyway, the stems of these miniature catapults were wrapped in this wire, all the way to the top where the wire enclosed the rubber band that acted as the projecting mechanism. The ammunition was more wire, cut into short strips, and bent into a horseshoe shape. So you needed a lot of wire to arm your friends with catapults, and then a lot more wire for the ammunition. These things flew like bullets, and you would never see where they went or could hardly ever find them for some element of reuse. On several occasions, children were left with horseshoe-shaped marks on their faces where they had been targeted unknowingly. It was surprising nobody ever lost an eye. So going back to the 'you need a lot of wire' part. It turns out there was only one place you could get this type of wire. Telephone junction boxes on the streets. You can see where I am going with this can't you? There was a version of 'Rock paper scissors', that South African children played called 'Ching-Chong-Cha'. The same principle, to decide out of a group which poor soul was going to do something that he or she would rather not. That thing, in this particular case, was to identify a suitable junction box, with an open door, and rip out a length of 'Scooby-doo' wire in one grab, and then run for your life. I regret to admit that being a novice at 'Ching-Chong-Cha' meant that I often lost, and had to fulfil the group's request. I hereby apologize to the South African telephony company responsible for services in that area circa 1980, and also their paying customers who were strangely, and without notice, disconnected mid-call.

I think my parents had got tired of me and my brother getting into trouble with the Hotel Management in the evenings, whilst getting up to no good with our friends. Usually, we were banished to our room. Especially if we had been caught playing in the lift, and even more so If we had broken it. This happened a lot with the single old lift, and often it was broken until an engineer could come and fix it. Maybe this was the reason why after a little while a television set was found in our room. Not sure if it had been rented or purchased, but we were excited to see it. We were used to three television channels back in England spouting content for most of the day and night. Our parents thought we were suffering from withdrawal symptoms, and that this might entertain us enough in the evenings to keep out of mischief. It was very early days for the South African Broadcasting Company. Very early days indeed. One channel, in black & white, shared between English and Afrikaans viewers. Starting at 6:00 pm and finishing around 12. One day was English viewing starting from 6:00 pm until 8:00 pm, with Afrikaans viewing from 8:00 pm onwards, and the next day it rotated. Within these small viewing windows, they managed to cram in the news and weather too. Leaving very little left for quality entertainment. Weekends were not much better either. Then there were the programs themselves. Nothing of much worth watching during English viewing for a ten-year-old. I struggle to remember anything, to be honest. The Afrikaans viewing slot was better if you didn't mind watching 'Battle-

Star Galactica' or 'Buck Rogers in the 21st Century', dubbed into Afrikaans. We usually endured this as it was better than nothing and helped us to adopt an understanding of the new language we were going to be expected to learn.

My brother and I had done well to escape school for our first month or so in the country and enjoyed every minute of it. Our parents thought we had settled enough, and very soon though we were going to get a very rude awakening, involving extremely early starts and two bus journeys to and from our new school. Brixton Primary was not your ordinary school. It was situated on the outskirts of Johannesburg and nestled directly under the Brixton Tower, a 237-meter concrete television communications tower. |This was quite a highlight for the pupils who spent many a break lying on the grass looking up at it, getting dizzy as they tried to track the clouds moving around it. There was a lot to learn about South African primary school life. It was nothing like the first year of Honiton Secondary School I had left behind. For starters, there was the respect that pupils were expected to display to teachers and the headmaster Mr. Raath. Any entrance to a class by either had to be met with the rapid, military-style 'attention' stance of all pupils behind their desks, and total and utter silence. Any failure to perform or any deviation from this ritual would result in a humiliation that would not be tolerated today. South African schools back in the 1980s were very hot on corporal punishment and dare I say it 'abuse'. If a boy of my age went through a day without getting punished, he had done very well for himself.

Every single teacher at Brixton had, what the Afrikaans teacher referred to as his 'planka'. A one-and-a-half foot long, 2 x 1.5-inch plank of wood, usually polished or stained. The older the teacher, the older the 'planka'. Those teachers who were nearing retirement had 'planka's' dark in colour and bearing the scars of many years of usage. The newbies straight out of university and teacher training had light-coloured 'planka's', cut fresh from the hardest South African timbers, and bearing no discernible marks. The punishment fits the crime. A giggle in class whilst you were supposed to be working would result in one strike. More severe acts such as getting homework wrong or even failing to do it could result in up to four or five strikes. You can believe me when I say that one strike was enough. Traditionally boys would get it on the rear, blazer lifted so that the only protection was the thin polyester of their school trousers. Girls, on the other hand, got it 'on the hand'. Being allowed to swap hands quickly between strikes. Looking back it was a cruel act. Barbaric in fact. Made all the worse by seeing the grins of enjoyment on some teachers' faces after dishing it out.

Starting a new school is always daunting. A frightening experience no matter how many times you have to do it. Those first few days, until you get accepted, are the hardest. Fortunately for me, there was a young lad who very quickly took it upon himself to show me the ropes, with a little push from our registration teacher. I accepted Harold as my new friend without question, even though he had shifty eyes that seemed to sparkle more than everyone else's, almost hypnotizing. He helped me mainly in Sotho class (a tribal language at the time spoken mainly by black South Africans and taught in primary schools), and Afrikaans class, where initially I had not got a clue what was going on. Identifying teachers and classes, attending school ceremonies at the right time, and introducing me to the National Anthem sung at assemblies. There wasn't much that Harold didn't help me with. One of my favourite things that Harold introduced me to was 'Vetkoek', which translates to 'Fat cake'. Made occasionally by a local mum and sold from a stall outside at lunch breaks, this delicious treat became one of my favourites. A cricket ball-sized, greasy, light, crispy, deep-fried doughnut, filled with savoury lamb mince, that was to die for. I still remember my first time like it was yesterday. Each mouthful was an explosion of doughy, crispy, savoury delight that you never wanted to end. I was as skinny as a rake when I was ten but had an insatiable appetite. It was not uncommon for me to put two of these delicacies away at lunch if I happened to have sufficient funds on me. Fortunately, Nan and Granddad visited often, and my palm would be graced with a Rand here and there. At 10c a pop I was often able to visit 'Vetkoek' heaven.

When I first started at Brixton, I was thrown in the deep end with regards to learning Afrikaans. It looked initially like they had nobody to teach immigrants the language. Not only those coming from England but also those fleeing Zimbabwe at the time. It took several weeks before we got information that a teacher had been found and that we would start classes soon. In the interim I was expected to sit in the main Afrikaans class and try to make sense of what was going on, depending heavily on Harold for interpretation of the teacher's ramblings, and homework assignments, which I was expected to do. These involved writing down several paragraphs of text from the board, learning it parrot fashion overnight, and then rewriting it from memory in your notebook the next day. Every day before this class, my fellow pupils could be seen standing outside the class door, muttering to themselves what they had memorized the evening before, like amateur actors learning lines before a big production. My first attendance at this class showed me why they were so keen to recite it perfectly. If a mistake was to be made, the first poor pupil that had made it had the honour of retrieving 'Planka' from the classroom cupboard, after which he/she would receive a strike for each mistake. This was no ordinary 'Planka' either. This was one of those teachers nearing retirement, with an aged piece of wood, worn and hardened, that was delivered to you with such expertise that it would inflict the utmost pain possible. Expertise that could only be obtained from many years of frequent practice. I witnessed many of my schoolmates hobble away from this hardly able to walk, especially after homework assignments involving complicated words, grammar, and punctuation that they had failed to memorize correctly. During my brief stay in this class, I took part in the homework in the same manner as my peers but was spared an introduction to 'Planka', due to the fact I had no idea what the teacher was saying or what any of the text meant. Eventually, I attended an immigrant Afrikaans class with a strict Jewish lady who had no patience for slow learners. Afrikaans was the kind of language you could only learn slowly. A mixture of Dutch, Portuguese, Malay, and some native languages, makes this a difficult language to learn. When I was learning at school, I was almost certain there were less than 26 letters in the alphabet. I am sure the letter 'C' was one of those absent, as all words that sounded like they should be spelled with a 'C' was spelled with a 'K'. The Mandela effect seems to have come into play over the past thirty years or so though, as all of the references I can find online insist there to be 26 letters, and 'C' is perfectly acceptable. I had to start from the very beginning. Letters and how to pronounce them, the alphabet, numbers and counting, and then pets and animals. Then it got harder. A simple conversation, talking through the preparation of a meal. Navigating through rooms of a house. It was all very strange. I was struggling with it more than I did first-year French back in the UK. It didn't help that my teacher had little tolerance for error. She used to make some very disapproving faces when I got it wrong, and her voice would get louder when she had to correct me. Not a great help at all when you are just starting. I found this with a lot of teachers at this school. As my brother and I were the only immigrants in the school, apart from those coming from Zimbabwe, there was little tolerance for us. Most of the teachers, although teaching in an English school, were Afrikaans speakers at home. To them, we were 'Rooineks', or 'Rednecks'. A derogatory term used to describe English immigrants, as most of the time we would get sunburnt on our necks until our skin got used to the additional potency experienced at this latitude. They had little like for us. The English had given South Africa independence long ago, and the English had left. Now they were coming back. If called 'Rooinek' in the street by Afrikaans youths, my brother and I would simply reply..' If it wasn't for us you would still be going round in your horse and carts!' (I think our Uncle Mike taught us that.) Believe it or not, there were some communities back in 1980 that still used horses and carts. Descendants of the original 'Voortrekkers' or 'Boers' still insist on living the same way as their ancestors. Still, even though we were not welcome in this part of Johannesburg, we did our best to pick up the lingo as best we could. Later that year we would make friends with the young Afrikaans girl and boy that lived next door to our new house and would spend hours talking to them, flexing our new ability to converse with the locals. We would end up learning a lot from them and be introduced to a strange and rather disgusting new fruit from their garden tree, which was encased in a crispy shell. I still don't like Lychee's today.

Apart from us two rednecks, and a few Zimbabweans, there were also a lot of Portuguese children at this school. These children fitted in perfectly on arrival, as they were no strangers to the sun, and bore the brownest of skins to prove it. It was not long after my arrival that children started to ask if I could run fast. I wasn't sure but thought I was OK. They informed me that the fastest kid in the school was a Portuguese lad in my class. He had won them numerous trophies in the past, at inter-school athletics, as he could beat anyone, anywhere, and barefoot. They tried to convince me that it would be good to match up against him, as they thought I could beat him due to my long legs, laughing behind my back as they knew what the outcome would be. I agreed to a race of a certain length on the grass playing field one break time. To my surprise a bigger crowd than I was expecting turned up. Word must have got out that another fool was going to be shown up. We lined up, with the organizer of this event starting us off. Now at this point, I would like to suggest that I had not yet acclimatized fully to the difference in sea level, etc., etc. so wasn't at my peak. Not that I ever had a peak. I gave it all the beans, but this kid shot off like a greyhound and left me in the wake of his dust. I hadn't a clue how he got his legs to go that fast. It was impressive to see him ahead of you, just making the distance between you wider and wider, and at a dizzying pace. He was superhuman. When I finally reached the finish line, I gave him a handshake of congratulations. All the while surrounded by the laughter of the audience who came to spectate.

Brixton's primary, at this time, was managed by the Headmaster Mr. Raath. Once again a man of little tolerance. A small, unreasonable man, with little stature who felt he had to make up for it by bullying the children at his school who didn't fall into line, and also having a good go at those who tried hard to fall into line, but occasionally failed. One such incident I have in memory is a prime example of this. It was every child's duty to keep an immaculate homework book, ready for inspection at any moment in time. Before the end of each class, and in perfectly neat handwriting, despite the pressure to get to your next class, you had to enter that teacher's homework instruction in detail. Sectioned by day, you would have to show your parents your homework and get them to sign next to that homework item. This had to be kept up to date, and god help you if there was a missing signature for a particular day or homework item. Not an easy task when you have hard-working parents who just want to relax after a long day, evening, or night shift, rather than be pestered constantly by their children for autographs. Now I had a slight misfortune on this particular day, in that during a certain class my pen had decided to dry up during a session where the teacher was dictating content to us. In a panic, I reached for my homework book and scribbled madly on one of the pages at the back of the book, in an attempt to coax ink back to the nib. Eventually, it did return but unfortunately, I continued scribbling leaving an impressive piece of art on the page. It looked like the Gods were not smiling at me that day, as low and behold who should enter the class several minutes later. You guessed it. 'Little Big Man'. It was amazing how a class of pupils responded when he entered the classroom unannounced.

The door was usually flung open quickly, and he would step in promptly with his hands behind his back as If he was trying to catch you all out doing something you should not be doing. This was the case. If he could catch you talking as he made his entrance, then you were nabbed. Every single pupil flew up at their desks and stood to attention, with impressive precision. All eyes forward, hands by your sides, not a whisper could be heard. Then from Mr. Raath's lips came the words 'Get out your homework books!'. It was not said at a reasonable level, it was neither spoken nor shouted. It was more like a shriek, under pressure, where the voice-box cannot handle the sudden request for volume and decides to omit the vocal sounds like a choir boy whose voice has just decided to break. 'Sit down!', he added. Next came the long wait as he paced up and down the central aisle, looking at each pupil in the eye, looking for any sign of fear, further clocking the contents of the desk to see if any items should not be there. The pace of the walk and the length of the step changed periodically, making each pupil think he was going to be the victim. I was sitting at the back of the class and watched nervously as he walked towards my desk. He reached me and then turned around as if intending to walk back the other way. Instead, he looked straight at me and picked up my homework book. Flicking through the pages to the current endpoint. Then flicking further to a page that looked disturbed. A page that looked used, but was not used in the correct sequence. He opened the page and stared at it in horror. I could see his blood start to boil, his chest started to inflate, and his head started to shake as he mustered up all his might to say 'What is this boy!!! A formula for a space rocket to the moon???'. It was delivered in the same shrieking manner as his previous utterances. Now, as I said I was new. How was I supposed to know that in asking that question, he did not want an answer of any sort? Was I supposed to ignore him, and be accused of insolence? No, I decided to answer him and be accused of insolence instead. I don't know how many of the words I managed to get out of my mouth to inform Mr. Raath of my pen incident, before being bellowed further, and told to get to his office. I stood outside his office for a long time. The bell went and I was still standing there. Break time finished and I was still standing there. At some point, he returned, after completing his rounds, and no doubt a coffee and some biscuits in the staff room. All I got was a 'Get back to the class boy!!', and that was that. Unbelievable. If it had been Vetkoek day I would have been fuming. Harold became a good friend of mine, and soon we started to mix outside of school, attending each other's houses to learn about each other's home life and ways. I quenched Harold's curiosity about England and English ways and Harold, in turn, taught me how to kill and pluck chickens. A fair trade I think? At school, we would continue our talks whenever there was an opportunity. There were always things to talk about, write about, or draw together. I introduced Harold to the world of sticker art and decorating one's book covers with Biro drawings and cut-out pictures of cars and motorbikes. Little did I know that my influences on Harold were being closely monitored, and more importantly, disapproved of! Enter Emanuella.

Emanuella Giangregorio. Harold's better half. It made sense. Harold was always perfectly smart. Neatly pressed grey shorts, crisp white shirt, tie perfectly straight like his mother had used a plumbline, buttoned-up blazer, and shoes you could see your face in. Emanuella was no different. The only girl in the school whose skirt was at regulatory length (not above the knee). Hair plaited and tied up tight against the cranium. Together they were immaculate, top-grade students and that is probably why they became Head Boy and Head Girl during my stay. Emanuella had seen a change in Harold since I joined. Not that I was a bad influence or anything, but I think Harold had seen a bit of a rebel in me, which he liked and wanted to mirror. Emanuella's fiery Italian blood was having none of it. One afternoon she came over to me and Harold and introduced herself to me as his girlfriend, continuing to point out that I was influencing Harold in a bad way. Teaching him to worship material things and idols, and effectively aiding him in straying from his Christian upbringing and beliefs. All this while displaying to me a face like thunder. I can't remember how I responded to Harold once she left, but I would like to think it was the ten-year-old equivalent of 'women, eh?'.

I think everybody has had a near-death experience in their life, whether it be an accident, near miss, or sudden entry into a dangerous situation. Those that have, all share something in common, they have all had that single moment of realization manifest in their brains, that fills them with dread, and fear, and also instantly makes them aware that their game is up. The next thing that happens is your acceptance of defeat, and you give in. This is exactly how it played out for me, but fortunately, my acceptance of defeat caused me to do something that would ultimately save my life. When not feasting on Vetkoek at break times, I would often indulge in my favourite Marmite sandwich. Break times were short, and there was often a lot to do like get a toilet break-in, a drink, socialize, etc. Usually, all of this meant that you had to hurry to eat whatever you had before the bell went. On this particular occasion, I did just that, leaving the devouring of my sandwich until the last minute. The bell went and I stuffed it in as quick as I could, trying to chew and swallow at the same time. Now South African bread back then was not light at all. It was the stodgiest loaf ever and thick and heavy as well. Take a ball of dough out of the middle of a loaf and squeeze it into a ball, and it forms this greyish, hard, inedible mass. This had happened in my mouth with what little moisture was available to it. I hurriedly swallowed and then attempted to take a breath. Nothing. Gasped for air but was unable to do so. My lungs were not moving as I attempted to breathe. I jumped on the spot. Still nothing. Panic was starting to kick in now. I signalled to Harold for help pointing at my throat. He and my other friends didn't realize what was wrong. Nobody had taught them about the signs, and they had not been on this earth long enough to know the 'Heimlich' manoeuvrer. I started to feel faint and in desperation ran like mad across the playground to the other end. When I got there, still nothing. I rushed with what little energy I had left to the nearest drinking fountain, trying to get water into my mouth without being able to suck it in. I stood up and took one last attempt to draw breath. Absolutely nothing. I felt like I had tried everything and had lost the battle. I turned the corner and looked back at the playground, seeing the backs of the last few children making their way back to class. It was at this point I admitted defeat. I had nothing left in me. It had probably only been a minute, but I had used up what was in my lungs by exerting myself. In my mind, I said goodbye to the world and then collapsed hard onto the ground. I don't know how long I was lying there, but all I remember in the blackness, was my body trying to take in a last breath and miraculously succeeding. Air filled my lungs; I took long breaths which helped to bring me around. It was the biggest relief ever. Without knowing it I had given myself the 'Heimlich' manoeuvrer. I got up and immediately went to join my class, to find them waiting outside for the teacher to let them in. Harold was curious as to what I was doing back in the playground but was unaware of the seriousness of it. He seemed concerned when I explained what was happening to me. To this day, forty five years down the line, when I am eating a Marmite sandwich, it takes me back to that time.

CHAPTER 3 - CHICKEN RUN

It was very surprising, especially after only living in the hotel Stephanie for around a month, to find out that Dad had bought a house. 18 Plunkett Avenue was a road off of one of the main dual carriageways out of Brixton, a few miles out of Johannesburg. It was a typical South African-looking set of houses down one side of the road, with their corrugated roofs, gated driveways, front gardens, and verandas, or 'stoep' as they were referred to out there. The beginning of the other side of the road housed a small set of shops, with some waste ground afterward. In the distance, about 500 yards away was the hospital, which turned out to be very handy a few months later when both myself and my brother (on two separate occasions), damaged our left knees requiring stitches. Our house was nice. It certainly beat all four of us living in the hotel Stephanie in a single room, or living above shops as we did back in the UK. It had a brightly painted red 'stoep' out before the front garden. A driveway along the left-hand side of the house leading up to a garage at the rear, the wall on either side laced with vine-like growth. Inside there was a large kitchen, a smaller front room, and a hallway leading to my and my brother's bedrooms, my parent's room on the other side. At the foot of the hall was the bathroom. Outside there was a small courtyard with a raised (and hardly grassed) area with a large aviary-like structure housing around eight chickens. These had been a gift from the previous owner. A sort of 'moving in' present. To the left of that the small outbuilding that was usually used as the maid's accommodation, if you were lucky enough to have one that resided with the family. This particular outbuilding had not been used in years, and only housed spiders, scorpions, flies, leaves, and dust. Inside we had basic furniture, as we were starting from scratch again, but had everything we needed. We had been living there for just over a month when news arrived that our Tea Chests had survived the many weeks' journey from the UK, had made port, and were winging their way to us. By this time I had forgotten what I had been allowed to pack, and so it was going to be exciting to get my only belongings back. My brother and I had to share a chest, and I cannot remember whose belongings were on top, but I can still remember peering into it, and reaching for my 'stuff', with an excitement level more fitting of opening a fifty-year-old time capsule!

My Dad worked late some nights and very early mornings on others. Being out in the sticks at night wasn't easy for my Mum, so Dad thought it would be a good idea to get a dog for security and company. One weekend my brother and I accompanied Dad on a trip to the SPCA (RSPCA equivalent). Here we were allowed to peruse the dogs and look for something suitable. I am pleased to say that I spotted something 'suitable' that after a week would become our family pet for our entire stay in South Africa. I remember looking to my right at some point and seeing him sitting in a large caged area. I went up to him as if there was something about him. He was different from the other dogs in that he was not barking, yelping, or making a fuss. Just sitting at the front of the cage looking at me. After a meet and greet through the cage wire, it was a done deal as far as I was concerned. I didn't hear the other dogs after that. This was the dog we were going to have. My brother seemed to agree, and I don't remember my father putting up much of a fight. Off to the office to sort out the paperwork. 'David' was his name and 'David' was a Dachshund. Albeit a Dachshund with a twist. That twist was a considerable amount of excess weight which made his belly nearly drag on the floor and a tail that rotated like helicopter blades when he got excited or pleased to see you. He was a Bassett Hound cross, and so a larger framed Dachshund than you would normally meet. Jet black apart from a slightly rusty brown chin and chest. 'David' was not a very suitable dog name I grant you, but it seemed to suit him and we weren't going to change it. David settled in fine and very quickly became one of the family, and a very close friend of the butcher just down the road. Somehow he had managed to strike up a relationship which meant that he could frequently escape from our garden, wander down to the butchers, and be presented with a bone. On several occasions that I can remember, we would call him from the house when he had gone missing, only to see a faint silhouette of a dog jogging towards you from the dark, and the direction of the butchers. Tail whirling incessantly as he did, with his large and prized possession in his mouth. Usually, both he and the bone ended up in his bed in the kitchen. Next time he was let out it would be time to bury it for a rainy day. Aside from bones, his other love was Moles. He would sit next to a mole mound and not move a muscle for hours. If you called him, he would look back at you by only moving his eye within its socket, with no movement or change in breathing pattern at all. You could almost see him whispering under his breath... 'GO AWAY... can't you see what I am trying to do here?'. Eventually, due to obedience, he would get up and come, but it often took a stern voice before he did. On the rare occasion that a mole was stupid enough to raise its head above ground level, he would get it. Now I saw David eat some nasty things in his time, some of which I cannot mention. Whole 'live' mice crunched up, and a lot more. I would have expected the same fate for any mole that was unlucky enough to be captured during one of his twilight mole hunts, but not so. Instead, he took them to his bed, for what seemed like additional company. When they wouldn't move, he would prod them with his nose and look disappointed when they didn't respond. Poor things always died of fright. David would have several other canine companions over the years, but it still would not stop him from hunting for mole-like companionship.

Now a warning about this next piece. I don't want to offend anyone, so if you feel you cannot handle reading about two ten-year-old boys taking matters into their own hands, and disposing of some foul, I would skip this next paragraph. It isn't graphic, but I have had to stay true to the event, and so there is talk of some actions that people may feel uncomfortable reading about. It is important to remember that this is 1980 when the world was a lot different from today, and it was the action of two, naive young lads in deepest, darkest Africa, who thought they were helping out. It was over dinner one evening I heard my parents talking about the chickens at the back of the garden. None of them were 'lay-errs', and they were pretty much becoming a nuisance. There was talk of getting rid of them, and even a comment about having to kill them and eat them, much to my mother's disgust as she believed them to be too old, and too tough. It was at school the next day that I happened to mention my parent's dilemma about the chickens we had been gifted to Harold. Straight away he was in with the suggestion that we should take matters into our own hands and solve the issue for my parents. Even at the tender age of ten, he displayed confidence when talking about the simple slaughter of these animals, convincing me that it was something he had done many times, and even bragged about the foolproof technique he had to ensure a swift conclusion to events. I have to admit Harold had not let me down at all since I met him, and that I had no reason to believe he could not coordinate the demise of these chickens. We talked about it over the next few days and drew up a list of the equipment that would be needed until Harold could get a pass from his mother to come to my house after school. Amongst other things, the equipment list required a length of rope, sufficient to strangle the chickens should the attempts to twist their necks prove too difficult. Once again Harold came up trumps, having a suitable length of sturdy rope in 'his' shed. This was a ten-year-old going on forty-five. Whatever you thought you needed Harold had it. I believe Harold only lived with his mother and sister. He didn't talk of a father, so I assumed he had either departed life or left his mother. Whichever of the two it was, Harold had stepped into the role of the man about the house, doing anything that was required. No job is too big or small.

Later that week Harold and I caught the bus home to my house. After an initial assessment of the livestock, Harold gave the go-ahead, and we started preparation. We had the length of rope, an extremely blunt penknife of Harold's, and a maid on standby to perform 'plucking' duties. That was about it. The first thing was to catch the first chicken. This was best left to the expert, and so a barefooted Harold dressed in nothing but shorts and a tee-shirt entered the chicken coup, and I closed the gate. Within ten minutes, and after the air in the cage had been filled with dust and feathers, Harold stood up victorious with our first victim under his arm. He exited the coup and attempted the 'strangle', which was point 2 on our to-do list. This proved difficult and I started to wonder if Harold was being honest when he had told me this was a 'piece of cake'. We lost the chicken repeatedly as it tried to escape, having to perform point 1, 'capture' again, several times. After half an hour or so an executive decision was made to skip to point 3 'rope strangulation'. This proved to be just as time-consuming, Harold stating that these were indeed 'hardy' chickens. Finally, the deed had been done, and point 4 'head and feet removal' came into play. Now Harold's penknife had seen a lot of action, previously belonging to Grandfather, and so blunt you could confidently run your finger along the blade without incident. Harold went in and found it hard going. We decided I should tag in and take over so he could rest for a few minutes. I found it equally hard going.

This knife was not up to the job. I went inside and looked for a replacement, emerging after a minute and brandishing the family bread knife. It was much longer, had very large teeth on it, and was a lot sharper. It made sense. I hacked away with this for a while, still having trouble. The combination of the large serrated edge and the dimply surface of the garden retaining bricks was making life very difficult for us. Still, persistence paid off and we got to two chickens completed and one in progress. Harold had to depart as it was getting into the late afternoon and he was expected back. I assured him I could complete the last chicken. Harold left and within a few minutes, my mother returned from work, coming through the rear garden gate. Now my mother had spent ten years with me, thought she knew me, and would never have associated me with a procedure of this kind...ever. I was scared of pretty much all insects, blood, the dark, and sometimes my own shadow. You would have not thought that I would have had anything to do with any such culling of birds that had taken place. There was a look and gasp from her when she arrived and asked me what I was doing. 'Killing the chickens', I replied. She was horrified and asked me to stop. I tried to assure her that I had not attempted this on my own, but had up until a few minutes ago, had professional help from a native with the task. I informed her how many we had already done by showing her the bucket of plucked birds so far. As far as I was concerned the fruits of my labour were going to grace the family dinner table that evening. After all, as my father always said 'man is instinctively the hunter...', and I had now taken my turn to provide. In reality, nothing of the sort was going to happen. The birds were offered to the maid to take home, and she was only too pleased to accept the offer. A phone call followed to my father, who was still at work. My mother didn't know whether to laugh or cry as she told my father 'he's killed the chickens'. I really couldn't see what all the fuss was about. A job needed to be done, and I had taken the initiative.

Now as I mentioned earlier, Plunkett Avenue, in Hursthill,

was decorated with several shops at its entrance. A Butcher, and if memory serves me correctly, an Estate Agent. This was not all though. On the very corner of Portland Street and Plunket Avenue was a corner shop. My father and mother had run several NSS Newsagents back in England, with stores full of toys, sweets, magazines, and much more. This corner shop was very different. Run by a young Chinese couple, who had lived in South Africa for around five years, it carried everything imaginable. Shelves tightly packed with every confection possible. ½ cent Sweets galore, fridges full of every possible fizzy and non-fizzy drink. Everything you needed to repair anything, wash anything, personal hygiene products, houseware, household cleaning products, alcohol, cigarettes, and pet foods. You could hardly walk through the aisles in this small shop. Where there was room, there were boxes of new items ready to go into any available place on the shelves. If you needed it, they almost certainly had it, and if it wasn't visible, it was probably out the back. This was my 'go-to' place if I managed to get my hands on any kind of money! And if I didn't have any money there were always places to find it in 1980 South Africa. Back then fizzy drinks like the popular cola brands and others were sold in glass bottles ranging from 330ml, 500ml, 1 litre, and 1.5 litre. You purchased the drinks at the store, paying an additional charge if you didn't drink it within the store, and handed the bottle back afterward. If you did take the bottle of drink away, you could return it empty to get your refund. For the 330ml bottle, this was about 10 cents at the time. All stores that sold the drinks, had to take your empties if you took them to them, regardless of whether you purchased them there. They also had to give you the standard refund back for those bottles. Most of the time people did this, but on the odd occasion, if someone trekking through the fields or wasteland couldn't be bothered, they would simply discard it in the grass. These areas were our hunting grounds, where we hoped to strike gold, maybe being fortunate to locate a bottle or two in the long grass. Africa was a hot country, especially in summer, and you were almost certain to find the prizes if you looked hard enough! If your efforts failed, there was always the option of you and your brother guzzling down what was in the bottles at home in the fridge, so you could take those empties back. Our father was always passing comments on why there was never any pop left in the fridge. Find a litre bottle in the grass (or the fridge), and you were looking at 30 cents. You can't imagine what you could buy in Aladdin's cave on the corner with that sort of wonga. I had a favourite that I could not do without. Cadbury's 'Crunchie' bars. Yes, we did have them in England, but these were different. In South Africa, they were made with white chocolate, and came in a shiny blue wrapper, instead of the standard gold. I cannot be sure but think they were about 8 cents. Then there was 'Chappies'. A small square of chewing gum selling at two for a cent. These were popular with everybody. I had witnessed children going into the store with a Rand (100 cents), expecting the young Chinese owner to count out two hundred of these things. If it happened too often you could see the frustration on his face, and hear the Chinese mumblings coming from his lips. Another favourite was the 5 cents 'Chomp' bar. Soft, chewable caramel with milk chocolate covering. Whatever change you had after this, went on drink, usually drinking it in-store so you could pay less. The young Chinese lady owner of the store was always welcoming to the children if they came in. Even if it was just to chat with her, which we often did. The man was less tolerant and would suggest we had homes to go to if we were not spending cash. We spent all our cash there, and he should have been more grateful for our business.

It was one afternoon, whilst sitting on the wall at the side of the house, chomping on sweets and chocolate that I noticed something moving in the vine growing on the side of the house. On closer inspection, I saw something I had never seen before. It was quite large and bug-like, green with an odd-shaped head. Sort of like an odd-looking cricket or grasshopper. It blended in with its surroundings so well that at first, I couldn't make out what it was. I had no idea what it was and had no means to reference it and find out, so I did what I normally did. Asked Harold. The next day at school I described it to him, and he knew instantly what I was talking about. 'Praying mantis', he said. I was assured they were harmless and that they would make a good pet if I kept it in a shoebox with some holes in and a portion of the vine. I didn't like the look of it that much so I said I wouldn't be keeping it as a pet. Harold suggested 'Silk Worms' as another option as they were not as 'creepy crawly'. He was a 'silkworm' farmer and could bring me some of his stock in a matchbox that I could take home. They would spin silk which I could collect. I accepted the offer and the next day I got my new pets delivered to me from Harold's inside blazer pocket. That afternoon I placed them on the side in the outbuilding, checking on them every few hours up until bedtime, to see how my crop was coming along. At this point, I have to say that silkworms take a long time to make silk of any substance. They take even longer when they are dead, which is what soon happened to mine after a period of neglect. Another friend at school had a pet Chameleon, which he bought to show us. This thing was amazing, it changed colour to whatever the colour was of its environment. Now that would be much more exciting! Just have to find one crawling through the vine.

It was about this time, mid to late 1980, that I started to take more of an interest in music. Missing episodes of 'Top of the Pops' and not having anything similar to watch in South Africa meant the radio was your friend. The only trouble was we didn't have one. Imagine my surprise when I am walking down the road one day, and there before me in the middle of the road is a crushed pocket radio. The black casing pretty much smashed, but the internal circuit board, electronics, and battery compartment looked in good shape. I knew nothing about transistors or electronics but decided to retrieve it and take it home for further investigation. It had a single earpiece attached to the socket on the side of the casing, so I was hoping that this would reveal any signs of life if I put batteries in. It worked the first time. That night when the reception was clearer I searched through endless stations on Medium Wave. Do you remember that radio band? The one where the signal used to drift out and then come back periodically. Some local stations had better reception but it still wasn't perfect due to the fact the aerial was cut off at a few centimetres. What was needed was some serious upgrading to make this a more suitable appliance for my new bedroom (which I didn't have to share with my brother!). The first thing was to get an old pair of car speakers that I had seen in the garage and some speaker wire which If I remember right Harold helped me to acquire. Some painstaking searching of the circuit board soon found a couple of solder points that blasted the sound through the speakers, albeit not in true stereo. The wires were secured with sticky tape initially, which often needed replacing. Next were some speaker cabinets made from two old shoe boxes, with a lot more use of sticky tape. I'd made myself a Hi-fi! The sound travelled well in my room from the new speaker cabinets, especially at night, but I was still suffering from limited reception. More wire, lots more sticky tape, and a trip onto the roof to attach the wire to the overflow pipe/lightning conductor thingy on the corrugated roof was all that was required to fix that. The result was a perfect setup and served me well for many months. Many an evening was spent in bed tuning into lots of different stations, from all over the world. This was my first attempt at fixing something, and I got a lot of satisfaction from investigating how to make it work. It stood me in good stead for later life, when I started to build my computers.

Before I left my school in England, I had struck up a friendship with a young girl called Caroline. When she heard I was moving abroad she insisted we became pen pals, and that at the first opportunity, I should send a postcard. I sent this first postcard when we moved into our first house in Plunket Avenue so that there was somewhere for a reply to be addressed. I was able to let Caroline know how things were going and the adjustments I was having to make to South African life, and Caroline could fill me in on what the second year of secondary school was like, and what options she was choosing for her third year. During the last few months, I had got to spend some quality time with my Uncle Michael who was a keen stamp collector. I had taken an interest in the hobby too, and Uncle Mike had kindly parted with some stamps and first-day covers to start my collection. Caroline on hearing of this new hobby did her utmost to send my letters on the first day of the issue of new stamps, which instantly added to my collection of first day covers. I still have them today, but sadly not the letters that were within them. I don't know what happened to Caroline. We lost touch after three or four years. I do still have a photo she sent me of her Spaniel her family got, called 'Jasper' if I remember.

My father was and still is a very hard-working man. Our family never went without what they needed. If times were hard, he would find a way to get what we needed, even if it meant working all the hours God made. He would not only do this for the things we needed but also the things we wanted. My mother too was working from the time we arrived to help with the family finances. I can't imagine the expense my parents must have been enduring over the months we had been in South Africa. Starting from scratch, and needing everything. A house, a car, furniture, school clothes, electricity, food, entertainment. All this and more my parents provided me with what seemed like relative ease. In reality, they were both working very hard to make our new future as great as possible. I guess my brother and I must have been especially well-behaved for some time, either that or they felt that as we had to leave so many of our belongings behind, it was time to provide us with some new ones. One day my father came home from work and my brother and I were summoned to the front room. I could not believe my eyes. The EK Kit, that I had drooled over at the shopping mall, that I had whispered to through the glass shopfront 'Oh yes, you shall be mine...', was now in my hands. It was like all my Christmas had come at once, and it wasn't even Christmas! My brother was equally chuffed with his present. An electronic chess computer. Right up his street as he had gone to the chess club a lot back in England. We were both over the moon and after some thank yous and hugs, we made off to our separate bedrooms to play with our new devices. I had no idea what I was going to make first. My kit was the EK-47 which came with a plethora of electronic blocks, and instructions on what kinds of circuits you could make with them. There was an alarm to tell you when your bath water had run up to a certain point. That looked tricky and so would be left for another day. Radio! Let's try that one. The set came with an earpiece that you could plug in to hear the sound, or you could use the built-in speaker. A length of electrical wire with a metal contact strip at the end needed to be placed within two of the blocks to act as an aerial. I made a Morse code device, a light signalling device, and much more all on my first evening. It was an amazing piece of kit that you could experiment endlessly with, and I did for many years.

In addition to spoiling us with presents, my mother and father also took my brother and me out a lot. Mainly family get-togethers at restaurants, or visits to the local roadhouse. Very similar to the American-style roadhouses, except no pretty, young ladies on roller skates delivering your food. I am surprised nobody has cottoned on to the fact that these could be winners here in England. Far too many branches of that popular so-called 'restaurant' with the big golden arches above it. They could do with some quality competition in the form of one of these roadhouses. People could choose to take their food away or on a nice day eat it off the tray attached to the window. If only I had the capital to build a test version, and then franchise it. 'But what would you call it Carl?', I hear you say. Only 'Fandangos Fast Food Drive-In...', I would reply. 'Fandango' comes from a nickname that friends have been adopting and calling me since I was knee-high to a grasshopper. Even when I have never told them that people called me it before at my last school or workplace. Everywhere I go, I go from 'Carl Williams' to 'Carlos Fandango', in a very short space of time. Anyway, enough about my dreams of becoming a fast food millionaire, onto the evening out which this particular time did not involve going to a roadhouse as such. We went on a trip out in the evening not knowing where we were going. My father liked playing with us. If we asked, 'Where are we going?', he would usually reply with our grandfather's standard answer, 'Here, there, and back again to see how far it is'. The first time we heard this expression, we looked at each other puzzled, trying to work out what it meant. Was it a riddle? Where was here, and where was there? And why did we need to find out the distance between them? Was it some sort of a clue? It didn't take long before we realized this was a statement to keep us quiet and to stop us from asking questions. It was no different this trip. It was a secret where we were going. The drive took us into Johannesburg and then just on the outskirts we started to travel up and around a large hill. Getting higher and higher so you could see more of the city with each circle. It wasn't long before we realized where we were. For some time, whilst on other car journeys in the dark evenings, we had seen the strange, morphing, colourful lights like televisions in the sky. It was, in fact, the glow of large movie screens in the distance, showing the latest films. Some at ground level, and some perched high above on what we thought were large hills. There were several all over Johannesburg and became a common sight. Depending on where you were in Johannesburg, you could sometimes see two at the same time in differing directions. These were of course 'Drive-in' movie theatres, and this is where we were going this evening. Our particular one was perched on top of one of these dusty hills. Hills that turned out to be made from all of the ground that had been removed from underground at the site of Johannesburg's goldmines. We were very pleased when we found out about our destination. We had been to the cinema many times, but never at night, outside, in a car, with fast food readily available. You couldn't do anything like this in England, but it was warm enough most of the year to do it in South Africa. We twisted our way up to the top, paid the entrance fee, drew the car up to a slot, and parked up. Mum wound her window down to accommodate the speaker, which you detached from a pole to the side and hung on the glass. Your window could then be wound back up leaving just a little gap. Advertisements were playing and the sound came into the car. Very basic I know, but we were impressed. If you had to go to the toilet, it sounded weird, hearing all the speakers from the cars in unison but slightly out of sync. It sort of echoed all around you. My father went to get refreshments before the movie started, which was to be one I hadn't heard of at that point. 'The Gods must be crazy'. The story of a bushman out in the wilderness getting hit on the head with a Coke bottle that has been thrown out of a light aircraft overhead. The bushman having never seen a coke bottle, thinks the gods have struck him with it, and he questions why, as he has lived a good life and not been bad in any way. He decides to trek through the bush until he gets to the Gods to ask them. His travels take him through the city where he sees all sorts of sights that he has never laid eyes on before, and all sorts of situations that he has trouble dealing with. It was a good film and we had a great evening out. Drive-ins were plentiful, and later on in life, we would visit them often, either by jumping the wall and hot-footing it to the front of the projector building, where you would find a long line of your schoolmates and their girlfriends, or occasionally acting as a paying customer and entering in a friend's car.

When you say home cinema these days, it conjures up images of huge widescreen 4K plasma screens, or digital projectors with Dolby quality 5.1 through some high-end surround system, with huge sub-woofers to boost the cinematic experience. Back in 1980, it was somewhat different. Blockbusters hadn't been invented, there was no rental of Video Cassettes or DVDs. None of that existed. South Africa seemed to be taking a step in the right direction though, with something that I hadn't seen available in England at all.

One evening I went out with my father in the car and we stopped at a store at the mall. Inside there was nothing on any shelves to peruse. A few film posters on the walls but that was about it. My father looked at a list at the counter and asked the man for something off of it, paid, and then we waited for a few minutes. The man behind the counter returned with a large, and heavy-looking suitcase-like box and handed it to my father. He also gave two round cases about 10-12 inches in diameter. We packed this lot in the car and went home. All was revealed when my father got the large device out of the case and placed it on the coffee table. It was a very big and very heavy projector. This was all new to me and my brother. We had never seen any home movies on a projector before. My mother got a white bed sheet and with the help of my father attached it to the wall in front of the projector. Then he got one of the film reels out of the case and attached it to the projector's arm. An empty spool was waiting on the other arm. The film was fed through the projector and attached to the empty spool. We were all set. 'What was the film?' we asked. 'The Wild Geese', my father replied. I had never heard of it, but it was an excellent film with many famous people in it. We all sat back comfortably on the floor, and my father turned the knob on the huge projector. A light turned on and a rectangle appeared on the sheet. Some adjustment was needed to the distance between the coffee table and the wall to make the rectangle bigger. The projector made a lot of noise, it was by no means a quiet machine. The next thing we saw and heard was an awful noise. Music playing but being distorted horribly. The screen wasn't much better either. Flick after flick of images going upwards, the images distorted up and down and sideways. Whatever it was it was unwatchable. We then had to wait while my father turned other knobs of adjustment to try and stabilize the picture and sound. It took a while but eventually, it calmed down, and some way into the film we began to be able to identify the plot. That is until the film broke. Everything stopped picture and sound-wise, with one reel flapping around like mad and the other slowly coming to a stop. My father wasn't going to let this ruin things. A quick fix with some sello-tape and we were off and running again. That is until the first reel finished, at which point we used the opportunity for a well-earned toilet break and then continued. The film was excellent. Full of action there were several famous faces I spotted, like Roger Moore and Richard Harris. It was the best thing I had watched in ages and beat anything that was served up on SABC hands down! What interested me was the fact that some of the film's scenes were filmed in South Africa. There was one scene at a runway at a deserted airport, where planes came down and bombed a bridge over a river nearby. This was filmed in the Kruger National Park. Somewhere that I would visit in the next few years, and be able to view the plaque next to that bridge that says that the film The 'Wild Geese' was filmed there. Movie nights would continue over the next few years, and we would watch other films such as 'Papillon' with Steve Mc Queen & Dustin Hoffman. My father got better at handling the projector, and he could deal with any mishaps regarding film reels snapping with ease. Friends were invited around, and the event was shared with snacks and drinks. It was short-lived though, as just around the corner something better was coming. It began to be the thing everyone was talking about, and those with enough money would be quick to jump on the bandwagon. I'm talking about the Betamax and VHS video recorders. Soon the projector shops in the mall would be replaced by stores full of shelves, stacked with copies of all the major movies, as well as US and UK television programs. My father would invest in a Betamax video recorder, which as it turns out was a mistake, but at the time it allowed us to receive tapes through the post from my sister back in England. All the good comedies, Russ Abbott, Two Ronnie's, Kenny Everett, Dave Allen, as well as episodes of Top of the Pops that I would tape and edit onto cassette to listen to at my leisure. Suddenly we didn't need SABC anymore. Our world had been opened to a plethora of entertainment, the majority of which would start to make us feel homesick. My father still has the Betamax video recorder in his shed. It hasn't seen the light of day for about 40 years and is probably wrapped up well along with a few tapes of 'Dynasty' episodes, whose hell my brother and I had to endure for what seemed like a lifetime! It might be worth a few quid now, so you should get it out and see if still works Dad.

David the Dachshund posing for a photo

18 Plunkett Avenue, Hursthill (My brother Chris, me and our Nan)

CHAPTER 4 - GOLDEN CITY ENTERPRISES

I am not sure how long we stayed in Plunkett Avenue. I remember being in the last year 'Standard 5' before we moved and changed schools. I got the lead in the school end-of-year play, and sadly we had to leave before I got the chance to take the stage and perform as a fat King, in a play whose title escapes me. I was an eight-stone weakling at the time, but the drama teacher had plans to fatten me up with the aid of several cushions. Due to my departure, an understudy had to take over the lead role. We will never know if first-night nerves would have gotten the better of me, or whether I would have consistently delivered an Oscar-winning performance each evening of December. Still, a new school awaited me, perhaps there would be a similar opportunity thrown my way there. That school was Norkem Park Primary School, and unlike my previous school, there would be some welcome friends from England to get up to no good with. We would end up talking about the good old days together and spinning a few yarns to teachers, which they would eat up hook, line, and sinker. Norkem was not too dissimilar to Brixton primary. The same levels of discipline, the same behavioural expectations. Sadly though it had very poorly run lunchtime catering facilities, with not a 'Vetkoek' in sight. Not anything in sight to be honest with you. I cannot even remember it having the most basic of tuck shops. Probably for the best, as if my access to those deep-fried delicacies had been prolonged, I would be able to play the part of the fat King at an end-of-year production without any additional aids from the wardrobe department. The one thing that Norkem did have though, was quite a neat green boy's blazer. It was much better than the Black-striped uniform of Brixton Primary. Gracing the pocket was a badge containing the brightly coloured 'Strelitzia'. The school's motto was 'Aim High', and these words accompanied the flower on the badge. The words also featured heavily in the school song, which we had to learn instead of the National Anthem that was sung at Brixton's school assemblies.

Our new house was quite different from the one in Plunket Avenue. A step up. It was gated at the front with a driveway and garage in the middle at the front. To the left, you could go around to another large waist-height gate, which went into the rear garden. To the right was a large lawned area with a side gate to a small courtyard giving access to the maid's quarters, garage, and the rear door of the kitchen. The front door was straight in front of the lawn. Inside was a spacious sunken living room with a door to the garden. Three bedrooms and a bathroom with a separate toilet and a small kitchen. There was something special in the large garden though, something I would take control of shortly. Our first swimming pool. It was a funny blob-like shape, with a bit extra containing a large step-down. A raised sun deck. To the right was all the sand filter equipment, partially hidden by a tall, thatched umbrella. The pool itself needed a bit of tender loving care, and indeed, later on, we would drain it, repair and repaint it so that it sparkled like new. It would be in this pool, despite its meagre five-and-a-half-foot depth, that my father would teach us how to do what he called 'Harvey Wall Bangers'. This involved putting your arms out and hurtling yourself forward whilst flipping yourself over, splashing the water as you hit it, soaking everybody in the near vicinity. I still have pictures where four of us are attempting this all at the same time. One other thing the garden had was a chicken coup. Fortunately, though there were no fowl left behind as a present by the previous owners. Much to my mother's relief. A small area reserved for vegetable growing, and a canopied terrace with a patio area completed the garden. It must have been like heaven for David. Our old place was just dirt and dust out the back, now he had a large, lush green lawn to run all over, well I say run but I mean wobble. Soon he would get a companion to share the garden with him. 'Lucy', a small black dog that looked like no breed at all. Once again Dad had a phrase to categorise her. 'Pavement Special', he used to say she was. The maid said she was a 'Skippetjie', but I never found out what that was. She was just jet black, small, and had a spring in her step that could launch her from the ground to around four feet in the air, continuously. Sometimes she even did this while riding on David's back. 50 Karee Street was the house that had everything we needed. I was sure we were going to set down roots here and not have to move again.

One Christmas my brother and I had received a pair of roller skates each. Mine were green and his were red. They were not the cheapest of skates. These had brightly coloured hard plastic wheels and a reasonably sturdy plastic mechanism for attaching to your trainers. Trainers for some reason were called 'Takkies' in South Africa. If you didn't refer to them like this, nobody knew what you were on about. We had used our skates quite a lot, and got quite good with them, being able to go backward, and sideways, do jumps, and stop instantly if needing to. We became quite addicted that year. We would stay out until late evening, skating on the large concrete patio that was in front of the swimming pool. It had an extra smooth, painted coating that made it perfect for the job. I say late, but I mean until it was a suitable time for a 13 and 10-year-old to go to bed, which In my eyes was far too early. We had to be dragged in, especially my brother who would always insist on doing one more circuit before finally agreeing to come in. Fortunately for us though our parents had a very active social life and would quite frequently go out to dinner, or events, leaving us in bed and asking our maid who lived in the outbuilding, to be there if we needed her. Never leave a 13 and 10-year-old in bed, and then go out and expect them to stay there. Ever. The first time it happened we chatted to each other for a while from our bedrooms. I think we were both thinking the same thing. We couldn't could we? We ruddy well could. The evenings were warm so we just kept our pyjamas on. Pair of socks, takkies, and the skates. Would you believe it? There was even a floodlight attached to the soffit of the house, pointing out towards the patio and pool. Floodlit, night-time, roller skating.. oh yeah... This was good for about an hour until I realized that something was missing. We had been to roller skating rinks before and knew that one of the vital elements to complete the enjoyment was musical accompaniment. A light bulb came on in my head immediately. I had seen that just underneath the floodlight, was a rectangle chipboard-like box with holes in the front. Looked like a speaker. I had also noticed that in the front room, behind my father's music center, was a pair of joined wires coming out of the wall. The small spool of wire was wound up on the floor. I got a knife from the kitchen and exposed the wire at the ends, at the back of the music center were terminals where the speakers plugged in, so I stuck the wires in the black and red terminals and used the speaker plugs to hold them in. My brother went outside so he could confirm if anything was coming out. I turned the center on and put on the radio station, 'Radio 5' if I remember right. Chris comes running to the door, 'it's working!'. I went out to hear. It needed some volume adjustment so we could hear it loud enough, but then we were off. Our home-made roller disco. If it had got flashing coloured lights, I think we would have been in roller disco heaven! This type of event happened frequently. We didn't need to say anything to each other. As soon as that car could be heard departing, skates were already being put on. Chris would be in charge of getting the flood light on, and I would set up that evening's music selection. Often from albums, I had purchased. Roller skating skills improved and we soon started learning tricks and getting so familiar with our surroundings that skating around the pool and jumping up the sun deck and down the other side could be done with ease and speed. Many a long evening was spent skating, so much so that the next morning our calves and backs would ache. Now I know what you are thinking. How did you not get caught? Mum and Dad always told the maid, and us what time they would be expected back. We would make sure that the nightclub had closed down well before they were expected home. We also could hear the front gate being opened, and hear the car in plenty of time to shut up shop and dive into bed, roller skates and all, pretending to be fast asleep. The maid never bothered us, she was too busy doing her own thing. I cannot remember her interrupting us ever.

I had got myself a part-time job at the weekends that was earning me some cash, and the temptation to start experimenting with cigarettes was at the forefront of my mind. To keep my brother quiet, I had to keep him happy with a pack of ten Lexington. These were the cheapest, and often only purchased by coloured men who had to watch the pennies. I, on the other hand, could splash out on 'Camel Lights'. Keeping them secret from our parents was the difficult part. I found an old black cassette tape case in the garage, and we hid the fags and lighters in there. It was then strategically placed in the guttering at the front left-hand side of the house, my brother making sure it was not visible from the ground. One thing I can't understand is why the neighbours never said anything to our parents about the fact we were both night skating, in our pyjamas. dragging on fags as we did so? Our music got louder and louder, and let's face it, our taste in music was not that of people from our parent's era! So if they did hear it, and were annoyed, I would like to take the opportunity to apologize to those residents living at 48 and 52 Karee Street, and the property behind (whose number is unknown to me), circa 1981. It wasn't long before the hidden cigarettes were discovered. As far as I remember, my father had decided to clear the guttering or tend to something on the roof, and that was the end of that. Well, it was the end of keeping our smokes in the guttering anyway. I think we considered burying them in the vegetable patch that wasn't used but decided against it as the dogs may have dug them up. In the end, my cousin Timothy provided the answer whilst we were visiting him. Tim had things he needed to keep hidden away too, and the perfect place was inside his speaker cabinet. For Tim, it wasn't his smokes he had to hide, as he was old enough to enjoy a puff in front of his parents. It was his magazines. Scantily clad young ladies, some baring all apart from conveniently placed *stars*. Back then total nudity was not tolerated in magazines. The only magazine like this that you could buy on the shelves in the newsagents was 'Scope'. More articles in it than women in various stages of undress. Tim's magazines had not come from the newsagent's shelves. These were imports. If I managed to get hold of any like this my speaker cabinets were going to come in handy. In the meantime, though, I was going to park my 'Camels' in them.

One day I came home from school to find a black Datsun car parked in the back garden. I queried my father about it when he came home and he revealed that he was looking after it for a friend. It sat there for several months before I realized that somewhere there would be a set of keys. After all, my father wouldn't have taken them to work with him surely? My first look was at the key hook in the kitchen. There were several bunches on there, but some new ones I didn't recognize. Looked like they belonged to a car too. I couldn't believe it when they opened it. Struck gold at the first attempt! At first, I used to just sit in and look at the controls, see what's what, and then lock it up. A few days later I got the nerve to start it. A while later the nerve to try and drive it. My brother sat in the passenger seat. He had to be involved, as I needed him to make sure that we put it back perfectly over the grass indentations it had made from standing for so long. At first, I would drive it straight forward for a couple of feet and then reverse it back. This helped me to hone my clutch skills and get familiar with the column change gearbox. A few weeks down the line we were taking trips right up to the pool edge, having to turn hard right to do so. My attempts at reversing back to the correct spot were getting better each day. It is probably a good thing that things were nipped in the bud shortly after, as I was making plans to open the back gate and drive out to the front of the house. Who knows where I would have gone from there? One day, returning home from school, all I was presented within the back garden was four deep depressions in the grass where the tires had once stood. That was the end of my self-driving lessons, well for now at least. Soon I was going to be presented with an opportunity to take things to the next level, and all for the price of a tenner.

Hard to believe, based on the above, that I was still at primary school, be it the final year. School life was OK, but some strange crazes were going on that were attracting my brother and me. The first was Yo-yos. Not any old Yo-yos. These were sporting the colours and designs from most of the popular fizzy drink brands. It was part of some promotion where you could collect the inserts from the glass bottle versions of the drink, and swap them for the Yo-yos at your local retailer. These Yo-yos were impressive. They were well-constructed and with high-speed spindles. You could do all sorts of tricks with them and my brother pretty much learnt them all. I don't think the string left his finger until he went to bed. Everybody seemed to have one, and it was driving the teacher's barmy. The school playground was full of kids showing each other the latest tricks at break times. The other craze that was sweeping the school nation was marbles. This seemed to take over the whole playground all of a sudden. It started with little games being played between a few children and quickly escalated into a full fair-like 'prize every time' event. Alongside the building, various children set up lanes with their marble challenge. Punters rolled up to take part, obeying the strict rules set out by the provider i.e. type of marbles that could be used, the distance away, and what had to be achieved to win. There were challenges of all kinds. Knock the pyramid of marbles down to win all of them. Hit a hidden marble under the sand to win a special multi-coloured, large marble. All marbles that were thrown were kept by the provider of the challenge if they did not succeed. It was a very quick way to increase your marble collection if you set up a challenge. It wasn't long before my competitive brother was carrying around a huge sock of marbles. The challenge providers hated him, as he could usually make their challenge with a few attempts. We used to compare marble collections at the end of the day and my brother usually filled the floor of his room as he had so many. Marbles of all colours and sizes, and most of the prized ones that everybody was after. He was the king of the playground games. My days of playing break-time games soon came to an end. It would seem that I had caught the attention of one of the girls in the class. She and her friend 'Staum', sat behind me in registration class. Notes started to be passed by Staum, to the guy sitting next to me. He then passed them on to me. It turned out that my new admirer was too shy to approach me directly, and that any communication had to be performed via this convoluted route. It was odd as she sat right behind me and could have passed the notes straight to me without getting the other two involved, but I went along with this strange courting ritual and directed my responses in reverse using the same channel. I was quite excited by it all, as this girl was the best looking in the year, let alone the class, and I had never had a girl show any interest in me before. After several note exchanges indicating that we were interested in each other, an agreement was reached that we would 'go out' together. The formalities of this contract negotiation were handled by those representing us. A meeting was to be held at break-time where we would seal the deal, and progress from there. Her name was 'Elsabe Eillard', and she to me was beautiful. Long dark brown hair to her shoulders, a sparkling smile, bronzed tan skin, and twinkling eyes. So good looking even then, so it was no surprise when later in High School she started hair modelling. I knew at the time I had won the jackpot. We sat up against the school wall at break-time, finding out about each other. We were in the same class but had not talked a lot, well not to this depth anyway. Just finding out about each other's families, interests, pets, etc. The usual stuff. Elsabe's birthday was soon and I was invited to go ice-skating with her and all her select friends, and then the Saturday after she was having a pool party. I was not very outgoing back then but she won me over easily and I agreed to go to both.

The day of the ice-skating arrived and I turned up at Elsabe's house. In the days before mobile phones, you had to announce your arrival at the locked gates by shouting, which I did, and attracting some attention that I didn't want. Instead of Elsabe rushing to the gate to meet me, her two Dobermann Pinchers did. Snarling and gritting their teeth through the mesh of the gate, drooling from their lips as they looked at the meal that had arrived before them. I was petrified. Elsabe came out and started to open the gate, assuring me that 'Zeus' and 'Apollo' (yes, I know... I had to go with the names of the two Dobermanns in Magnum PI as I could remember the names of hers), were fine and weren't going to take a chunk out of me once I stepped through. She conveyed this message to them but I think it must have been lost in translation, as they both snapped at my legs as we walked towards the backdoor of the house. It turned out I was the first to arrive, the others would not be coming for a while and Elsabe's parents were not home yet either. It's almost like she planned it. After a drink in the kitchen, she took me to see her room. We sat on the bed and she looked at me, and I remember thinking to myself, 'I wonder when everybody else is going to arrive?'. It's obvious to me now that this was supposed to be an opportunity for our first kiss and cuddle, the scene had been set, and she was sitting ever closer, gazing into my eyes, but unfortunately, I was oblivious to it. Yep, been kicking myself ever since. In my defence, I was youing and fresh from the playground, dealing marbles on the markets. This was new territory for me, and I was unprepared. Anyway, the moment passed and Elsabe's mother turned up with some of her friends. We all congregated in the kitchen, where Elsabe's mother said 'OK, which one is he?'. She seemed surprised and pleased when I was pushed forward to meet her. Unlike her two dogs who were still pacing outside, awaiting the return of my white, bony flesh. The thought of ice skating didn't faze me, even though I had never done it before. I was a seasoned night-time, roller disco king, so how different could it be to that? A lot different as I was to find out. Everybody else had been many times before and took to the ice like Torville & Dean. On the other hand, there was me, who took to the ice like Bambi. Pushing away from the side, my legs going in all different directions, and my arms changing from outstretched above my head, to outstretched to the sides, to outstretched to the floor, and then back to the beginning again. It must have looked hilarious. After seeing the struggle, Elsabe took me by the hand and led me out to the centre of the rink, very slowly. By now I was bent forward, half over, my other arm to the side, legs apart, just gliding next to her. Then she left me, skated back, and told me to skate towards her. I was going to give it a go, after all, I didn't want to look like an idiot the whole afternoon. I was going to crack this, and we were going to be skating around the rink hand in hand like all the other couples there that day. So, at this point, I have to explain something sensitive, so you can get the full gravity of what is about to happen. Elsabe, although just a young girl, was endowed pretty much the same way as a young woman in her twenties would be. Developed more than her age. This was probably why not only I was attracted to her, but pretty much every boy in the year. This day she was wearing a tight sweater, looking as gorgeous as ever, and coaxing me towards her with open arms. I started well with a little push against the ice from one of my blades, forward motion-activated, and then it all went pear-shaped. It went from graceful skating to 'running on ice', to stopping and standing up, to then bending forward and propelling myself at speed in

Elsabe's general direction, where she was still waiting with open arms. Next, I lost my balance completely and lunged towards her, totally out of control, reaching out for anything available to prevent me from wiping out on the floor. In essence, reaching out and grabbing two things that were available, and looked like they were sturdy enough to prevent my collapse. It was one of those moments where time stood still, and then you realized you had kept your hands in a place they didn't belong, for far longer than the owner would have liked. There were embarrassed looks in both directions, but nothing was said apart from my very quiet 'Sorry'. I would like to apologize to Elsabe for the inappropriate placement of my hands on this occasion, especially since we had not even kissed yet. We didn't stay boyfriend and girlfriend for very long. Something I would regret as we grew up in High School together. We would end up in the same class again, still being good friends. I would even get myself into difficulty whilst trying to protect her from a bullying schoolboy a few years older than her. She grew ever more beautiful in her later teens, ever more popular, and eventually found herself another long term boyfriend.

My father was and still is the 'Entrepreneur'. I think that is what attracted him to South Africa. I am sure he would have done his research and found out about the wealth of diamonds and goldmines, the opportunities to get in on the ground floor and introduce innovative business ideas, or products to those that matter in the city. After all, Johannesburg was the 'Golden City'. A title that oozed possibilities for those seeking fame and fortune. It wasn't long before my father started networking, and built up a portfolio of associates. My brother and I started to find literature lying about. Headed paper, business cards, business magazines, etc. Something was going on, something big. It turned out my father had decided the time was right to hit the world with his ideas. The first is a regenerated toy from the 50's. The company that was to bring this toy to the masses was appropriately titled 'Golden City Enterprises'. Not only a toy company but the umbrella for several import/export opportunities, the main one being African artifacts. My father also had the ideal base from which to grow his operations. 'Jan Smuts' International Airport. As Manager of all of the retail outlets, he had contact with a manufacturing and supply chain that would come in very useful. He seemed to spend a lot of time at the airport, so much time that occasionally my brother and I had to spend the evenings there. Usually, we would go off and find quiet departure lounges where we could play on the trolleys, watch planes landing and taking off, or talk with those shop assistants who knew of us. When it got dark though, we started to feel tired and bored, wishing for it to be time to go home. We could be there until nine or ten some nights, and with having to get up early for school the next day, were eager to get to our beds. I saw a lot of African carvings, sculptures, precious stones, and sadly ivory artifacts at the airport. I also saw them at home and being stored in the garage, so putting two and two together knew that there was a money-making venture at hand here. In addition to the African artifacts, 'Golden City Enterprises' had its first product in secret development. We started to find evidence of what was being created whilst clearing the garage. First, we found an old wooden spinning top. Next lots of concept drawings, packaging, and advertising media for Expos. If I remember correctly we quizzed our father about these items, at which point he divulged the operation and enlisted our help. The product in development was called the 'Q-Top'. The 'Q' stood for 'Quiz', as you didn't know what it was going to do next. This was a 20th-century version of the old wooden spinning top from my father's youth. There was a handmade, clear, solid prototype that my father demonstrated. Even at the weight it held, my brother could do tricks with it and was quickly given the go-ahead to become fluent in these tricks for demonstration at toy fairs to come. In the meantime, a deal was being made with a manufacturer to produce the lightweight, plastic injection moulded versions for the market. These couldn't come quick enough, as I had already damaged the expensive prototype, rendering it useless, in a tricky manoeuvrer that had gone wrong!

One weekend my father took my brother and me to see the manufacturing operation. On some old industrial estate somewhere on the outskirts of Johannesburg, was a factory spitting these tops out. Those with the skills had produced the prototype and then tooled the mold to create them by the hundreds. My brother and I grabbed a couple of these for testing. It had been said all along that they were virtually indestructible, and that sounded like a challenge we should rise to. It was very surprising to find that these things could not be broken. You could stand on them, stamp on them, crush them, throw them in the air to land on a hard surface, throw them against a wall or hard floor. Nothing. Not a scratch. The challenge had to be taken to a wider audience i.e. our school friends, and that is what we did. Trying to drum up future customers by showing them the sheer magnificence of this product. It impressed. Mostly by the ability to knock off any attempt to destroy it, but also by what it could do. As young as I was, I distinctly remember thinking that this was going to be the next playground craze, replacing the yo-yos and marbles currently occupying everyone's time. There were supplies of these packaged in white boxes stacked in the garage. These were ready for toy expos, but we were allowed to get the 'word out there' by selling them at R3.75c. One evening we overheard conversations about the top. It seemed there was a design flaw with the point. It had been made of nylon but was proving to wear out quicker than was expected, after heavy use on hard surfaces. After a short period, we started to see 'Version 2' of the top appear with a replacement brass end, that was going to last for ages. It was this version that my brother and I would try and sell at the school fetes being held at the time. Tee shirts were made, which my brother and I wore for marketing purposes, but one evening a visitor turned up at home wearing one of these tee shirts, and none of us expected him to butt in on the show! As I said previously, my father was a hard worker and would often come home late in the evening. One evening my mother was in bed, and my brother and I were talking to her to keep her company until my father returned home. We heard the front door being opened with keys, and my mother shouted out 'Who is that?', to which my father replied, 'It's us...'. 'Who is us?' my mother bellowed out. After a reply of 'Come and see!', my brother and I rushed to the front door. There, standing around four feet tall, on top of a green box, was the scariest-looking clown you have ever seen. The clown of children's nightmares. Think of the clown that hides under the young boy's bed in the 'Poltergeist' movie. That kind of scary. Trailing behind the green box was an electrical plug. The clown itself was wearing one of the Q-Top tee-shirts. By now my mother had arrived to see it, and so my father plugged it in so we could witness the wondrous marketing tool, that he was convinced was going to get the children flocking towards the toy stall, and not running away from it screaming. There was the whir of some sort of compressor starting up, followed by the continuous noise of a small jet engine beneath the clown, and then the moment we had been waiting for. The clown started to jump up and down in quick succession, half a dozen times or more, before relaxing for a small period, probably to gather up more steam from below before setting off again. It's arms flayed about as it did so, bringing it even closer to life than I wanted. Enough was enough and my mother asked for it to be shut off. Then it was off to bed for everybody. What I didn't realize was that this monstrosity was going to be spending the night in the hallway. Not just that night either. Every night. Every night until its rental period had run out, which seemed a long time. I don't think I got out for a wee all night. The thing freaked me out, and to be honest, I was glad to see the back of it. At this point, I would like to apologize on my father's behalf to all the children who laid eyes on it at toy fairs, expos, and school fetes, circa 1982, and as a result, have been scarred for life. I didn't get the opportunity to attend the toy fairs and expos that my brother and father went to at weekends as I had a weekend job. This took me out of play on

Friday afternoons, all day Saturdays, and sometimes Sundays as well. I was around 12 and a half, coming on 13 when I started. My father had been instrumental in getting me the job, and it was a job I turned up for without fail for three and a half years until it ended quite abruptly.

My brother and I never knew we had an 'Uncle Frank'. We had never heard of him before. He had never been to any family gatherings and wasn't on the current Christmas list as far as we knew, and yet our father was talking about him like he had been part of the family for years. We were both very suspicious, as we had been caught out before by miraculously appearing family members our father had thought up. There was the time we were told about our Irish Uncle Shamus McFlaherty. So hooked by that one we were, that we told teachers at school for years that we were English, but quarter German with a dash of Irish thrown in. Our father was a bit of a joker on the quiet, and had spun many yarns, including being the author of the book 'The Wooden Horse'. Of course, I took great pride in telling my English teacher this but was shocked to discover that the man with the same name as my father looked entirely different on the rear cover of the version in our school library. It was based on these previous experiences, that my brother and I took 'Uncle Franks' existence with a pinch of salt. It was announced that we were all going to Uncle Franks' farm, whose location was secret, and that Uncle Frank had said to bring our swimming trunks as he had a pool. I of course pictured a nice outbuilding containing a heated pool, with a sun deck, spa, and Italian tiling surrounding it. After all, these farmers had loads of land and made loads of money. It was quite a journey there, being once again in the middle of nowhere, with very little population in the surrounding area. It was revealed to us that Uncle Frank was a 'business associate'. What sort we didn't know, but by the abundance of African Artefacts around I guessed that he was supplying them to the shops my father managed at the airport. It was a working farm with livestock, which was evident from the cows and sheep on the land, but there was some sort of manufacturing operation going on as well, producing wooden, and stone, sculptures, jewellery, and ornaments. Frank was a typical South African farmer, living on his huge estate with his wife and two young boys. Acres and acres of land that must have been worth millions. I couldn't wait to see the pool we had been told about. We left the women back at the ranch and headed off with towels underarm. Frank and his two little boys came along as well. We passed the buildings surrounding the farmhouse. No, it wasn't in there then. Went out into the fields. Ahhhh, he has built it well away from the farm, so it's more peaceful. Good plan. We started walking along the hedgerow of another field after climbing a cattle gate. Something is up. I questioned the whereabouts of the pool, and both my father and Frank were smiling, telling us it wasn't far. That sinking feeling started to come across me as I realized I had been swindled again. I wasn't going to come originally, and the pool promise had swung it for me in the end. I shouldn't have bothered. We pulled up alongside a round cattle watering trough, and the two young boys climbed in. 'You what?', I exclaimed. 'This is the pool?'. The young boys were enjoying themselves, splashing around in the Zambezi swamp water that this so-called 'pool' contained. There was no way either I or my brother were getting in there. That part of the trip was very disappointing but the next day or so would make up for it.

After their swim, we went back to the house for lunch and then were taken to Frank's armoury. Quite a large building, with a very secure door not far from the farmhouse. Once inside you could not believe what you saw. There were enough guns and ammunition in there to weaponize a small army. Every type you could imagine, rifles, handguns, and automatic weapons, some in specialist cabinets, and some in even more secure safes. Back in Johannesburg, there was a gun culture. Every citizen, if they were white, could at age sixteen carry a weapon or four, having a license stamped into their 'Book of Life'. This was a green book of

ID, that carried details of your birthplace, photo, marriage license, vehicle license, and of course gun license. I knew of a lot of people that had guns, my cousins for example, but I had never seen anything on this scale. This guy's collection would have made some American gun enthusiasts weak at the knees. Later on the next day, I was going to get my first introduction to weapons, but for now, the trip to the armoury was just to supply his two young boys, and my brother and me with air rifles and enough ammo to keep us happy for the afternoon. Outside the armoury were targets for us to practice on before we went out onto the farmland to find objects to fire at. These were good air rifles, with good sights. You could hit anything with them. Even though the two young boys were half our age, they were seasoned gun handlers and showed us up by executing the perfect shot nearly every time. We took the opportunity to shoot down anything we could lay our hands on. Using up all the ammo we returned to the farmhouse and swapped the rifles for fishing rods. In the rivers passing through the farm, we had several bites that afternoon, but no catch. Maybe we should have kept the rifles and shot the fish out of the water. That evening it was BBQ time. This was my favourite part of the trip. Give me dead meat, charred within an inch of its life back then, and I was a happy teenager. Franks BBQ area was in an enclosure, with a huge firepit in the wall. We ate, and drank, and Uncle Frank entertained with songs on his guitar. Not the sort of day or evening we City boys were used to, but we enjoyed it. Later that evening, drinking, for the parents, continued on the veranda outside the farmhouse. We boys sat around talking. Then Uncle Frank had an idea. He emptied his side-arm of ammo and gave the pistol to his oldest lad. The youngest had a toy pistol. He then asked them to give a display of the 'Buddy' system to the rest of us. The 'Buddy' system consisted of one gun-toting person running forward at a diagonal, whilst covering fire was provided by the second person. Then the covering person would break forward in a diagonal, whilst the other issued covering fire, and so on until they reached their target. Now this was impressive enough to watch when executed by a five and six-year-old, but throw in a few 'Mission Impossible', or 'James Bond' forward rolls at suitable points, and you could see this system had been taught to these guys from an early age. My brother and I even had a go and picked it up quite quickly, dispensing with the 'peeooww' sound effects that the younger two were adding in. In around twelve years these two were going to walk their basic training in the army.

The next day my father and I were going to have an introduction to some further firearms, this time a lot more powerful. We were going to go guinea fowl hunting in some of the fields later on, but first I had to get to grips with a Winchester pump-action shotgun. Before that Franks eldest son showed my father how to handle a Luger. I didn't have a go, instead Frank told me I was going to have two shots with the shotgun before we headed out to the fields. He explained to me that it gave a hell of a kick, and said that first I would be firing it at waist height. Then if I handled that it would be against my shoulder at head height. I had never shot anything like this before, and so didn't know what to expect. Waist height went OK, and the head height against my shoulder too, Frank explained that I had to push the rifle butt hard against my right shoulder and squeeze the trigger slowly. As all had gone well and I had proved myself, the rifle was emptied of cartridges, and stowed in the open-top wagon. Then we were off. Off onto other areas of Frank's land far out from the farm. The aim was to get a guinea fowl or two for supper, and I was going to be the one to get them. Frank drove us near to a wheat field that he said had loads of guinea fowl nesting in the middle. I was to arm the gun and walk into the field slowly, and quietly. Once they saw me near the middle, the rest would scare the guinea fowl out. I was to track one of them as it flew out and give it both barrels. Dinner would be served. I got to my position and waited nervously for the commotion to start. Gun at the ready and pointed towards the sky, with the butt firmly against my shoulder. I wasn't going to risk getting hurt like Frank said I would if I didn't hold the gun properly. I waited and waited. Nothing. Waited some more. Still nothing. After about fifteen minutes I decided to go and see what the delay was, first cocking the gun open, and carrying it over my arm with the barrel pointing downwards. When I got back out of the field, they said the guinea fowl was not here any more, and so they waited for me to come out. My first proper hunting experience didn't get off to a good start. We had better luck with the 2.2 calibre, knocking Meerkats off as they poked their heads up out of their holes. Meerkats in South Africa spread Rabies, and it was essential to cull them to stop the spread to livestock. We had dinner before leaving that night, although there was a distinct lack of meat present. It had been a good weekend, where we had got to take part in several things we wouldn't normally get the chance to do. I was glad I went in the end, and when we had the chance to go again, I didn't hesitate to join the rest of the family.

The roller-skating and pool area at Karee Street, Kempton Park

Family & friends performing harvey-wallbangers into the pool in Karee Street, Kempton Park

Me in my bedroom at Karee Street playing an electronic game

Evening at Uncle Franks farm complete with firepit, whiskey and song

Uncle Frank and Dad doing some woodcutting

TALES FROM THE GOLDEN CITY

The huge expanse of Uncle Franks farmland

One of Uncle Franks sons - A highly trained South African army operative in the making

CHAPTER 5 - 'THE LITTLE CHEF'

If you heard the term 'Little Chef', your mind would immediately turn to the motorway services restaurant, that served up hot meals to order for many years, to tired and hungry holidaymakers and travellers. Either that or you were thinking of Ronnie Corbett in the kitchen, making a soufflé for one of his dinner parties. The 'Little Chef' I worked for in South Africa was quite different. It could not make its mind up what it was. Takeaway, cafe, bakery, or supermarket. That is why the signage outside said 'Welcome to the Little Chef Bakery & Food-centre'. It started as a single store and then grew to two more, one outside of town, and the other who knows where? Owned and run by three Armenian brothers, Myron, Steve, and Harry. Steve was the youngest brother, with Myron next and then Harry the oldest. Myron was a late 50's, balding, greyed-haired man with large dark glasses, and the boss at my store. Steve was a slightly younger, skinnier ex-boxer, who fancied his chances with the ladies, and the young girls. Harry, or 'grandpa' as we used to affectionately call him, was an older-looking version of Myron and only spoke through his cigar, which never left his mouth. If Harry said anything, you would usually only pick up on one or two words from the sentence, the rest were undecipherable as they left his vocal cords and tried to emanate from his mouth, impeded by the tightly wrapped tobacco leaves of his Havana.

My first remit at The Chef was to work behind the takeaway counter. At age 12 and a half I was already a dab hand in the kitchen, so it didn't take me long to get to grips with frying the fish, chips, frankfurters, Vienna, and Russian sausages that were on offer. Aside from that, you had to make toasted sandwiches to order, including the rarely ordered 'Dagwood'. This was a monstrosity of a toasted sandwich. So big it needed a box of its own. Between the toasted slices of bread lay everything you could get your hands on. A fresh beef pattie (grilled to order), lettuce, tomato, cheese, fried egg, mushrooms, onions, sausage, ham, pickles and sauce. I used to add in anything extra I could find in the fridges that were suited to a place in such a savoury feast. You could not quote any prices for any of the items from the takeaway counter, as there were none advertised. Customers took their takeaway over to the till, where Myron would instantly decide on today's price. If you had to shout over and ask a price for a customer, he would reply almost instantly without any delay, giving the perception of a fixed price, but we always knew it fluctuated with as much frequency as the FTSE 100. The price was based on what he thought he could get away with charging.

Behind the takeaway counter for the week and weekends were two young black guys who became good friends of mine. Johannes, and Gope (not his real name but the name was given to him by the other employees). These guys worked hard. All week and long hours for a pittance of pay. This is how it worked in South Africa. Exploit the black man for the white man's gains. These guys had families back in the townships, and god only knows how they used to survive. Having to be at work for opening at 5:30 am meant they had to leave their township, however far away they were, at ridiculous times in the morning. Travelling to work by whatever means was available, often walking huge distances. They would often get back home very late at night or opt to stay in the crowded underground barracks that Myron had supplied for the live-in bakers. Work was often mixed with laughs, and we all got on well. Never a cruel word said, and never any falling out. These guys also had your back and would intervene if a black customer came in stinking of booze and looking for trouble. Considering the life these guys were living, and how little time they would have been spending with their families, they always wore a smile and were jolly and full of life, brightening your day if you had been dealt a bad one. Johannes especially, was always singing songs in his native tongue, and dancing, but aspired to be a musician or artist. One time he asked for my opinion on his song that was going to be a hit once he got it out there. I can still remember the two of them reciting it. 'Come on brother, come on sister, we make the world'. 'Too many people suffer, so come on brother, come on sister we make the world'. It came accompanied by a dance routine that I too had to pass judgment on. It wasn't going to get an 'It's a yes from me' on the X-Factor, but I gave them the thumbs up and said how I was looking forward to buying the 7-inch.

I must have been doing quite well behind the counter, improving quality and the like because one evening my mother and father called me and showed me the local newspaper. Inside was a full-page advert for the Little Chef, along with caricatures of all the main staff. There were Myron and his brothers, Jeannine who worked behind the tills, Simon who was head baker, and low and behold me! A very English-looking gentleman dressed in top hat and tails, with a monocle, and alongside the words 'Carl an Englishman who knows his fish and chips'. I was famous! My parents sent my other Grandparents who were still in England the newspaper cutting. I believe my Grandmother still has it to this day. Very soon I was asked if there were any mates I had who fancied a part-time job as well. I had a Scottish friend at school called Alan Bradley, and so I asked him. He joined for a short while until he got fed up with missing out on his social life. He also worked behind the takeaway counter, continuing there when I was promoted to the tills. Alan was a small kid, at school, he was called 'Wee Alan Bradley'. His best mate was of similar height and stature but worked out at the gym a lot. The girls aptly named him 'Popeye'. So, it wasn't surprising when Johannes and Co. decided that Alan would be referred to as 'Small Boy'. From my position at the tills, I often heard the giggling as Johannes and Gope had cornered Alan and had him down on the floor for a tickling. Out the back was the bakery area, Managed by Simon. Simon and the other bakers made sure there was a constant flow of fresh bread rolls coming from the oven for most of the day. No sooner had they come out of the oven, than people were bagging them in large brown paper bags, burning themselves in the process. The queue waited for the next batch. They were quality rolls if not a bit on the sweet side. When bagged hot, they steamed themselves until they were almost flat. All manner of other bread was baked alongside. In a long fridge on the other side of the room were the cakes. The bottom shelf was full of individual cakes, eclairs, and the like. The middle tier carries the small-sized round cakes, with the largest gateaus at the top. Some had chocolate 'hundreds and thousands' covering their circumference, and others had toasted almonds. Aside from these Simon used to take his hand to speciality Birthday cakes, and the occasional Wedding cake.

The Little Chef was the first store within the entrance to a shopping mall that housed a 'Pick & Pay' supermarket, chemist, liquor, and various other independent stores. As the Chef was housed on one of the internal corners, it had glass windows all the way around with cabinets on the inside. These were the display for every kind of coloured individual meringue you could imagine, along with some baklava and other Armenian and Greek sweet pastries. If you fancied a sweet treat this was the place to come, and most people did, making Myron and his brothers more and more money. Even though the Chef had the monopoly in the area, as far as bakery and takeaway goods went, and was raking in some serious takings, the wages for the guys working there were poor. They weren't much better for me either. I didn't realize it at the time, but it was just another option of cheap labour for Myron to exploit. My hours were about 3:00 pm to 6:30 pm on a Friday, and then all day Saturday 7:30 am to 6:30 pm. For that, I got R18.00 initially, which was about three or four quid. Over the three and a half years I was there, it only went up by a couple of Rand. I used to get lunch on a Saturday, being able to have something from the takeaway. It was very much like being at school though as if you hadn't finished what you had taken, you had to show Myron your plate so he could decide to take it out of your wages or not.

I used to keep some of my wages and give some to my mother to put in a savings account for me. I had a couple of things I wanted, and not being good at saving I needed help to stop me from spending it all. My first purchase was a new racing bike. I needed this to make the trip from school, back home, and then onto the Chef on Fridays. It didn't take long before I had a brand new, silver 12-speed racer. Next on the list was a music centre. I had records and tapes but nothing to play them on. In the evenings I had to sit in the front room with my father's headphones on, listening to my music played at his old music centre. He would always complain it was too loud whilst he and my mother were watching the television. I needed something similar in my room so I could listen in private and not disturb them from watching their episodes of Dynasty. I had saved about R110.00 and was starting to look out for something when one evening my father came home with a music center he had found advertised. He had bought it with the money I had saved and I was pleased as punch. It was a sleek-looking center in black and silver, with a perspex lid that covered the turntable and tape deck. At the front were all of the controls as well as the radio band viewing window. There were two large speakers in wooden cases, which sounded amazing. I borrowed my father's headphones for a while when it was late so as not to disturb anyone. I hardly took them off listening late into the evening.

When I came home it would go on loud through the speakers. From that day forward, most of my money went on records. There was a good record shop in the city which I could take a train to get to. The train journey for us was simple and comfortable, the carriages being mainly empty. For the black countrymen, it was very different, especially at rush hour. The segregated trains for them were always packed to the brim, with hardly any standing room left. Imagine those pictures you see of the trains in India or Asia where the people are hanging off it from every angle, and you are not far from what they had to endure. I hate to say it but sights like these were becoming the 'norm' for me and having grown up for a few years with this segregation, I didn't question it. Much like the people on those crowded trains, I would sometimes stop at the Kentucky Fried Chicken store near the station, getting a box with two chicken pieces, a bread roll, and gravy mash. My brother would come with me in the school holidays, scraping as much change as he could from around the house, so that he too could indulge in the chicken and gravy. There wasn't one nearer to home, so we made the most of it whilst we could!

As I mentioned earlier, after a year or so Myron said he was promoting me to the till. I wouldn't have to work behind the takeaway counter any more No more going home smelling of nothing but chip fat. There were two digital tills, side by side next to Myron's desk with a counter-top in front of them. Behind was a wall of every brand of cigarette and some cigars with... yes, you guessed it... no prices. Much like everything in the store, which meant you had to memorize Myron's prices... all of them. You also had to try and second guess what prices he would charge for those items where he made them up on the spot. Now from the time the store opened, Myron worked the till. The main till person would then arrive at about 8:00 am, so he didn't have to work very long. After 6:30 pm he would again man the till until he decided to shut up shop. So for most of the day, he just sat at his desk, drinking some extremely strong, thick, mud-like

Armenian boiled coffee, smoking endless cigarettes and cigars, and reading the papers. Only lifted his head occasionally to respond to our questions of 'How much is this?'. Sometimes he would get bored and stand up for a stretch, trying to strike up a conversation about the state of the country, how the government was taxing him too much, or how much better the country would be if a certain majority of the ethnic population were not here. This transformation into a grumpy old man usually happened when he indulged too much in coffee and cigars and could end up escalating into the abuse of some of the staff if they put a foot wrong. He didn't have to do too much else. The odd cake needed boxing for a customer but that was about it. I just think the early starts and the late evenings did not agree with him. The most effort he would have endured was counting all his money each night, in his office under the ground. This is a place he went to ritually every night after he had extracted the day's takings from the tills. Sometimes I was asked to give him five minutes, and then to go down with the takings. It was a long way underground, and I often wondered why the developers of this shopping centre had bothered to create such weird underground bunkers. Myron's office wasn't the only bunker. The bakers and their girlfriends who lived on-site had several rooms in an underground complex on the other side of the Chef. It was a good staircase and a half down to the door to Myron's office. I would knock and wait to be told to go in. Once I opened the door, there would be Myron in front of you, sitting behind a huge wooden office desk, the room dimly lit by a lamp. Much like Scrooge Mc Duck, he would be there counting his collection of R10 and R20 bills on his desk, making sure that he hadn't miscounted the night before, and probably hoping that by some strange fortune, they had magically replicated overnight. I would give him the brown bag of bills to add to the collection. This is the only time you would see a smile come to his face unless we had been subject to a bad day, and the bag did not look suitably bulked. The office looked quite homely, there were a few pictures up, some desk ornaments, and other furniture around, and behind him his large wall safe. I used to wonder how much more money was in there because his desk was full. I also used to wonder if he had firearms. Most people over 18 had a handgun of sorts and given he worked early until late I assumed he would have something for protection. If he had a gun anywhere it would be there, so that he could pull it out and surprise any thieves that had asked him to open the safe. Money was everything to Myron, every cent was sacred, and you would need to watch out if you ever came between him and his first love.

On Saturday afternoons, just after lunch, Myron would go home for a bit of shut eye. Returning just before I had to go home at 6:30 pm. Sometimes he would oversleep, and I would have to phone his wife Jenny to wake him up. Jenny was from England, and I would guess in her late forties. There were times when the place was short-staffed, or when Myron believed that he could not afford to pay for staff, so he would tell Jenny she had to come in and work. Much like Myron, she would end up complaining about her feet and then have to sit down at his desk with a magazine, a fag, and a cup of tea. One Saturday Myron had gone home as normal leaving me entirely on my own, as he did often. Difficult if you needed the toilet as you were acting store Manager and till operator. Around three or four o'clock a black man stands in front of me at the tills and says to me 'Boss, can you help me? Another bad man in the fields out there has stabbed me. Please help me, boss!' He then proceeded to show me a very deep wound on the right side under his collar bone that was oozing thick dark red blood, which had stained the white shirt he was wearing. I didn't panic but told the man to sit at Myron's desk and I would call an ambulance. Johannes came over to talk to him and find out what happened, extracting more detailed information in their mother tongue. I scurried through the yellow pages looking for the number of the local hospital and rang it. 'Someone has come into our store in the shopping centre who has been stabbed', I said. After taking our address and telephone details, I asked, 'Can you send an ambulance?'. The man on the other end of the phone replied, 'Is he white?'. 'No, he is black' I replied, failing to realize the consequence of what I had just said. The man told me an ambulance would be sent straight away. I came off the phone and reassured the guy and Johannes that an ambulance was coming. In the meantime, Johannes got some tissue to hold onto the wound and we gave the guy a drink to settle his nerves. The guy must have waited for a couple of hours before he decided to leave and try and make his way back home. The ambulance never arrived. I should have known it would never have come. The hospitals were only for white people. They didn't care what happened to any black man, woman, or child back then. I would have thought, much like today, that people in the medical profession, no matter what part they played, would help another human being who needed assistance. On reflection, I was extremely naive to think that would happen in 1980s South Africa. Johannes was sad that the guy had no option but to leave and try to get to a township where he may have been able to get some medical attention. I, on the other hand, was ashamed to be white at that moment. I had let my friend Johannes and his fellow countryman down. For years this incident played on my mind. In later years I played out how I would have handled it if I had the chance to do it again. To the question 'Is he white?', I would have replied 'Yes' and then insisted that they help him when they arrived and found out he was not.

My time left on the tills alone on Saturday afternoons was short-lived. Jenny, Myron's wife, used to come and work occasionally, and it was good to have a fellow Brit to talk to, helping to pass the time. One weekend I turned up and there was a new guy behind the tills. This turned out to be Jenny's younger brother visiting from England. He would come over, stay a few months, work while he was here, and then when the heat got too much, return to England. By 'heat' I mean the authorities getting wind of the fact he was staying. You see Steven left when he was supposed to go into the army, and now and then would return for a while. I would see him three separate times in the three and half years I worked at the Chef. Somewhere in his thirties, Steven was the spitting image of his sister, apart from his gingery-blonde moustache that is. Much like his sister, he wasn't one for hard graft. The Chef was an easy option, that could fall in his lap to earn a bit of cash, without having to do too much as he was 'family'. It was nothing for Steven to grab a handful of 20-cent pieces from the till and go over to play the arcade machines at the back of the store. Nothing to pocket a few packs of Chesterfields or take a tenner from the till to fund the purchase of that evening's alcohol from the liqueur store right next to us. He would also insist on giving me a handful of 20-cent pieces now and then to play the arcade machines when it was quiet. At the time I thought this was to give me a break and keep me quiet about his arcade sessions, but I realize now it was probably to preoccupy me whilst he dipped his hands in the till a little deeper. He had seen his sister do it when Myron wasn't around, and so thought it was acceptable for other family members to earn a few perks too. I turned a blind eye, because what can you do when the boss's wife is helping herself to profits? Nothing. I knew Myron would have blown his stack if he had known though, wife or not, brother-in-law or not. One thing I did approve of was the way they treated the staff. Being from England they were well aware of the way black people were treated, and how they were exploited. To their credit, they used to give the guys two packs of fags for the price of one sometimes. Or just give them the one pack and decline the cash completely. When alone with the guys I would do similar for them to help them out. This would never have happened in the presence of Myron. If I had dropped a 1 Rand coin, whilst taking cash from a customer, and it had rolled under the counter, I would have been accused of trying to bankrupt him. This would have usually been shouted, several times along with various expletives and a mention of our Lord and Saviour. I remember dropping a bottle whilst filling the drinks fridges once. You had to balance a package of 24 small glass bottles on the side of the fridge, try to open the thick plastic with a Stanley knife, and then place the bottles one by one into the fridge whilst trying to stop the packaging from collapsing with the remaining bottles in. I had a bad afternoon and broke two bottles in two separate incidents. The torrent of abuse came in floods. Myron was spitting blood and gasping for breath whilst also trying to air his frustration at his future bankruptcy, which of course was going to be caused by me. I paid for the breakages instantly so that he had no cause to explode. On reflection, I should have left him to give himself a coronary over it. Future incidents were going to show me that despite my loyal service and hard work over the years, I didn't matter at all, wasn't trusted, and was expendable.

One year an Afrikaans girl of around twenty started working behind the tills with me. We used to get on quite well and would chat throughout the day. One Saturday evening when Myron arrived back, we did what we usually did and prepared to go home. This meant putting the day's takings in a brown bag to give to Myron for his daily ritual counting session down in the office. The girl was about to give him the takings when he got distracted by a customer and had to help them get gateaux from the display cabinet. The girl put the takings under the counter towards the back on top of some sweet boxes. We served several other customers and then left for the evening, forgetting entirely about the stash of money under the counter. I got home and then very shortly was called to the telephone by my parents. It was Myron on the phone, asking where the takings were. I told him where the girl had put them but he said there was nothing there. Panicking I told him I would cycle back down to show him. When I got there, the girl was also there. So were the police. The girl and I had to undergo an interrogation separately. I had shown exactly what we did and explained why the money was put there. Also including the fact that we were seen off after our shift forgetting that the money was still there. It would seem that we were both under suspicion. I because I had recently bought a brand new racing bike, and the girl because she was due to get married in a month or so. We were both allowed to go home, but I could tell there was something not quite right. There was probably between R500 and R1000 in that bag, yet Myron seemed unusually calm about the whole thing. Considering how he normally would be close to exploding after losing a single Rand of profit, something didn't smell right. I saw his wife Jenny a few weeks later and she spoke about the incident saying that Myron didn't suspect I had anything to do with it. Instead, he thought the girl had something to do with it. She didn't come back after the incident, and I don't know what the outcome was in the end.

My time at the Chef ended abruptly one Summer. I turned up at work as normal on a Friday, attempting to wheel my bike out to the back through the shop. The guys on the takeaway counter beckoned me over as I came through the door, stopping me from passing the tills. I went up to the counter where Johannes said, 'He has gone!'. 'Who?' I replied. 'Maglassa', he replied. 'Maglassa' was the nickname they had for Myron, and how they referred to him. When questioned about his nickname they said it was a way to describe a 'Dirty old Greek man with glasses'. Sure enough, when I glanced over towards the tills there were two new people behind the tills, and a new man standing next to Myron's desk. I approached him and explained who I was. He told me that he didn't need anyone now as his family was running the place. That was that. Three and a half years of faithful service and not even a phone call to let me know that I wouldn't be needed any more Instead, I had to suffer the embarrassment of going down there and finding it out from strangers. I said goodbye to my friends behind the takeaway counter, and rode home, upset I have to admit, choking back tears as I made my way down the road. I wasn't going to let anyone treat me like that again, but the reality was that I would work part-time at other establishments owned by Greeks, where I would still allow myself to be exploited.

My brother was very social at nine going on ten. He would disappear for hours after school, that is if he came home from school before dark. His usual haunt was a house further up the road, where he had made friends with an older Afrikaans lad 'Eckard Jansen' or 'Echie' as his mates called him. Now you may find it a little strange, but Echie was 17, considerably older than my brother Christopher, but back in 1980 Afrikaans teenagers were a lot younger than their years. This, coupled with the fact that Echie endured a strict upbringing, being protected heavily from the outside world and its influences, meant that he was of a similar maturity to my brother, and they enjoyed each other's company. Aside from that, Echie's parents had a large, top-class pool, deep enough to dive in, and my brother spent a lot of time enjoying this perk from his friendship.

Mr and Mrs Jansen were unlike most Afrikaans parents I had met. They had no ill feelings towards English immigrants and welcomed us into their home frequently. On several occasions, they would ask about how we felt about South Africa. I always told them I liked my new home, and at every opportunity would ask them to switch to Afrikaans instead of English to help me learn. I think they appreciated this and they helped to put our language correct if we struggled. Usually, both Mr & Mrs. Jansen would say to me 'Wat se je Englesman?', (what do you say Englishman?), when I came into their house. My usual reply would be 'Niks' (nothing). Not normally because I wasn't up to much, but because it was too difficult to reply about what I had been up to.

Even after being in immigrant Afrikaans classes for over a year, I was still struggling with the language. It didn't help that my current immigrant Afrikaans teacher hated me. I wasn't keen on Mrs. Venter either, although a young woman, she had a face like a smacked behind that oozed nastiness. Evil eyes and feisty too. She had a lot of time for the Zimbabwean girls in my class, but none for me and my English mate Andrew. Any excuse to get us out of her class and she would make it. One day, on the day of the school photographs, whilst we were waiting to be called, she refused to let me be photographed with her and the rest of the class. I had heard the Afrikaans kids that used to live next to us in Plunket Avenue use a certain Afrikaans word to refer to their posterior, which I believed to be an innocent word as it had come from the mouths of babes. When Mrs Venter was getting frustrated with the class and was searching for a word, and could not find the right one to use to finish her sentence 'Sit op jou.... sit op jou...' (sit on your...sit on your...). I helped and finished her sentence with the word I had heard, expecting to be praised for knowing it and using it in the correct placement. 'Gaat', I shouted out, waiting for Mrs. Venter to look at me and nod with approval, and maybe even offer a reward of a sweet from her jar. Instead, her lips uttered a torrent of abuse, first in Afrikaans and then translated for my benefit, as she could see from my face I was confused. Her face I could understand. It went bright red, and the angry eyes started to go angrier and as red as someone demon possessed. It turns out that I had said 'Sit on your asshole'. An honest mistake I thought, but not as she saw it. So I missed out on being photographed with the other members of the group that day. I do have a photograph of the class though, as I got a camera for my birthday and took my own of the group, whilst on an immigrant Afrikaans trip to the 'Voortrekker' monument. I even let Mrs. Venter be in it, so now I can look back at it and remind myself what an Afrikaans witch looked like.

In South Africa, schooling was quite different. Whereas in England you proceeded through the years uninterrupted until you eventually left school at around 16, in South Africa your migration pattern could be impeded if you failed to perform to the required standard. Before the end of every year, in primary school too, you had end-of-year exams in every subject. Coupled with your performance in mid-year exams, as well as marks for assignments and coursework throughout the year, this would finally decide whether you had achieved the grades required to move up a year. The end of the year was a stressful time for all pupils everywhere, as they collected their end-of-year report and opened it nervously. The majority were lucky, but there were the poor few who didn't make the grade and had to endure the embarrassment of re-doing the year again, whilst their friends and classmates moved upward. Fortunately for my 'Standard Five' year (the last year of primary school), I scraped through by the skin of my teeth and awaited my start at 'Norkem Park High School', just a stone's throw away. I had passed the mandatory subjects English and Afrikaans (although immigrant Afrikaans), which were instant failures, and also passed the majority of other subjects. Not History or Art though, This was a pattern that would follow me through high school, with the addition of Accountancy. In Standard Eight, I would be able to drop these subjects and change my curriculum to include subjects from the 'Natural Sciences' field of study, which would appear on my final 'Standard Nine' certificate. 'What's that? Didn't you get your Standard Ten certificate after matriculation?', I hear you ask. No, I didn't, and the reasons why are revealed later in this book.

Christmas Day at Karee Street with Nan & Grandad visiting

My fathers homemade spit roasting a suckling pig on New Years Day at Karee Street

Jumping in with a lit cigar is against Karee Street pool rules Grandad! as is still wearing your clothes!

CHAPTER 6 – NORKEM PARK HIGH SCHOOL

Remember me saying that we would hopefully be putting down roots at 50 Karee Street, and staying there for a while? No such luck, but I wasn't going to mind moving again. My mother and father had decided to have a house built on new land that was reserved for house building further down the dual carriageway (Mooifontein Road) from my new high school. We had seen architects or builders come to the house and spend a lot of time with our father and mother in the evenings, but we didn't know what it was about. One evening we took a drive out to the location and were shown the foundations and the beginning of brickwork. It was in the middle of nowhere. There were inactive streetlights around and a few other houses in the process of being built, but a lot of empty fields where other houses would eventually go. After this visit, I used to cycle down the road after school every day. Just to check on the progress and to see how my bedroom was coming on, as I had already chosen it before the walls went up! I'll be honest progress wasn't as fast as I would have liked. Some days it looked like they had not done anything at all. I'm not sure how long it took to complete, but the day eventually arrived when we could move in. It was a lovely house. Large porch and front door leading to a small hallway. From there you could go left to a sunken, second lounge which led onto a games room complete with a brick-built bar. To the right of the hallway was the main part of the house. A larger lounge and separate dining room with breakfast bar, and off the lounge, patio doors to the garden. Another hallway with an entrance to the other side of the breakfast bar and the large kitchen and laundry room. Further down the hallway were my and my brothers' bedrooms, with our bathroom and shower. At the end of the hallway was Mum and Dad's bedroom with en-suite. There was a courtyard outside the laundry room with access to the garage and maids' quarters.

Back in Karee Street, we had a pool, it was a little small and not very deep but very welcome in the summer months. Of course, the new house was without one when we moved in during the winter. It didn't seem long though before, once again a man was visiting our parents in the evening, this time to discuss pool designs. My brother and I were always listening on the periphery but didn't hear anything regarding timescales. Both of our parents didn't give anything away when asked about the pool either. It came as quite a surprise when a month or so later I returned home from school to find a huge hole dug out in the back garden. At least 25 feet long, and what looked like 6 and a half to seven feet deep in the deep end. They had started it, and we pictured it being completed in a month or so. On the second day, the walls and floor had been reinforced with iron rods, and electrics, sand filter, and pool light were all present. I was impressed at the speed these guys worked. I never saw them. By the time I returned home from school, around 2:00 pm, they had already left for the day. There was a pause for a few weeks where nothing seemed to be happening, at which point I was wondering what the Project Managers' excuse was. This was unacceptable to me. What were they doing that was more important than building my pool? I wanted it finished, even though it was only May, and it was way too cold for outdoor swimming. Fortunately, a couple of weeks later things started to move again, with the addition of the surrounding tiling, service hatches, and 'slasto' paving around the outside edge of the pool. As far as I was concerned all they needed to do now was gunite concrete it, paint it blue, fill it with water and the job would be finished. A week at the most, or so I thought. Unbeknown to me my parents had said that work could stop at this point as there was no point in completing things until just before Summer. For the next couple of months, might have even been three, I came home from school each day to check on progress, expecting to see some improvements somewhere and being very disappointed when nothing was evident. I questioned my parents at this point to find out the reasons for the delay, only to be told it was 'intentional'.

I think it was a cold, early August afternoon when my brother and I returned home from school to find the workers on site. This is what we wanted; some action. Let's get this thing finished! They were busy spraying on the 'marbelite' white coating, covering the horrible grey gunite underneath. It was beginning to look like a pool now. Whilst waiting for the coating to be completed I spoke with the foreman asking when it would be painted blue. All pools shone and sparkled blue, so it must have been the paint colour underneath the water right? Apparently, not. The white-coloured marbelite was all that was going to be put on. I can remember thinking that it was going to look awful once the water was in, and not like everybody else's pools. My parents had been talked into this white coating, probably due to cost, and I thought that was going to be a big mistake. The coating was finished and immediately the workforce started filling the pool with water from the garden tap. This was normal apparently and would take well over a day before it was filled. I had heard that some people hired the Fire Brigade to fill it up, so it could be done in an hour. My parents had opted for the garden hose approach. More delays. Like I hadn't suffered enough delays already? Most of the evening and night, as my bedroom faced the pool, I kept an eye on the filling process. The level didn't seem to move at all, and it looked like this process was going to take ages. Indeed, it did, another whole day. When my brother and I returned home from school it was still filling but had gone a little too far over the mandatory 2 to 3 mosaic tiles from the top. We turned the tap off and ran back inside to get our swimming costumes and a towel. It was still August, it was still winter, there was hardly any sign of the sun in the sky, and grey clouds covered the majority of it. We were both prepared to try out the pool but knew there would be no sunbathing afterward. We felt the water with our hands and were surprised to see that it was indeed a lot colder than other pools we had 'felt'. In my naivety, I decided that the best thing to do would be to jump in, directly off the side, so it was over and done with and our bodies would adjust to the temperature difference quickly. I went first, plunging into the pool about midway down as I wasn't sure how deep it was. It may not have been deep, just up to my chest, but it was cold. Very cold. Too cold to swim. Too cold to do anything. I don't know what happened but as soon as I was in the water, my lungs refused to work. I couldn't breathe. It was like something was pushing against my chest, and I could not draw breath in any manner. I had to get out quickly and was relieved when normal breathing resumed. Of course, I wasn't going to tell my brother it was this unbearable, oh no. As far as he was concerned it was perfectly safe if a little cold. Based on the lies I had attached to my assessment of my first dip, he promptly did the same, enduring the same panic as I did whilst gasping for breath. After his quick and hasty exit, we agreed it was a little too cold and we would wait for a few months. Maybe it would be better in October? I would like to take this opportunity to apologize to my brother, circa 1982 for not coming clean regarding one's inability to breathe, whilst submerged to chest height in the pool.

Well, October came, and it was much warmer, and the water in the pool had a chance to increase in overall temperature. There was one thing wrong though. Whilst swimming we noticed that the white marbelite coating was coming away from the walls. It got worse so our father had to call out the contractors. The diagnosis wasn't good. More disappointment ensued as they had to drain it, painstakingly chip off all of the marbelite, and then re-coat it all over again. What's more, we had to wait until it was filled up again, and of course by garden tap.

South Africa was a country of motorbikes. It was the ideal land for it. Loads of space to roam, beautiful weather, and quiet roads. Nowhere was this more apparent than at school. Once a young man had reached the age of sixteen, the world became his oyster and a lot of female attention to boot. At sixteen you were allowed to get a provisional license, after a brief theory test, and then take to the road on two wheels, as long as those wheels didn't exceed 50cc capacity. At eighteen, you could upgrade if you had taken your full test, get any size motorbike, or opt for a car. Those lads who were the eldest in the last year of high school had this privilege and the luxury of taking young women in their year off on jaunts in the evenings and at weekends. I had just over a year to go until I could get my first road bike. Some lads in my year were older and had got their first brand-new 50ccs. Time seemed to go so slowly, and I couldn't wait. I had been to some expos and also gone into the bike shops to drool over the shiny Suzuki's, and Yamaha's. These are what I had my eye on. In the range of 50cc bikes, the main contenders were those two, and of course Honda and Kawasaki. The television and radio were filled with adverts about 'Smoking them on your 'Suzi'..', or being 'on the road with your Yamaha'. The morning at school was torture. You had to stand and watch as all those who had come of age rocked up on their bikes. So many that pretty much all schools had large, secure areas allocated for motorbike parking. It seemed like further torture, as you had to watch the girls swoon over every guy who was carrying a motorbike helmet around class after class. It would be a year and then some before I would be able to get similar attention. A surprise came along though coming up to my fifteenth birthday. My parents had noted the torture that I was going through and seen the endless occasions where my dribble had touched the floor whilst admiring any bike that I laid eyes on. One evening my father took me out in an open-backed truck, stating that we were going to look at a motorbike he had seen advertised. This was going to be the best birthday present ever. We turned up at a guy's house who was selling a 1976 Honda CR125 off-road scrambler. Yep, that's right. No piddly 50cc nonsense for me. Straight in with the big boys at 125cc level. It was dark but we got an idea of the general condition, and it started the first time. It sounded a lot louder than I expected but I wasn't worried about that. It turned out that the majority of the exhaust pipe was missing. All that was left was a cut-off just behind the right footrest. The section that rose from there, and then went along the rear mudguard to the silencer was all gone. Everything else seemed OK, and I pictured being able to clean it up nicely. It ran on a 20:1 mixture of petrol and two-stroke oil, and the guy advised on how best to mix that up in an old pool chlorine bottle. My father paid for it and we loaded it up on the wagon and headed home. It would be too late in the evening to ride it off-road somewhere, and I was advised to wait until the weekend when my father would help me. Yeah right. Like that is going to happen.

The next day after school I rushed home quicker than I ever have. I had spent most of the day showing my mates the manual that the guy had given us with the bike, and they were already making plans to come over after school to have a ride. A stone's throw from my house was Tembisa, one of the main black townships. Before that, there was a stretch of no more than 500 yards of dual carriageway. In the distance, just over the border so to speak, there was a quarry of sorts, which I could hear was already being used by other off-road motorcyclists. The border crossing consisted of a six-foot or so mound or wall of earth, with a pathway made by motorbikes to get over. It was blind, so you had to close your eyes and go for it if you couldn't hear anything. A mile up to the left from there, on the white side of the border, was a motor-cross track that had been carved out with a circuit, camel jumps, and wild turns by other off-road enthusiasts. Just simply loads of wasteland, probably government-owned, for you to explore, and I was going to!. I think I must have sped through the house like the Tasmanian Devil that afternoon, changing quickly into rugged jeans, boots, and a jacket. The bike had no keys. It was just a kick-starter, with an engine kill switch. I wouldn't have to worry about fuel as it was fully laden with it. The night previously we had parked it in the pool area for safekeeping. What I hadn't noticed was that my father had added a padlock to the gate, so it was impossible to get the bike out. I searched through all the keys I could find, on the key rack, in all the drawers and cupboards. Nothing fitted. This called for desperate measures, and as they say in South Africa 'A Boer maak a plan', or 'A Boer makes a plan'. This Boer had come up with his plan to save the day. It was going to be risky, but I was confident I could pull it off. The plan involved trying to lift the bike into the front room via the patio doors, wheeling it through the front room, and then very cautiously negotiating the tight squeeze around the hallway corner, with a final and further tight squeeze through the front door. This coupled with having to do it in reverse later at a time before my parents arrived home from work. 'You never managed it', I hear you cry. I did, and for several weeks until the correct key was identified for that garden gate.

I had been given a second-hand helmet by the guy we bought the bike from, so I was all set. First off I used to walk the bike down the carriageway until I reached the wasteland. There were often a lot of police cars about, mostly chasing black men who were heading towards Tembisa. I have no idea why. Often they would be put in the back of the police truck and taken away, presumably for not having the correct papers. Once I was off-road, I turned on the petrol tap, kicked it until it started, and then road up the hill towards the border crossing. A quick listen to see if anything was coming the other way, and then up and over, which was quite daunting due to the height and steep angle. Then I was off in the direction of the quarry. The bike was loud. Very loud and not surprising due to the lack of an exhaust pipe. It was just a single section of a foot and a half coming off the cylinder. I didn't realize at the time but was informed on several occasions by my brother and the maid, that you could hear me all the time but could not see me. The sound from this motorbike transcended time and space and could be heard when the source was miles away. The quarry was an excellent place to scramble around, and I did it constantly for hours when I was out. The bike though used a lot of fuel, and I had to come up with a way of transporting additional fuel with me. My refuelling station was mainly based in our garage. A series of 21 milk bottles alongside the garage wall. One filled with two-stroke oil, the rest with petrol. This would be poured into an old pool chlorine bottle, mixed gently, and then used to fill the tank of the bike. I would then estimate how much two-stroke oil to put in the chlorine bottle to perform a further mix. A mile or so up the road was a petrol station, and there was no way I was going to push the bike up the dual carriageway in the heat, so I made a dash for it on the bike, got the petrol station attendant to fill the chlorine bottle, paid up and then dashed straight back to the quarry. It was a very quiet area, and I think if I had been unfortunate and got caught, it would have been a rap on the knuckles at the very most. I carried the bottle inside my jacket which I tucked into my jeans at first but soon got a rucksack to make transport easier. I could leave the chlorine bottle in sight, whilst I raced around the quarry, and take it with me when I ventured further out. I have very fond memories of racing that bike around. I also have fond memories of making a new head gasket out of cardboard and fitting it under my grandfather's instruction. Parts were hard to come by, even though I had money so when the throttle cable started to break at the throttle end, I had to come up with quick and ingenious ways of soldering on new parts to make it work again. I suffered a puncture in the rear tire once and had to wait weeks whilst the mechanics at my father's work sorted it for me, but apart from that the bike served me well for the next year or so until I could get on the road and 'smoke them on my Suzi..'.

When it rained in South Africa, it rained. I witnessed roads turn to rivers in minutes and then dry up an hour or so later like it never happened. It was only supposed to rain in Summer. In Winter there was not supposed to be a cloud in the sky at all, and so no chance of a sudden and treacherous downpour. It was this rule that allowed kids of my age to indulge in a certain pastime, without fear of drowning. Reports were always coming in of children drowning whilst investigating storm drains during the wrong season, but this did not stop us from doing it. We were doing it at the right time of year, and there was nothing that could go wrong, or so we thought. A friend of mine was a seasoned storm drain investigator. A pastime where you would navigate yourself through the maze of underground tunnels until you reached the point where the pipe shrunk down in size, so you could no longer go any further. The entrance to the storm drains was usually on waste ground, with a small water outlet, stream, or river beyond it. It was covered in iron bars, which were insufficiently close enough together to prevent thin children from getting through. I was in a group of four that day. My friend had done the pipe to the length several times, knew the route well, and assured us under his guidance that we would make it there and back. Before we entered, we checked the sky one last time. Completely blue from horizon to horizon, not a cloud in sight. No sign of anyone else around. It was just us in the vicinity. Our lighting for the trek was not torch-based. Instead, we opted for candles, placed in coconut halves. Our pockets are packed with lighters and backup matches. Even though we were in our teens, you still had to make your way through the tunnel 'ducked' down or you would hit your head. We used to jog at quite a pace, as it was a long way to the end, and if you misjudged your head height, you would hit the pipe joins at junctions hard, and it hurt like hell. It was quite a long way, and we all had to remember the direction we had gone at the two junctions we encountered along the way, so as not to get lost on the way back. The candles went out a few times and had to be re-lit along the way, but they always did, showing that there was plenty of ventilation. I would say at a pace we had taken 2 to 3 minutes before we reached the end., A small clearing where you could stand, where smaller pipes, about 12 inches or so in diameter, fed in from various locations. We decided to stay for a few minutes to rest before the trek back when suddenly everybody's candles went out. Repeated attempts to light them failed. Then panic stepped in as we all started to feel difficulty in breathing. You could taste smoke in the air, and it started to fill the space quickly. I don't think anyone suggested that we should get out of there, they didn't need to. We all started running as fast as we could in a bent position back towards the entrance. You only tried to take a breath once, and then didn't bother again. The air was toxic with smoke and burning, and it hurt your lungs. It was just a case of leg it as fast as you could, trying to see where you were going and holding your breath. Following the sound of the rapid footsteps in front of you as they echoed on the pipe. Adrenalin certainly kicked in and took over me that day. I don't know how I managed to hold my breath for that long, whilst running my heart out. I could not tell you how long it took either. All I remember is the relief when I turned a corner and saw the light coming from the end of the tunnel. As you approached it, you could immediately see what the cause of all the smoke was, and what nearly caused our suffocation. Someone or some group had lit a fire at the entrance, using dried grass, twigs, and small pieces of wood. Somebody had seen us go in and had decided to teach us a lesson. I was last to get to the end, launching myself through those bars so I could take a beautiful, deep breath of fresh air and revive myself. We all had to sit on top of the pipe for five minutes or so to regain our composure, as we had all thought it was going to be curtains. There was a lesson learned that day. It doesn't have to be Summer and raining cats and dogs for you to get killed in a storm drain.

Every year, Johannesburg puts on its biggest show. The 'Rand' show was a huge event, where every company could showcase their products, every radio station, every housebuilder, every pool manufacturer, every car dealer, every food company, every everything. You name it and it was there, with lots of entertainment options for the family too. We didn't go every year, but on the years we did, I made sure the route through this Goliath event included areas I wanted to see. Any motorbike dealers, and of course the 'pee-wee' 50cc racing motorbikes, which you could throw around a small hay bail enclosed race track, with three or four other participants. I was also interested in swimming pool manufacturers. Even though we had a pool, I was extremely interested in the many automatic swimming pool cleaners that were available. I was the main person who had to clean our pools, taking care of balancing acid and chlorine levels to keep them sparkling, which involved a small chemistry set and some tablets. Also, having to painstakingly clean the bottom with a brush on a long pole which you had to hook up to the filtration system. It used to take ages, as you could not move the brush any more than an inch a second, otherwise, the silt at the bottom would just lift and mix into the pool, rather than get sucked up and transited to the sand filter. It wasn't a job that I looked forward to. On the show this particular year was something I had my eye on, having seen it on television and hearing about it on the radio. The 'Kreepy Krawley', was the elite of automatic pool cleaners, and the demonstration of it that I watched convinced me even more that we had to have one. It was an alien-looking piece of kit. A 14-inch in diameter rubber disc, with a plastic housing containing moving counterweights, and attachment for the hose to the filtration system. The amazing thing about this cleaner was that it was autonomous, being powered entirely by the suction through the filtration system. It made a light 'phut, phut, phut' sound as it moved through the pool, sucking up all silt. It would climb the walls of the pool right up to the mosaics, and then fall to the bottom of the pool, going off in another direction. The manufacturers stated that it would cover the entire surface of the pool in around 24 hours, stopping or starting when the timer for the filtration system kicked on or off. It even collected debris from the surface as well. Safe to have in the pool whilst you are swimming too. It wasn't long after our new pool was built that my father purchased one, and my days of pool cleaning were over, apart from the weekly chemical analysis that is. It even came with a gift. Two inflatable pool horses, a ball, and two ringed nets for either end. My brother and I had a lot of fun with those, once we had mastered the skill of staying on them. Apart from the interest in the pool equipment, and the motorbikes, I also managed to get the autograph of two American stars that were visiting South Africa that year. For many months I had been watching one of the best English-speaking television shows that were available on SABC. 'WKRP and Cincinnati', was an American sitcom about a struggling Cincinnati radio station. Starring Howard Hesseman, and Tim Reid as 'Venus Fly-trap', it was one of my favourite shows at the time. I managed to meet them and get a signed autograph picture from both of them, at one of the radio station stands. It was the first time I had ever seen someone famous and something I will never forget.

I didn't have many friends at Norkem Park High. Those that you thought were your friends soon turned against you when the going got tough. I had it particularly tough, as I was a constant target for a guy in my year. He was three years older than me as he had failed several times. Unluckily for me, he started passing when I started high school and followed me up as far as Standard eight before I left the school. John O'Connor was from England and was having a hard time at home. The only way he could deal with it was to pass on the punishment his father laid out to him, back to us at school. Some of us got more than our fair share. He worked out at the gym regularly and was smoking and sniffing all kinds of substances. This made him very unstable, and the wrong word or look in his direction could end up being brutally punished. Sometimes it didn't even take that. I used to dread going to school every single day. You would be waiting outside of registration class and see his bus arrive. Then you watched as he approached, wondering what sort of mood he was in, and whether you would be on the receiving end of his size 10 'Doc Martins' or a fist. John used to perform a special attack move on his victims sometimes, which involved a scissor kick in the air, similar to what the 'Karate Kid' used to knock his victims out, which was swiftly followed by a punch to the chest, face or arm, accompanied by a shout of 'Qua!'. Any retaliation of any kind, whether verbal or physical, would be a big mistake. Sometimes the guy would completely lose it when the teacher had left us alone in class. He had no scruples, dishing out abuse to boys and girls in the class. I saw him once after he had stepped over the mark with an older guy outside of school. He came in the next day looking like he had taken a thrashing from Mike Tyson, with black eyes, cuts, bruises, you name it. You soon learned that you did what John wanted, whether it be parting with cash, your lunch, or your dignity. One of his favourite things to do was go through everyone's bags stealing their lunch, whilst they were not looking. This used to cheese me off something chronic, especially If I had gone to town with my lunch that day. I was talking to a couple of the other guys in my class and they told me about how they were dealing with it. They both stated that they brought in a 'decoy lunch' for John to find in their bags, keeping their proper sandwiches and crisps in their inside blazer pockets. This sounded like a great idea as I was getting fed up with going hungry all day. I put the same plan into action the very next day. I would give John plain peanut butter sandwiches, usually on the doorsteps from the bread. I would have my signature polony and Mrs. H. S. Balls peach chutney in my inside pocket. It worked like a charm. Well for a while. John eventually noticed that the standard of sandwich making took a nose dive pretty much across the entire class. He wasn't fond of peanut butter and started to question why everyone else had taken such a liking to it. We soon got frisked and then it was game over. The only thing to do then was bring nothing in and bring money to get something from the tuck shop. When you did, you scarpered and hid, devouring whatever it was as fast as you could, risking heartburn or choking. This was short-lived as well as John and his mate from another class would wait around corners to surprise you with a citizens' arrest and confiscation of whatever delicacy you had purchased. I say delicacy but it was mainly burgers, hot dogs, or pasties, absolutely no sign of a Vetkoek.

The day I found we were moving again; it was more welcome than any other move we had made. I couldn't wait to escape this school and one pupil in particular. Unfortunately for me, I have a memory like an elephant, as you can tell by this book and my accurate accounts of my life forty or so years ago. I have been in touch with a couple of school associates from this time in the last 20 years, having found them via various social media networks. John was one of them. Now living in Australia with his family, he has absolutely no recollection of any of it. I suppose I should be happy for him that he made it through whatever he was going through and is managing to live a normal life. The second pupil was Richard Scott who I located after seeing him work as a Marketing Director for a software company. Richard was always extremely good in art class, and at the time I was convinced he would do something artistic later on in life. If you search for him on the Internet now, he is a well-renowned artist in South Africa, mixing with high society and getting very large amounts of money for his unique artwork. Richard and I fell out at school in Standard Eight, the outcome of which was an after-school punch-up on the fields down the bottom of the school. I went in hard and fast but lost at the end, which arrived very quickly. Speaking with him some time ago, he too has no recollection of events. It's almost like I am the only one with a memory. I didn't end up having scraps with everyone I encountered at school. There was the odd few who were happy to enjoy school life alongside me and encouraged me to take part in extracurricular activities that I would never have dreamed of doing. Two of these 'odd few' were Dean and Johnna. From England at around the same time as me, they were joined at the hip. Dean was from the Midlands somewhere, and Johnna was a scouser. Together they formed an unlikely comedy duo, performing excerpts from UK comedies such as the 'Young Ones', or 'Russ Abbott' whenever you ran into them. Dean was tall and lanky, whereas Johnna was short and plump. It was like watching 'Little and Large'. They both had an odd diet too. At lunchtime, you could find them sitting somewhere hoarding the ten bags of crisps they had purchased from the tuck shop, and getting through them quickly before the bell went. It wasn't long before I and a couple of others used to meet up with them every break time so that we could get a recital of the latest sketch they had watched and mastered. There was the occasion when they had run out of fresh material, and we were subjected to a further rendition of 'Neil' singing 'There's a Hole in My Shoe', or acting out Rowan Atkinson's 'I am a mime... my body is my tool', from 'Not the nine o'clock news'.

Despite what you may think, I was very shy at school. A lot of the time I kept myself to myself, and it was unheard of for me to get involved in anything that involved physical exertion, except for football on the school playing fields. Dean and Johnna though embraced adventure and went on lengthy excursions, some of which were in the school holidays. It was two of these excursions that I let them talk me into doing with them. One of them which I regret, and the other, that although was hellish at the time, I look back on as a great time, with lots of laughs. That great time and those great laughs were had whilst hiking through some of the most remote areas of Southern Africa. We all go through life crossing paths with certain individuals who are a bad influence on us. I am ashamed to say that I let Dean and Johnna do just that with me. Initially, it started by purchasing an extraordinary amount of tall lager cans called 'Long Toms', sometimes a dozen apiece, and retiring to some quiet spot in the wilderness to drink them and put the world to rights. Accompanying the drinking would be smoking our favourite brand of cigarettes or partaking of some 'Zohl' if Dean and Johnna had managed to get hold of some. 'Zohl' was a seedy plant that grew out in the wild and apparently could be found flourishing by the train station. You always picked out the seeds before mixing it with your tobacco, as legend had it that it made a man infertile. The dried plant though was supposed to give a high of some sort. This was a poor man's 'Dagga', another plant-based, smokable drug that was said to have an even better high. I never tried Dagga, so could not comment, but as far as Zohl was concerned, the stuff Dean and Johnna got hold of never did anything for me. They told me tales of Saturday night's sitting inside derelict buildings where they had UFO encounters, or so they claimed. We did, however, get extremely drunk together and wandered the estates looking for items to help ourselves to. For the other two, this included finding a closed petrol station and shaking the 4-star contents out into a milk bottle, for inhalation purposes. Once again not for me. There weren't much these guys would not try, including glue at school if they were bored. The beer we would buy was 'Castle Lager', which was the strongest available and a favourite with the black men of the country. Walking through the bush you would find endless 'dumpies', a small chubby brown glass bottle that Castle would come in as well as tins. These empty 'dumpies' were ideal for one of Dean and Johnna's other pastimes, which was 'bomb' making. Not the sort of bomb that causes a fiery explosion, but more like a pressurized smoke bomb. The contents were chlorine, sugar, and water, and I am afraid I cannot be specific about the quantities, but put in together, capped, and then shaken violently. The next thing you did was run. Once left, some magical chemical reaction took place, and this would eventually end in the bottle exploding. You had a further option of making a grenade version, which was the same minus the violent shaking. This you would do seconds before you launched it forward in the air. If you had got it right, when it landed it would explode on impact, sometimes very impressively. Although Castle Lager was quite a strong beer for lads our age, it didn't satisfy Dean and Johnna's quest for the ultimate high. Instead, they would venture deep into the bush to find and barter with the owners of, the strongest brew available to man. At night, and if you knew where to go, (they did know where to go), you could stumble upon a 'Shebeen'. An illegal pub set up under a tree somewhere remote. You knew you were getting close to one, as you could see and smell the burning fire that was keeping the patrons warm. There would be black African music playing on an old boom-box, men dancing with prostitutes, and some large receptacle containing the 'home-brew' that was on offer. The most common receptacle was an old bath, which punters would dip their mugs into once they had paid the price including them in the festivities, sort of an African punch bowl if you like. Now you would think this would be a dangerous place for white South African lads to venture late in the evening, and you would be right if the wrong people were there, or if the party had got to the point where too much of the brew had been consumed, and 'Stella' wars were about to break out. On most occasions, we were welcomed, as white people had cash, and they would do everything in their power to swindle us out of what we carried. We would have to part with at least R10.00 to be allowed to leave peacefully. This amount would secure a mug each, that being a mug of the most disgusting stuff you have ever tasted. Too strong to drink and keep down. God knows what was in it, or how long it had been brewing in the hot South African sun. It was so nasty even Dean and Johnna would not drink it. In the future, these establishments would be reserved for negotiating Zohl trades, and we would stick to the Castle Long Toms, or 'Amstel' if you fancied a lighter night.

It was one evening in 1985 that my father came home with a large box under his arm. All I could see was the word 'Commodore' written on it in large font. When quizzed by my mother he revealed it was a home computer, a 'Commodore

VIC20'. Now at this time, home computers were taking off big in the UK, but in South Africa, they were only just starting to emerge. My brother and I didn't know anything about computers, or what they were capable of, but like most teenagers of the time, we would very quickly find out through experimentation. That first evening when my father agreed to get it out after dinner, got me hooked. I am not sure about my brother. We loaded and played a few games that came with it on cassette tape, and entertaining they were, but I wanted to know what made this machine tick. How were these programs written, how did you write the code to make sounds, change colours, move, and animate graphics? Little did my father know that his purchase that week would go on to inspire me to become a Software Developer later in life, and I am still enjoying designing, and writing software programs professionally today after over 30 years in the industry. This new machine had to stay in my father's wardrobe after we packed it away. We would be allowed to get it out again when my father would free up the television set in the evening. The home computers coming into the market were mostly without dedicated monitors, and so a lot used a television set for output. It was the Winter months, so I did not go motorcycle riding a lot after school, but it didn't matter, I had something new to take my interest. Once again though, I had to be underhand about it. Getting the computer out of my parents' wardrobe, setting it up, playing for a few hours, and then packing it away before they came home. I did this for about a fortnight.

One weekend I asked to get it out and borrow my parent's portable black and white so I could play in my bedroom. That computer never went back into the wardrobe again, and I hardly ever came out of my bedroom. There was a lot to learn, and without tuition of any kind it was going to be hard to decipher all of the details in the manual and learn this language called 'Basic', that the computer seemed to work from. By now I had been talking to friends at school, and we had found out that many of us had recently become users. I had a friend 'Bruce', who lived about 200 yards from me whose parents had bought him and his brother a Sinclair ZX Spectrum 48K. This was the home computer invented by Sir Clive Sinclair, which was extremely popular due to its many games, and easy-to-use keyboard. Other school chums had the Oric Atmos, Atari 800XL, or Sinclair ZX81. Everybody played games on them, but a lot like me wanted to know how to program them to do more. Bruce was already subscribed to a monthly magazine from the UK called 'Your Computer'. South Africa could get this magazine about a month behind back then. I went around to Bruce's house after school to see the ZX Spectrum in action, and also to assist in typing in the free games listings that were at the back of the magazine. There was usually a small program or game for the most popular home computers. I used to read the listing out, and Bruce used to type it in, as the ZX Spectrum keyboard interface took a while to learn. Rather than being able to type a word such as 'print', you used a small number of key combinations, e.g. Shift 'P', to produce the word as the computer program required it. I never got to grips with it, and I much preferred typing on a standard QWERTY-style keyboard, such as that built into the VIC20. The ZX Spectrum used any standard cassette player of the time to save program listings on, so we could save, and then load and continue the next day if the listing was long. The VIC20 I had at home had a dedicated Commodore cassette player, where you did not have to bother playing around with sound levels to load the digital information back into the computer. Most of the computer code I was reading to Bruce was gobbledygook to us. We didn't know how it did what it did, but we knew the answers were in there somewhere. Bruce's magazines contained listings for programs and games for the VIC20 too, so I asked if he could come round to my house so we could type one into my computer. We would take turns reading and then typing the large listings into the computer throughout a couple of days. The first listing we tried was 'Tron Light-Cycle'. Pages and pages of machine code were entered and then the final moment of truth. 'Error in line

###', or words to that effect. No matter how many times we checked the code, or tried alternatives, nothing worked. Now Bruce knew that this was sometimes the case where there had been a printing error, and usually the next month they would post an apology and a fix in the magazine. Sure enough, after a wait of a month, we were able to complete the code correctly and play 'Tron Light Cycle'. It was a bit disappointing, to say the least. An awful lot of typing to see two coloured blocks race across the screen, you control one of them with keyboard buttons to avoid smashing into the boundary walls. It did have sound though, which was a bit more impressive than the beeps of the ZX Spectrum. I started to order the magazine from the newsagent and spent many hours into the night typing in listings. The time came though when we got bored with this, and we wanted to get more creative. It was time to hit the 'Basic' manual and learn how some of these code lines worked. At first, we were doing the simple repetitive print statements, then making screen colours blink, changing font colours, and adding random aspects. Simple stuff. Then we started to work on creating large font graphics using lined-up print statements.

One evening in my bedroom, I came up with a concept for a game and started to design not only the title sequence and gameplay but also the design of the cassette tape that would contain the game. My creation was to become 'Viper Tactics', a game based on the fighters in 'Battle Star Galactica'. I didn't realize but at this moment in time, all over the world, but mainly in the UK, young teenagers like myself had got bitten by the same bug, and as young as they were, had started designing games for these home computers. Some of them would grow up and own successful computer game companies, becoming millionaires in the process. It could have very well been the same for me and Bruce, as we later formed 'Tornado Software', and worked simultaneously on the VIC20 and ZX Spectrum versions of the game. I would like to have thought that had we been back in the UK, we would have made better progress. We were very isolated in South Africa and got knowledge and information later than everyone else. What also didn't help was that both our sets of parents got itchy feet again, and moves away were on the cards for both of us. I also suffered VIC20 technical issues with hardware, that could not be resolved, meaning that I was unable to store and retrieve any code that was written. It wasn't meant to be I guess, but that didn't stop me from continuing to experiment. It may have not happened for me back in 1984, programming in my bedroom, a mile away from Tembisa, but it did happen for me back in the UK some years later. In my twenties, I took aptitude tests for programming and got excellent results. I continued to experiment with the 'Commodore Amiga' range of home computers. I moved onto PCs and ran them for my father's wholesale bakery business, finally going to college and then getting a trainee programmer position with a company producing software for the publishing world. 'Tornado Software' the computer games company, conceived all those years ago in South Africa, never made it off the ground, but 'Tornado Software Publishing Ltd', did around 1998 when I formed it so I could contract my services out to various clients such as Royal Mail, and WHSmith. It's strange how things work out. If my father had not purchased that home computer or discouraged my use of it, would I be where I am today? I think not, so I have to thank him for making that purchase all those years ago, which opened my curiosity box, and drove me towards an endless journey of discovery in the wonderful world of computing.

South Africa didn't have much to offer recording artists in the way of venues back in the '80s. If anyone famous came to do shows, they would usually do it at 'Sun City'. Just inside the border of Bophuthatswana, Sun City was the South African gambler's dream venue, as back then the practice of casino gambling was illegal under the National Party government. A more apt name for the place would have been 'Sin City'. It took about three hours to travel to Sun City from Johannesburg or Pretoria, but this didn't stop South Africans from doing it, especially if there was the opportunity to gamble, dine in style, or see their favourite artist. I had only been once before when my parents wanted to see what the place had to offer. My brother and I, way too young to gamble, were given some cash to spend on food and the arcade machines, of which there were plenty all over the complex. I can't remember finding my parents at the Craps or Roulette table, but this was obviously what they were doing, as well as having a drink and no doubt something exotic to eat in a restaurant somewhere. Usually, we were given a meeting point and a time to meet up with our father, just so he could see we hadn't been kidnapped. This was the only opportunity for my brother to extract some further cash from my father, as he went through it at some sort of pace. My brother was an arcade junky, who couldn't hear a sound from the world around him once his eyes were fixed on that screen, and his hands were stuck to buttons and joysticks. His inability to walk away from a machine he could not conquer meant that endless 20c pieces came from his pockets and were deposited in them, and over a short period. I, on the other hand, knew my limits, and if I could not master something I moved on to something I could. Once he was of age, my brother moved on to one-armed bandits, or anything with a cash payout, studying the form of the machine to such a level, that he could predict if a payout was due.

Our next visit to Sun City came as a bit of a surprise. I think my father had got hold of some Rod Stewart tickets, as we had about a day's notice that we would be going one evening. What's more, we would be going in style, as my father's boss had lent him his five-series BMW company car to take us all in. I had never been in a BMW before, and all I remember was how technically advanced the dashboard seemed, and how comfortable and quiet it was. Back then electric windows were a luxury of the elite, and also something my brother could not stop playing with. I think our parents had pre-show dinner booked, as my brother and I were given significant cash for food and entertainment, and once again set on our merry way. There would be no midway meeting arranged, we would simply meet after the concert, at the arena exit. Of course, pre-show dinner, drinks, and the event itself took many hours and didn't finish until late. My brother and I were exhausted early, not only of money but also energy and enthusiasm. We waited around an hour before the concert was due to finish by the exit. An hour that seemed to take a day. When they finally came out, late I hasten to add, they looked like they had a good time. A special guest even made an appearance with Rod. Elton John was there too, so they had a surprise at the concert. We got back very early in the morning the next day, and so with a little persuasion had a day off from school to recover. I would only visit Sun City once again, and that would be with a mate from school. His father just said to us one afternoon 'F*ckit, let's go to Sun City. I've got some cash burning a hole in my pocket'. I went home to clear it with the parents, and a little later on we were off. Mr. Burrell treated me to dinner with his wife and son, so the evening got off to a good start. More cash for arcade machines and one-armed bandits (I was eighteen then and could indulge). Mr. Burrell and his wife hit the casinos and came out a few hundred down. More about the Burrell's later on.

Not much else around... construction starts on the house in Mooifontein Road, Birchleigh, Kempton Park

Starting to take shape - my bedroom is third hole from the right

Family & friends round for a BBQ once the pool had been completed at Mooifontein Road, Birchleigh, Kempton Park

Dad, me and Uncle George christening the new homemade, brick-built Braai (BBQ)

CHAPTER 7 - TO THE DRAKENSBERG MOUNTAINS...AND BEYOND!

One lunchtime at school Dean and Johnna brought up the fact that they were interested in going on a school-organized excursion that was coming up in the middle of the year. It surprised me to find out that this ten-day excursion was happening during the school holidays. I wondered why two young teenagers would volunteer to go on such an outing when school would have finished for the holidays, and what's more with teachers, and deputy headmasters of all people. Were they insane? If I am honest, I do think that their parents had got wind of it and insisted they go to get rid of them for a week or so. They didn't strike me as the sort of guy's who would willingly drop freedom for a week, to spend more time in the company of school authority. According to them, this was going to be an adventure, and far better than sitting at home bored during the holidays. Dean gave his usual wide-eyed smile of encouragement as he tried to convince me to come and join them on this once-in-a-lifetime adventure. I told the pair of them that under no circumstances would they talk me into joining them. It was over 140km of hiking, through a mountainous region, carrying a heavy H-Frame with everything you needed for the ten days, through all sorts of weather. 'You guys have fun', I said. Over the coming week, they continued to warn me of the deadline date for application and convinced me of the hi-jinks we could get up to whilst sitting around the campfire and cooking our food. It was also pointed out that the deputy headmaster and the accompanying teachers would see us in a 'different light' afterward, and we would potentially be treated better. I don't know what came over me, but I dropped my guard and said at some point I would consider it and ask my parents about funding the few hundred Rand fee. These two swindlers had talked me round, with their beaming smiles and enthusiasm. I bet anything you like they both left school and became second-hand car salesmen. My parents didn't take much convincing to let me go on the trip. They were more than happy to pay twice as much to get rid of me for ten days, including paying for all the necessary gear I would require. Now if they could only get rid of my brother too, they would be sorted.

Once the payment was made at school, word started to get out, and the teachers who were accompanying us on the trip approached us to talk about our up-and-coming adventure. My art teacher Mrs. Moolman and her husband, My English/PE teacher and her husband, the deputy headmaster and his wife, Dean, Johnna, me, and a few girls from our year, would all be joined by a couple of teenagers from a nearby Afrikaans speaking school. Several from another English speaking school, and some other teachers from those schools would also be coming. Preparations had to take place quickly. The school had provided a checklist of all the mandatory items you needed, along with some optional. First and foremost was the 'H-Frame' backpack into which all of the items would be packed for the ten days. This frame had a place at the rear bottom to secure your sleeping bag in its watertight packing. Feeding one's self would be the individual's responsibility, so dried and dehydrated provisions, for all three daily meals, would be required for the entire ten days, as well as suitable camping gas equipment to prepare hot meals and drinks. Billy cans and cutlery, first-aid equipment, hiking boots, warm clothing, plenty of underwear, waterproofs, water bottle, Swiss army knife, and torch. You name it and it was on the list. When packed into the H-Frame, the whole thing weighed a tonne. This thing was going to hurt my shoulders on these 30km hikes we were going to be doing in the first few days.

On day one I was dropped at the school by my parents, where everybody from our school was waiting for the mini bus to arrive…all that is except for Dean and Johnna. For one moment I felt this feeling of dread come over me. Had these two swindlers stitched me up like a kipper? My mind wandered back to the school ground chats we had about the trip. I could see Dean in my mind laughing, repeating over and over about how great it was going to be, then the pair of them laughing. Had these two comedians pulled off the greatest dupe ever? Time ticked on, getting ever closer to departure, and still no sign of the pair of them. I started to think how I could get out of this if they didn't turn up, however, I didn't have to put any plan into action as a car pulled up with minutes to spare. It was the pair of them, thank God. I think they could see the worry on my face turning into relief on their arrival and found it extremely funny when they realized I had thought I had been stitched up.

The mini-bus was loaded, there were some last-minute checks and then we were off on a drive of many hours to the Drakensberg mountains. On the way, we would pick up the two Afrikaans boys and some other guys from neighbouring schools. The bus was full, and we were on our way. Our starting point would be near Nelspruit, that is as far as I can remember. A lot of places have changed names since 1984. For example, I used to live in the Transvaal province, but it was renamed 'Gauteng', shortly after Apartheid ended. The trek would take us towards the Three Rondawels, Mount Anderson, the Blyde River Canyon, to God's Window, eventually ending up at the final camp at 'Bourkes Luck', where there are some interesting potholes formed from water movements through the rock layers. We arrived sometime after mid-day at our starting point, where we were going to spend the first night, with a very early start to the day the next morning. There was over 30km to cover on this first day, and it would be a true test of character.

That first night we slept in a room full of bunk beds, girls and teachers separately. Most of the evening was spent comparing the contents of each other's H-Frames. Foodstuffs, snacks, and cooking equipment mainly as well as the cash we had on board. This would be used at Bourke's Luck to feast on whatever was available at the tuck shop they had there. We didn't explore our culinary skills this first night as a meal was provided. That would come tomorrow night after the 32km trek to the first camp. It was an early start, with teachers waking us up at 5:30 am. At 6:30 am we would be off, stopping for a first breakfast along the route a little later on. We loaded up and shipped out making our way up the first trail. It was a bit of a shock to me at first. It felt comfortable carrying the H-Frame although a little heavy, and I wondered what I would feel like by the end of the day. I also wondered what my feet would feel like as I had made a very stupid mistake. I had brand new hiking boots, made of tough, waterproof material, and had not started wearing them until yesterday. They had been fine for the mini-van journey here of course, but now they were being put into action, they were eating away at my heels something chronic, and only after a few km. I had also been even more naïve and failed to bring any other footwear with me. At the lunchtime stop, I decided to check on my heels as they were extremely uncomfortable. As I feared, most of the skin had been worn through, and I had to open my first-aid kit already to plaster them up. Moving on it became even worse. I was not getting on with the boots at all. Fortunately, Dean offered a solution. He had brought a pair of trainers with him, and as he wasn't suffering at all at present, offered them to me, so I could continue more comfortably. It was like a sweet relief, and so I had to barter with Dean to secure them for the rest of the trip. I didn't care, money, sweets, snacks whatever it took, I couldn't go back to walking in those boots. They would come in handy a few weeks later though, as an ideal pair of off-road motorcycling boots. We were trundling along after lunch up high on the veld in the open. The weather had turned, and the temperature had dropped. Icy streams were in our path, and we had to cross many of them. A slight wind had pulled in and cloud coverage started to increase. Cold moisture was in the air and you were very glad of your thermals and waterproof. I know, South Africa is supposed to be hot all the time. No such thing. At the time of year we went, up high and exposed, it could still get bleak and cold. Although some of the women, girls, and a few of us skinny Brits were feeling a little chilly, two guys weren't. The Afrikaans lads. Now Brits and some English-speaking South Africans referred to the Afrikaans-speaking lads as 'Rocks'. You would often hear talk in the playground about running into a bunch of 'Rocks', or seeing a couple of 'Rocks' down the park. It was our term for referencing them, much in the same way they called us 'Rooineks' (Red-necks). The collective term was applied to them purely for the fact that they were hardened, nothing scared them, and no task was too big. It was nothing for 'Rocks' to run around barefooted on the tarmac, or any other surface for that matter. Think 'Zola Budd' here. Our two Afrikaans lads were no exception. Yes, they were wearing adequate footwear for this trek but were showing the 'hardness' of their central nervous system by wearing shorts. This was a great source of amusement to us whilst shivering our way down the trail, and even more so when they were questioned about their choice of attire, stating that it was warm for the time of year. It was a little later on whilst negotiating one of these icy streams that our deputy headmaster stumbled, losing grip on his prized, expensive, SLR camera dropping it straight into the stream, and stumbling down the grass verge himself until his boots hit the water. There was hardly time to take note of the situation, hardly time to blink before both 'Rocks' had sprung into action. As If they had worked as a team all their lives, and without any verbal communication whatsoever, one of them plunged one way into the icy water, shorts and all, to retrieve the sunken camera. The other with his in-built six sense, plunged the other direction into the water, soaking himself from head to foot whilst he proceeded to push the deputy back up the bank. Indeed, a 'Boer maak a plan', but the speed at which these guys executed theirs was impressive. Despite being drenched through, water seeping from their footwear, they insisted all was OK and nobody was to worry about them. The pair of them were indeed as hard as 'Rocks'.

Arrival at that first camp couldn't come soon enough, as I desperately needed to see to my heels. Despite more comfortable footwear and the added protection of plasters, they were singing to me, and loudly. My entire body was in agony. Shoulders hurt from carrying a heavy load over 30km. My feet had never seen so much walking, over such diverse terrain. I, like many others, had underestimated the toll that this sort of hike would take on our bodies. It was only day one, and we had many more camps to trek towards. The good news was that the distance tomorrow was going to be about 10km less, and boy was I looking forward to that. The camp was a very long hut divided into two separate areas. The one contained bunk beds for the teachers, their partners, and the two girls in our squad. The other one was for everyone else. We all quickly grabbed a bed. I went to the bottom of the first bunk next to the door leading to the other unit. Johnna decided to bunk next to me in the next set, with Dean on top of him. The accommodation was dry and looked like it would be warm that evening. It was the best accommodation we were going to encounter on this trip. The rest would get more and more hut-like, more and more stone-like, in a nutshell...basic. There was one thing though that stood out, and that I didn't like the look of. In the corner of my side of the room, opposite me, up high next to the rafters was a huge hornet's nest. Now we had been assured by the teachers that these posed no threat. They would come and go about their business as long as we didn't interfere with them. All was quiet with the nest at this time so I believed every word of it. As it was early evening we decided to go for an explore before sunlight fell. First on the agenda however was a nice cup of English tea. We needed a reviver, and only a cup of PG was going to do the trick. We all got our gas stoves out, made our welcome brew, and then departed outside to see what was about. There were some old outbuildings and a campfire with a roof overhead. We quickly got collared to get some firewood from the surrounding area so that the teachers could circle the campfire and chew the fat. There was plenty around, and we managed to gather loads for them, which they appreciated. 'More brownie points earned there..', said Dean. We made our way back to the accommodation, as we were getting hungry by now. There was a right ruckus going on. The girls were screaming and running out. This attracted the attention of one of the teachers who came over to investigate. He opened the door and looked in to find a swarm of hornets circling madly throughout the room. Hundreds of these large winged creatures were going bananas, trying to escape the room. The teacher immediately smelt and spotted what had caused the hornets to become extremely unhappy and irritated. It would seem that Johnna had made his brew earlier on, and left leaving his camping gas stove still running, but unlit. The hornets being aware that someone was trying to gas them out of their lair, had exited the nest in a panic. This may have been the first time, but it wasn't going to be the last time Johnna would attract insects with his tea brewing. We had to leave the room for several hours before they settled down enough for us to return. When we finally did, none of us could sleep and we talked and joked for hours. The only trouble was that the teachers had all been hitting the whiskey hard, especially the deputy, who was irritable and loud-mouthed. He could not tolerate the noise that late at night, and we had several visits to warn us what was coming if we didn't shut up.

The next day's trek was OK. My feet were comfortable, and we seemed to make camp a lot quicker with more time to explore before it got dark. We spent a lot more time with the 'Rocks' at this next camp, finding out about them and their school. Whilst talking about my blisters they explained why they would not be suffering in the same manner. Each of them had cut a pair of their mother's stockings down to shin size and was wearing them under their socks. This was a great source of amusement to Dean and Johnna, who had never heard of anything so ridiculous. They explained why this would help as the fabric moved and did not allow boots to rub against your heels so much. I took note of this for next time, even though there was never going to be a 'next time'. The night before I had knocked up some dried, savoury, soya-like, mince concoction out of a packet for my dinner. The thought of having it again bored me already so I decided to make a cottage pie. Dean and Johnna looked on eagerly, as their culinary talents were pretty non-existent. I had been invited to Dean's house before with Johnna and our other friend Bruce when his parents were out. Despite Dean saying he would 'make us all something for dinner', he served up a batch of buttered rolls filled with cold baked beans. Now I was going to show them all how to cook bush style. In one Billy can I cooked the dried mince, in the other a batch of that popular dried potato brand. I let the mince firm up a bit and then covered the top with the dried potato. Put it back on the low gas, and covered the cottage pie with the other Billy can lid to help it brown on top. When Dean and Johnna clocked eyes on the finished article and saw how much I was enjoying it, they set about making the same, occasionally asking for help as it was extremely difficult to cook two things at the same time. Deans came out alright but Johnna was showing he was a novice to the kitchen, with some sort of white slurry floating around inside his dried mince base. He ate it though and seemed to enjoy it. If this was impressing them, wait until tomorrow when I am having soya mince cobbler!

Our third night at camp three was very different from how the first few nights had been. The weather had worsened, we were even further into the wilderness, and the accommodation had changed from dormitory style to stable style. Stone walls, stone floors, and you shared the barn-style room with other creatures. It was cold. Very cold and we were all struggling to keep warm. The wind was blowing outside and rattling the twin door shutters that were up on the wall in front of us next to the door. It looked like this particular dwelling had consisted of two floors in the past, as the doors were up high and too far to reach. Apart from the creatures inside, there were also creatures outside. We had been warned not to leave anything outside, as the thieving Baboons would make off with it in the night. We were also told to stay in the room at night, and not venture outside as the Baboons were vicious. To help keep warm we all decided to make a brew, as the sleeping bags were not keeping out the cold. There were a couple of lads from another school sharing this barn with Dean, Johnna, and myself, and they had opted for a different mechanism to keep warm, which shocked and surprised all three of us. They had zipped two sleeping bags together on the top bunk, stripped off completely naked, and were snuggling up. According to them both, the transfer of body heat in this manner was a tried and tested way to keep the extreme cold at bay. Practised in the military they said. Yeah right. Dean looked directly at Johnna and said 'Don't get any ideas..'. As Johnna was on the top of my bunk, yet again, he came down to sort his brew out on the ledge of my bed. I was surveying the rest of the complex and could see him take several bags out of his H-Frame. You could see this was Johnna's first time camping in the wilderness and the first time his mother had packed rations for such an event. First, there was the retrieval of one teabag from a large plastic bag containing around a thousand. This seemed overkill considering we were only going to be gone for ten days, but not as 'overkill' as the second and third large plastic bags that contained several kilos of sugar, and a similar quantity of milk powder. There couldn't have been room for much else in his H-Frame. Dean and I looked on, creasing up with laughter as we saw the huge quantities Johnna was trying to get to grips with. The second two bags were particularly flimsy, and due to the excess weight they were carrying, big-time 'spillage' occurred. The one thing his mother had forgotten was a teaspoon, which was probably a good thing as he would have been carting around several pounds of stainless steel as well. When I got back to my bunk, the stone floor was covered in sugar and milk powder, as well as some of the hot water from his Billy can. The side of my bed was covered in sugar too. I complained to him about this but settled down for the night. The rain was coming down hard now, and the poor excuse for a roof had given up trying to keep it at bay. Next to my bed, I could hear the 'plink', 'plink' of rainwater hitting the stone floor, the sound slightly muffled by the impact on sugar and milk powder. I sat up and switched on my torch to find a sea of sweet milk powder pooling alongside my bed. This didn't worry me, but what did worry me was that the side of my bed, the floor, and me was covered in ants. They were everywhere. Having smelt the sweet nuggets that Johnna had so kindly sprayed my bed with, they had come out to investigate and collect, in their thousands. More merriment from Dean ensued, as he looked on at the mess of the floor, and the look on my face as I realized I was being eaten alive. It was difficult to get to sleep that night, but I eventually dozed off. Later that night I was awoken by a disturbance and a sight that would burn a disturbing image into my retina forever. It was the fumbling about in the dark that stirred me from my sleep. Not the wind or the rain. My bottom bunk faced the front of the barn, and from lying down there I could see the door to the right, and central to that, the two wooden shutter windows that were doing their best to protect us from the outside elements. My blurry, watery eyes opened and were immediately drawn to the windows that were not taking on their normal appearance. As my eyes started to clear I noticed a small figure silhouetted by the light coming in from the moon outside. That's not the only moon I saw either, as perched up on high, very precariously, with his tracksuit bottoms around his ankles, was Johnna, with the shutters wide enough open to allow him to relieve himself out of the window. I had to rub my eyes just to make sure I wasn't dreaming. Nope, it was him alright, and judging by the amount of steam and the duration of the continuous stream, he had taken down a lot of tea before bedtime. Johnna had scaled the wall like one of those extreme climbers who do not use any equipment, as there was hardly any jutting-out rock to hold onto. The next morning I told Dean all about it as he had slept right through. Trying not to laugh or cry he asked Johnna why he was doing it out the window. Johnna reiterated what we were told about leaving the barn, and the vicious Baboons that lay in wait for him outside. He said he tried to hold it until morning but couldn't any longer. There was no way he was going to be attacked by wild baboons, so his climb to the shutters was the only option. He didn't see the funny side of it at all. It's one of the stories we would tell when we got back to school, giving us endless amusement whilst doing so.

I was slowly starting to enjoy being on this trek with Dean and Johnna. It was starting to turn out to be exactly what they said. A complete laugh. I was, however, being lulled into a false sense of security, as unbeknown to me the two of them were plotting several schemes, of a comedic nature to give them endless laughs at my expense. The first was whilst climbing Mount Anderson, an elevation of over two thousand meters. At one of the most inclined parts, only an hour in from leaving camp, Dean and Johnna who were walking to my right, pointed out that my sleeping bag was currently making its way down the mountain having departed from its secure location attached underneath my H-Frame. I had tied this so tightly to the frame that morning, that there was only one way it could have worked loose so easily, and that is if helped along. I put my H-Frame to the ground and darted down the incline. Fortunately, I didn't have to go far, as about twenty-five meters away it had got caught on the side of the hiking track. As I made my way back up, puffing and sweating, and gasping for breath, the two comedians were trying to stop themselves from laughing. They swore that they had nothing to do with it, but their faces and smiles could not conceal the truth. The following day we were hiking once again and I have to admit I was struggling. I couldn't understand why after so many days, and utilizing lots of items from my H-Frame, it seemed to be getting heavier. The penny dropped when Dean just started asking me off the cuff, how hard the going seemed today, and how heavy his H-Frame felt. He further added how he could not explain it, as he had eaten a lot of his food, all whilst brandishing his normal 'giveaway' grin. I stopped in my tracks, took off my H-Frame, and opened it up. Not one large rock, not two, but four as I rummaged around through my belongings. The pair of them creased up, apologizing and laughing at the same time, as they could see the red mist coming over me. I asked them when they put them in and they replied it was done under the cover of darkness and that two of the rocks had been in there for several days! I'd like to say that I learned a lesson about these two, but it turns out they did a lot of their best work at night. You will hear in a later chapter about how they managed to get me again, once again performing their shenanigans as night ninjas.

I said how we were accompanied on this trip by several teachers and their partners. One of those teachers was my art teacher Mrs. Moolman. In her late twenties, Mrs. Moolman was every lad's dream teacher. I won't go into details but let's say she was often the topic of conversation and pretty much every lad held a candle to her. Mainly because she was stunningly attractive, but also because she was a fairly laid-back teacher, who didn't mind us listening to music during art classes. I had only been sent out of her class once in a case of mistaken identity. She was mortified when she found out I had been carted off by the headmaster, who was doing his 'rounds' whilst lessons were in progress. After class she took me aside and apologized, saying that she did not want that to happen, and was shocked when she opened the door a few minutes later to see I was gone. I held no grudges and accepted her apology, a young man could do no more when confronted with those glistening, hazel eyes... whoa!! What happened there? Back in the room.

Later on, that afternoon, we were climbing a steep incline within a forest. All had gone ahead and were out of sight except for Dean and Johnna on the right-hand side, Mrs. Moolman on the left and me struggling at the rear. Dean had already turned around once to look back at me, making a silent 'Phwooarr' gesture behind his hand, and pointing his eyes left at Mrs. Moolman whilst doing so. Seeing that I was struggling to keep up with the pace, Mrs. Moolman stopped in her tracks and held out her right hand towards mine smiling and saying 'Come on Carl'. I took hold of it, and we continued to walk up the incline hand in hand. I couldn't believe my luck. This was the stuff of dreams. I glanced to the right of me where Dean and Johnna were staring back at us, jaws nearly hitting the floor. The grin had been wiped off Dean's face and had been replaced with a look of disbelief. He was now mouthing over to me 'What the hell? How the hell...? and 'you Jammie bastard..'. I just gave them both a look that said, 'See it, remember it, and don't forget to tell all your friends...'. Well, they did, and there was a considerable amount more 'Jammie bastard' comments sent my way when we returned to school. My float on 'cloud nine' came to an abrupt end when we could hear the voices of the rest of the squad up ahead, including Mr. Moolman. Then came the quizzing from Dean and Johnna as to how I had managed to get that to happen, along with questions about whether anything was going on.

Our next day's trek was taking us to God's window, and on this particular day, God had decided he would open the heavens like never before, so much in fact that God's window was going to need windscreen wipers for you to see through it. We had all set off early that day, intending to stop and have breakfast along the route. Something had happened though. With the bad weather, and everyone's eagerness to get to shelter, we had become split up. Johnna, Dean, and I had struggled to keep up the pace at the rear and as a result, found ourselves making our way not knowing where we were going. Cold and hungry, we stopped at a clearing outside of the tree line and next to the roads. There was a concrete seating area, so we decided to use this to serve up our breakfast. It was no use considering getting a stove out, as it would have been impossible to light. The rain was coming down harder and we were exposed to the full force of it. With water streaming down our faces, and kagools, all three of us got out our Billy cans and started to prepare a bowl of cornflakes, shivering as we added the flakes and then milk powder. Almost at once, we all started to laugh and then burst into fits of laughter, shaking our heads. The Billy cans were already full to the brim with water, in less than a minute. On this occasion, we were not going to have to open our water bottles to make breakfast. More laughter ensued as we tried to finish our breakfast, all the time the Billy cans filling up faster than we could get through them. Cornflakes were now falling out over the edge. It was hopeless and we emptied our cans and packed up. It was a moment of sheer ridiculousness, that raised our spirits and allowed us to continue.

We could see people in the distance making their way up the road and so made our way in that general direction. We didn't keep an eye on them as we were too busy talking and soon realized we had lost sight of them. Other people were hiking up the road, but not from our party, and in the distance, we saw them cut off the road and head into the forest. Assuming that this was where our party had headed, we did the same once we reached this entrance to the forest. We followed the trail for ages. There was no sign of anyone. We couldn't hear voices from any direction anymore, so just followed the trail. Deeper and deeper into the forest we went, starting to get concerned that we were lost. We were lost, and once again panic started to set in.

The forest had become dense, and there was no further indication of where a trail was going or had been followed. We stopped in our tracks and listened to see if we could hear anyone. Nothing. Dean started to bellow for help at the top of his voice to see if anyone answered. After a few shouts, people replied. We ascertained which direction the response was coming from and immediately headed in that direction. Now at a running pace, all three of us were shouting and making directional changes when we heard the replies. After some minutes, we sighed a huge relief as we surfaced back onto the road again, and fortuitously right at the point where the two girls from our party were hiking. It was them that had heard our cries and responded. We had come out onto the road at a different location from where we entered the forest, but that didn't matter. We were further along the trail and back with some of our group, that's all that mattered. The rain was still coming down hard, and the two girls were finding it tough going, much as we were. It wasn't far though until we reached the tourist area of Gods Window. God had shut up for the day, drawn his curtains, and put up a sign saying 'closed'. Apart from a load of cars in the car park, and a few brave souls looking in the gift shop, everybody else seemed to be taking shelter in whatever outbuilding, or under whatever cover they could find. Dean wanted the toilet and so we waited whilst he used the public restrooms. A few minutes later he emerged, beckoning us over. 'We can camp in here until the rain eases off'. I instantly rejected the idea saying we wouldn't be allowed, but Johnna and the girls were straight in, as they were soaked, freezing, and desperate for a hot drink. I wasn't going to stand out in the rain alone so I went in as well. It was certainly a lot warmer, and drier than outside. There was just enough standing room for the five of us and our gear. 'See? It's alright in it?', Dean said. I remarked how hungry I was, and how it would be disgusting to prepare any food in here. Johnna though had different ideas, his Billy can and the stove were already out on top of the toilet seat, fired up and he was preparing savoury rice. We watched as he cooked it, and started to eat it. It did smell good. The girls were disgusted at the thought of cooking and eating in a male public toilet. Dean and I were initially, but decided 'If you can't beat them..'. I went into one of the other stalls, or 'Carl's Kitchen' as it was now known. There was no way I was firing up my gas on the toilet seat, so instead, I balanced it on the cistern at the back, and boiled water from my bottle, so that I could eventually indulge in soya chili con carne. Dean was now a fully-fledged cottage pie convert and expert, even at making it in the confined space of trap three. The girls soon gave in as well, making hot chocolate to warm themselves up.

We stayed inside, peering out through the door every half hour or so to see if we could spot any sign of the teachers and the rest of the group. We stayed in there for about two and a half hours before the door opened and one of the teachers from the group rounded us up. They had been looking for us but had taken shelter in one of the buildings until the rain eased off. We joined the group and made off to the next camp. The rain had eased off a lot, and it didn't take half an hour before it stopped altogether. Arriving at camp was very welcome. A change of clothes and a hot drink and we all felt much better. What's more, there was a huge fireplace undercover which the teachers lit once we had collected firewood. Everybody was gathered around it talking. Dean, Johnna, and I decided to explore a bit though. The area around the camp was different from previous camps in that it had a lot of very large boulders, some about twelve feet off the ground, all laying at different angles, and with differing inclines. This seemed like the perfect opportunity to test out our climbing skills, so we took turns to scale whatever height we had chosen. It wasn't long before our English teacher came over and joined us. She was our PE teacher as well, so was keen to take part in the climbing as well as pass on some tips.

The day finally arrived when we were making our last trek towards 'Bourkes Luck'. This was a very short trek, and we would be there sometime after midday. Proper accommodation awaited us once more. Warm, dry, with access to spending our money at the tuck-shop, and a proper meal to boot. It was something we had all been looking forward to. It had been a great time, a wonderful experience, and we had made some good friends, but we all missed the creature comforts of home. Tonight I would be able to have a hot shower and wash away many days of grime. It was a great thought to be able to feel human again.

On arrival at 'Bourkes Luck', the teachers spent far too long showing us what was essentially holes in stone filled with running water. Yes, it showed thousands of years of erosion by the river...blah blah blah... now, where's the tuck-shop? I and others had some serious snacking to start. I had not had a bag of crisps for over a week and was getting serious withdrawal symptoms. We all had saved money for this event, and the day had come. When we got to the accommodation, forgetting most of us had not washed in over a week, we dumped H-Frames and made off cash in hand. There was a scene in that well-known film 'Planes, Trains and Automobiles' starring Steve Martin and the late great John Candy, where they have fallen out and JC is outside, sleeping in the car in the cold. Steve Martin's character feels sorry for him and invites him into the motel room. The next scene shows them laying on the beds, laughing and joking, chewing the fat, whilst gorging on various snacks from the vending machine, as well as dozens of miniatures from the bar. When I think back, this is what this time reminded me of. Exchange the mini bottles of vodka, whiskey, and gin for cans of Coke, Fanta Orange, and 7-up, and the rest is pretty much accurate. Everyone relaxing, putting their differences aside, and having a bloody good laugh whilst making themselves sick from overeating. The laughs came from reminiscing about our journey through the wilderness. Johnna and the hornet's nest, Johnna and the midnight window pee, my sleeping bag, the rocks in my bag, and much more. We all laughed about everything even if it was you that it affected at the time. We went on laughing at school when we returned, as Dean brought various people up to speed on the events that had occurred. I am pretty sure that some of them when hearing of our shenanigans, had wished they had signed up. I'm certainly glad I did. Perhaps that is why I let both Johnna and Dean talk me into doing something else. This though turned out to be a different kettle of fish, and an experience I would not look back on with such fond memories.

CHAPTER 8 - VELD SKOOL

Dean and Johnna had gotten wind of the fact that there was going to be another school excursion planned, of sorts. This one was regular each year for boys of our age, and it was considered a good idea to go on it, as it would prepare you for the harshness of Army basic training that was to await us all at age 18. Disguised under the name 'Veld Skool' (or 'Bush School') for want of a better phrase, this fortnight away, during school time, was designed to turn young boys into young men, and was essentially, 'Army Preparedness Camp', if you went in Standard eight. An easier and less intense version was enjoyed by pupils at the end of primary school in Standard five. Dean and Johnna were selling it differently though. 'A great crack..',' Going to be as much as a laugh as the hiking trek...', t hey said. Once again I wasn't receptive, but in the end, gave in as it made sense to get a taste of what was to come in a couple of years. It was a mixed school affair, with the usual mixture of boys from both English and Afrikaans-speaking schools. On departure day it was a coach taking us all to the camp, and not a minibus. Our kit was very basic. A rucksack, a sleeping bag, a pillow, several changes of clothes, a torch, washing gear, some money, and a piece of thick plastic sheeting of a precise length and width. Everything else we needed would be supplied. The destination was also very vague. Somewhere near the Mozambique border was what we were told at the time. I have looked on maps over the years and I couldn't say with any accuracy where we were but would hazard a guess at being near the Mozambique border in Steenkampsberg, as conversations with the military guys at the camp seemed to confirm this at the time. It was a good three hours or more journey, from Kempton Park near Johannesburg, by coach, regardless of the location.

It was announced that we had arrived and we turned off the main road and started down a dirt track, wide enough for two coaches to pass each other easily. The ground was rich and orange, and the dust rose as the coach wheels made their way through it. On either side of the track was thick vegetation, so you could not see any sign of where you were going to end up. After about a mile the track ended in a clearing, and we were told to disembark and line up, standing to attention. A largish South African man dressed in camouflage gear, and wearing a military-style casual cap, asked us to stand at ease. This sort of expected behaviour came naturally to all boys in secondary school. We had to perform marching drills on the playing fields regularly, usually before an unannounced hair and uniform inspection. These drills and inspections could span the length of a couple of lessons in some of the secondary schools I attended. The man introduced us to himself and his team and then sprung a surprise on us. Before even getting our bags from the coach, we were going to go on a 'run'. At the entrance off the main road, two colleagues were waiting in a Land Rover with badges. We were to run the half mile there, collect our badge, run back, and show it to the colleague here. The last ten back would be drilled hard on return. Anyone who returned without a badge would be drilled hard on return. You hardly had time to take it all in before he shouted 'Go'. In the shock, nobody seemed to move, until he shouted 'Go!', again louder. At this point, I looked and some boys had processed the message and had started to move. That was my queue to get my skates on. I had never run a half-mile, let alone two, as would show when I arrived back. I used up all my energy pretty early on in the dash, was impeded by a stitch, and was well down the pack by the time I got to get my badge. Knowing what I had already been through, I wasn't looking forward to the return sprint. Fortunately for me, there were a lot of guys in worse shape, a lot of obvious smokers, who were pretty much coughing up a lung when they got back. I was having trouble breathing, and my heart was pounding so fast in my chest that I thought it would explode, but at least I was back, and out of the cut. We stood and watched as the last ten performed their punishment in front of us. Fifty push-ups, which they all struggled to do within any reasonable time frame after their impromptu sprint. That all over, we were shown to the camp where we would be staying for the first night. I say camp but it was just bush. The only thing that made it resemble more than wasteland, was a large circular area, with some seat-sized stones placed around it. Apart from that, we hadn't a clue where we were or where we were going to end up. Everybody was told to find somewhere to lay their kit down in the bush, leaving about a two-meter gap between each of us, and then assemble near the circular area for a briefing.

The name of the camp escapes me, but let's suppose for argument's sake that the ex-sergeant introduced us to it as 'Welcome to camp "we are going to break you bastards"...', as he might as well have done seeing what was coming up. A further introduction to the other ex-military personnel, as well as some details of the brief service for the South African army. Then the rules and regulations, of which the main point was that we would be left alone in this camp overnight, which was five hundred yards or so from the main camp, where we would be going tomorrow. This camp was currently full of girls on a trip and was being guarded. Any attempt to infiltrate the camp for whatever reason would be punished severely. Once in the main camp, we would be sleeping together in an outhouse and were not allowed to exit it after lights out for any reason, unless instructed to do so by any of the staff. We were told about a map reading and navigation exercise, a local assault course, a night hike, as well as a long hike into the mountains to do a more extreme assault course, that was coming our way. After our initial ordeal on arrival, none of us were stupid enough to believe that this was going to be anywhere near as easy as they made it sound. Dean was naive though, still grinning in expectation, saying to me 'Cheer up mate?', ' It's going to be like the Krypton Factor!'.

That enthusiasm and that grin were soon to be wiped off his face. We believe we were nestled within mountains somewhere near the Mozambique border. This was further confirmed as we were shown the cable car system that was appearing out of the low clouds, in the distance, and slowly making its way across the camp. It was some five hundred meters in the air, towards some base somewhere in South Africa. When I say 'cable cars' you have to think primitive. These were just large wooden crates, with sackcloth covering them, attached to the cable with skyhooks. Spaced every minute or so apart, it was anyone's guess what they contained and where it was going. The staff told stories of the guys at the South African end finding frozen dead bodies when they opened the crates, where some poor soul had tried to defect into South Africa, not being aware of the huge drops in temperature that they would have to endure, crossing the mountains at height for some considerable time. There were further stories about arms being intercepted that were on their way to wreak havoc somewhere in South Africa. You would think the answer to all this would be to shut it down. But for some unknown reason, the South African government was happy for this primitive transport mechanism to run day and night. We would see them for the entire two weeks we were there. They only stopped briefly on the odd occasion. Every time you looked up at them you wondered, what on earth was the bulge under that sackcloth covering the crates?

At 6:00 pm a cook was going to come to camp with that

night's meal. We were to bring our Billy cans over at that point to get fed. Those of us who still hadn't realized what we were in for conjured up images of barbecued meats, jacket potatoes, and maybe some bread rolls to go with it. All washed down with a nice cuppa. There might even be a starter. Some soup maybe? I wish I had partaken of my last meal in Civvie Street with a bit more thought. Maybe realizing that I wasn't going to get fed properly for a fortnight, and taking the opportunity to bulk up on meats and carbs. The cook arrived carrying a single pot, with a ladle in it. Probably all he could carry, wasn't it? He'll go back and get the rest now, won't he? No, he won't. He rang a bell and that was it. A long queue of thirty to forty ravenous boys formed. We three were quite a way down the queue but could see lads coming back down the line with disappointed and disgusted looks on their faces. We couldn't see what they had in their Billy cans. There weren't any nice savoury smells in the air either, so who knows what it could be? What it could be was a single ladle full of mixed beans and nothing else. That mixture of chickpeas, kidney beans, haricot beans, and the like. All swimming in their juices. Not a piece of meat or vegetable in sight. I wasn't too keen on it but wasn't going to leave any of it. I didn't know when I was going to be fed next or what I was going to be fed, so common sense kicked in. Polish the lot off and lick the Billy can clean. Dean was sitting next to me with Johnna, the pair of them staring blankly into their Billy cans, stirring the contents around aimlessly with their forks. A few expletives came out of Dean's mouth as he did so,

'What is this effin sh*te?',

expressing his concern at facing up to two weeks eating stuff he didn't like or want. Now you would think that a Billy can of lukewarm, mixed beans would be right up his street, as he often indulged in a can of cold beans in a bread roll for 'dinner'. Not these beans though. These were 'bush' beans and not the same as the '57 varieties' he enjoyed at home, bathing in tomato sauce. His disappointment was my gain though, as he didn't take much persuading to let me have them rather than tipping them in the bushes. Johnna, like me, was seeing sense and finished his. This was probably not a million miles away from the pot of 'Scouse' his mother served up, except for the lack of beef, vegetables, gravy, and above all flavour. Dean, however, was from more affluent stock, having everything at his disposal, and spoilt by his parents, so there was no way he was going to like the catering facilities at this establishment.

A few hours after dinner we were given further instructions on the sleeping arrangements and warned of the early start the next morning. Lights out were going to be announced shortly and it had to be adhered to otherwise there would be ramifications. All was revealed about the large plastic sheet we had been told to bring, conforming to a length and width that had been specified. You were to find some long grass to lay it on, place your sleeping bag in the centre, and then draw the sides up so they were vertical, up against the long grass. You would be lying in a sort of plastic-lined box, not being able to see over the edge when lying down. The reason for this? To stop snakes from being able to join us for the night. According to sources, they would be unable to successfully climb the walls of the plastic sheet, over the edge, and into our sleeping bags. This seemed a bit hit-and-miss to my liking, and so what little sleep I did get, I did with one eye open. If it did protect us from snakes, there were other night wandering creatures that may not look upon it as an obstacle. I survived the night, waking early just before the first light. I lay there in my cocoon, waiting to hear if anyone else was stirring. I had woken up a lot in the night, so had not got much sleep. It was fairly cold and there were a lot of animal noises I didn't recognize, so most of the night lay awake for fear of getting attacked by something. God knows what was out here with us. Not long after sun-up the staff arrived. We were told to pack up our gear as we were moving to the main camp, where breakfast awaited our arrival. With packs on we were root marched for about ten minutes until we reached the accommodation. I use the word accommodation loosely. This was a large building with a concrete floor, and a few concrete pillars holding up rafters in the ceiling space. A thatched roof lay on top, with one length of the building exposing us to the elements. Chicken wire for windows, with the odd wooden frame placed at meter lengths. That was it. No bunks. No hammocks. Find yourself a space on the floor big enough to lay your sleeping bag out and that was where you were going to live for the next fortnight. I found a spare spot quite near the 'window'. I would be alright there as the overhang of the roof and thatch would prevent any rain from coming in. Dean and Johnna were more central in the room. One guy had even opted to sleep upright against the pillar, ten feet or so in front of me. It was a bit disappointing, to say the least. The concrete floor was going to play havoc with our backs, with little to no comfort being supplied by the thickness of our sleeping bags. Breakfast was not much better either. Minimal rations of cereals and tea. After breakfast came the opportunity to form groups of four or five. This would be your team for the next fortnight, and as a group, you would be competing for a prize to be given out at the end of this two-week ordeal. Points being accrued for your successes in the various exercises that were going to be set out. Most of the morning and afternoon, post-lunch, were spent looking at mental problems, coming up with solutions within your group, and then presenting them to everyone at the camp. This included singing your group song to everyone, that you had come up with to represent your team. We spent a highly embarrassing couple of minutes on a stage with a badly prepared team-building song that repeated itself over and over again, increasing in volume with each iteration. Ridicule followed from the rest of the onlookers. Our efforts to solve the problems presented to us that afternoon were met with similar ridicule. You got the feeling that you were going to be in the losing group at the end, as none of us had any confidence. The teacher in charge of our group must have been thinking to himself how he got landed with this lot. Things started to look up with a half-decent, hot meal served up at dinner. Then out to the bush where an enclosed bush amphitheatre was the setting for a campfire and talks on everything dangerous out in the wilderness. This included details of what animals and reptiles could outrun you, and how to assist your colleague if he was bitten by a snake. This amounted to the indirect application of urine, before seeking further medical attention, with extreme emphasis on 'indirect'. There had been questions about what to do if someone gets a snake bite in the eye and whether it was acceptable to urinate in their face to save their sight. This talk went on for several hours into the night, and then we returned to the barracks.

Most of us took the opportunity to visit the washing block, to enjoy one of the ice-cold showers that they so kindly had laid on for us. Believe me, you didn't stay in them long. Just long enough to get the grime off yourself. We relaxed and talked about the day, and were settling down ready for bed when one of the staff came in banging a dustbin lid loudly and shouting for everyone to get outside and line up. The tone of the staff had seemed to change. They looked angrier than they had previously, and their voices were raised constantly. Orders were being issued and at very close quarters to our ears. What the hell was going on? It would seem that our time at the 'holiday camp' had come to an end, and now things were going to change. We had been a little bit premature in thinking we were going to be allowed to settle in for the night. Grouped into a squad of three per line, we were marched in the darkness along the dirt road. There was more staff around as well, and no teachers to be seen. Some of us were targeted for abuse as we root marched. If out of step or looking like you were struggling, one of the staff dressed in their military attire, weapon by their side, would jog through the group and shoulder barge you to the floor. You had to get up quickly and carry on otherwise face more verbal abuse, and punishment in the form of making the entire group do push-ups. Things had changed and changed for the worse. I could have handled the marching alone, as it was only exhausting, but after a while the real reason for our night jaunt became apparent, and I wasn't going to like it. We stopped on the dirt track about a kilometre or so away from camp. To the right of us was bush ground, and to the left a large cliff of earth and grass. The head of the staff barked his orders quickly and we had to jump into action.

'One at a time, on your knees, enter the cliff through this hole!'. 'Crawl through to the other end, do not stop, or you will be stopping the rest of the group behind you!'. ' Go!'.

I didn't know what to expect after entering the hole in the cliff. It was extremely claustrophobic. On your knees, your head scraped against the earth at the top of the tunnel. You were right behind the guy in front and trying to keep up with his pace, the guy behind you following suit. You couldn't see because of the dark. You couldn't see anyway as the guys in front were masking any light that may have been coming into the tunnel. Cobwebs, insects, water, mud. It was all in there. Panic set in as you realized you were in an enclosed space, within a cliff, with no reinforcements to the tunnel roof or walls, and it was damp. If it had collapsed at any point, we would have been buried alive. Adrenalin kicked in and kept you going, so nobody was aware of your inner panic. Ahead of me, the line stopped. Angry shouts of 'keep moving' came from those ahead of me, urging whoever had stopped to get the rear into gear again! I was relieved when the line started again. You hardly knew when the end was coming. It was so dark out there that there was no light to indicate you were coming out of the tunnel. We were in the middle of nowhere, with no street or city lights to illuminate the atmosphere. Just the light from the luminaries in the sky, which were numerous. I can't tell you how relieved I was to get out of that tunnel. The root marching afterward, however long it lasted, was welcome as long as I did not have to go back in there.

The next morning it was the first outing to the local assault course, if not the ideal weather for it. Unbeknown to us a storm was on its way and would hit us at an inappropriate time in the next few days. Today, light rain was already starting to move in and would make life difficult, and extremely messy out on the course. Good job I had just put on a new set of clean clothes to do it in eh? First up, leopard crawling, under the barbed wire just above your head, down into a muddy pool, and then back up an incline and out. That was all it took, to coat me in muddy water, that would later dry like glue onto my jeans, tee shirt, and hoody. Good job I had a set of clean clothes left in my bag. The next one I had to insist I skipped. There was no way I could do it. I have never had a head for heights. Even going up a small ladder I get vertigo. This jungle gym in the sky that faced us would have ended up with them calling an ambulance when I had fallen to the ground after passing out. I was fortunate that the teacher in our group wasn't bothered. Had it been one of the staff, I don't think any of us would have gotten out of it. Some marching followed to the next activity, which once again I had to bottle out of. I know, I am ashamed of myself and wish I had done it now, but once again it involved height, and there was no way I was going up there. Tree to tree zip line, across the river, which we were told had crocodiles in it. I certainly didn't see the heads of any sitting in the water awaiting the falling prey, so you don't know if it was a myth or not. The funny thing is that at age forty-nine I went to Costa Rica on holiday, and did a Zip Wire experience there. Two hours of zip wires with the biggest travelling at huge speeds over nearly a mile of ocean view. I guess later in life phobias don't affect you so much?

This assault course was an easy introduction, and we had been warned that something, bigger and more extreme was waiting for us in the mountains where we would be hiking the next day. Stories were circulating about previous groups that had been to this camp, and how they had to swim underwater, underneath a concrete block, with just enough body room in one of the items. I didn't like the sound of this either and was praying for some kind of miracle to prevent me from having to do this. The next morning before our 15km hike into the mountains, we assembled for breakfast as normal. This time though there seemed to be a distinct lack of pots and pans visible on the table in front of us. Maybe we were just getting a cup of tea now and then would stop somewhere on the way for a hearty breakfast? It was going to be a 20km hike, the assault course, and a night stay before the 20km hike back, so we envisaged being fed well to survive the trip. We envisaged wrong. Very, very wrong. The staff got our attention and then gave us the bad news. We were each getting a black cup of tea to drink now. In addition to that, we would each receive a small plastic sandwich bag containing the following contents. A handful of cornflakes, with milk powder mixed in, a boiled egg, and one slice of brown bread. That was it, and not only that, this was all we would have to eat until lunchtime the following day when we would return. We were advised that we should make one of two decisions, the first being to eat it all now, the second being to eat it at intervals throughout the day. Jaws dropped to the floor, and you could hear expletives being broadcast from several areas around the line of unhappy campers. This was the end of the line as far as Dean was concerned. I would imagine he would be having words with his travel agent when he got back. I used this opportunity to remind him, 'It will be a great crack, as much fun as the Drakensberg hike!'. A few of us got together and planned an escape from the camp, as this was the last straw. Dean was right at the head of this mutiny, exploring various possibilities for suitable times to action the plan, and where we would go. Our plan was set in stone, but there was one major flaw in it that had to be resolved and resolved quickly. That was where the hell are we? And which direction do we go in, and using what transport? The cable cars were quickly ruled out. We had heard how men had frozen riding in those, plus we didn't know if we would end up in South Africa, or worse still, Mozambique! We had plenty of time to work all this out on our 20km trek, whilst we pondered the question of how to make the delicious, and plentiful packed lunch they had given us, last thirty hours.

The rain was coming down still when we left. Our wet

weather gear was keeping it from drenching us, but it was getting colder, and we were getting more miserable by the minute. We had the occasional respite as we entered the forest, getting protection from the elements from trees and shrubs. Many of the trees along the route were covered in moss, and some interesting conversations were going on about how the feel of the moss on the trees resembled the thatch atop a lady's private parts. There were a lot of lads agreeing with this prognosis after rubbing a hand across the trunks. I, of course, had not had the privilege yet of being able to confirm this as true and accurate. Even to this day, I have yet to find a lady who is graced with thatch like 'dew-covered moss'. I can only assume that these lads had all had the misfortune to associate with ladies with a particularly rare fungal condition, either that or they were complete liars. Talk of lady moss soon died down as we exited the forest area, and moved into more open ground. The rain was coming down a lot harder now. That hard windscreen wipers were a requirement for your eyes. We had to cross several small streams, that were starting to run quite rapidly. Streams turned to rivers, which were a lot trickier to cross. Rivers turned to new rivers, where there previously had not been rivers. These rivers became more frequent in our path as they created new meandering flows throughout the countryside we were working our way through. No concern was shown by the staff or teachers about the hazardous crossings we were making, that is until the last one we attempted. We stopped at the edge and looked forward at the torrent raging in front of us. There was no bank to the river, it had just been created that day and was already fifteen to twenty feet wide. Water flowing so fast you could hardly keep track of it. Some of the staff went in first and tried to create a barrier for us to walk in front of. The first few lads that went, could barely stand, losing their footing a few times. One guy's rucksack was ripped from his back and went flowing down the river, unstoppable and irretrievable. The rest made it across until it came to the last few of us. I was second from last and got swept away from the men forming the barrier. I just caught the leg of one of the staff near the other side as I went, and hung on for dear life, trying to drag myself out of the water and onto the grass. It took some effort but with the help of the staff, I got out, leaving us with everybody across. One of the members of staff had been sent ahead earlier in the day to the new camp, to prepare things for our arrival. He met us having left there. It was announced that the camp had been washed away, as things were much worse closer to it. He was making his way back to warn us to turn around. The rain was heavier up in the mountain, and worse flooding was on its way down. The assault course was not visible any more. The staff and teachers had a quick crisis meeting, and the decision was made to go back to the main camp before we all got hyperthermia. My prayers had been answered, and I wouldn't have to undergo the ordeal of swimming underwater, in a confined space, under concrete. I'd done enough swimming for the day, and it had been perilous enough for my liking.

Back at camp, we decided to get out of our wet clothes and warm up by having an ice-cold shower. It was good to be dry now, but most of us were still shivering. The warmest place to be fully clothed in your sleeping bag. It had been an exhausting day and most fell asleep quickly, including me. Two guys who were suffering from insomnia, and were deciding to use the opportunity for tomfoolery, were Dean and Johnna. As if the ordeal of the day hadn't been enough, they thought the time was right to inflict some uncomfortable times, and what I didn't know was they had come prepared. A few nights previous I had witnessed one poor guy fall asleep and then have a toothpaste moustache and beard applied by some other guys. I had been warned by Dean and Johnna that I was going to be next, and they would be doing it to me. I tried to keep my eyes open as long as I could. Now and then I would realize I was dropping off, and wake with a start, looking over at the other two who would be grinning back at me, waving a tube of Colgate in their hands. 'Don't fall asleep!', Dean would whisper as he laughed. I had been through it that day, and I am afraid I had to threaten violence to the pair of them if they dared to disturb me or give me that 'ring of confidence' all over my face. I lost the battle with my eyes shortly after and must have dropped off. The next thing I knew I woke up suddenly, shouting with pain. The shit twins were creasing themselves with laughter, waking others up in the process. Something had bitten me hard on the foot and leg. I jumped out of the sleeping bag and opened it so I could see what was in there. Holly!... Bloody Holly!... Where on earth had these two got Holly, in the middle of nowhere, in South Africa, in July? And what's more, how the hell did they unzip my sleeping bag, put it in carefully enough, and zip me back up without me noticing? You had to take your hat off to them, they were professionals at this sort of thing. The planning that must have gone into it. They had got the Holly ages ago and had brought it with them, to use in the ultimate prank. I wondered what on earth would be next. I found out what would be next when I looked in my rucksack for some tuck shop provisions we had been allowed to buy when we got back from the mountains. I searched my bag but they were gone. I looked over at Dean and Johnna, who were grinning back at me once again, this time with their cheeks full of my Tuc biscuits and crisps. Making a point of showing their enjoyment of my items, despite having eaten theirs earlier. I hadn't the energy to pummel the pair of them, so I gave up and went back to sleep. They could not pull it off twice, could they? I don't have to tell you what happened next, do I?

The next day, despite being soaked the day previous, a lot of the guys had skipped the offer of a cold shower, as they had done for the entire trip. I think the smell must have got to the staff and they announced suddenly that everybody should strip to their y-fronts and congregate around the corner from the sleeping quarters. There was a very large, round, Cattle washing? Cattle drinking? Concrete pool, probably around six to eight meters in diameter. Within it was water of such a colour, that it looked like animals had not only been washing in it but may also have died in it. Insects, water scorpions and all, and what else God knows, had made it their home. This contraption was affectionately called 'The Washing Machine', and the staff had decided that we all needed to go on a thirty-degree wash cycle for twenty minutes, with a fast spin, followed by an air dry.

'Form a circle around the perimeter and follow the guy in front of you until we say stop', were the instructions. Speed adjustments were made to sufficiently aid the water in reaching areas above the thigh height it came to. Round and round you went until they saw some improvements in the skin colour of the soap dodgers. Then out and a quick check for any insect-like hangers-on such as ticks or leeches. As bizarre as it was, it did lift spirits amongst us a little. We still hadn't stopped thinking about our escape plan though.

That night we were going to do two activities. The first was a drop and return activity. After dark, your group would be given a compass, a map, and a flash light. A Land Rover would take you out into the middle of nowhere and leave you there. Your group had to find their way back to camp but get back into a checkpoint without being seen by security personnel that would be placed around the camp. All groups were going to do this at the same time, being dropped in different places. The second task was just for our group, as it had come around to our turn to perform it. Whilst everybody else slept we would guard the camp all night, taking turns every hour to be on watch duty. The first activity was hard. None of us were map readers, and it does help to know where you are at the start, to be successful in navigation via a map. We did make it back to camp though, an hour or so later, being captured by security before making the checkpoint. The use of a torch too close to the camp was our downfall. As soon as we made it back, we were taken to the area we had to guard for the night, which was at the other end of the camp. We set up camp on a strip of ground that faced a large cornfield. The corn was over a meter and a half in height at that time, and if you looked out you could only see the tips in the darkness. Behind us were the start of the wash block and then the sleeping quarters further on. It was eerily quiet, with just the sound of crickets in the air. The cable cars passing overhead made no noise at all, and there was no noise from the camp. I decided to go on the first watch. I thought this a good idea, as I could then get my head down for four whilst the others took their turn. Most of the time I sat down on my sleeping bag, just watching everything. If I heard a sound I investigated with a torch. Half an hour in, and I heard rustling in the cornfield. I couldn't see anything with the torch, and none of the corn was moving, so put it down to wildlife. The rest of the guys were right behind me, lying aligned in their sleeping bags like sardines in a tin. Suddenly we heard a thud. One of the guys sat up and showed a rock that had landed on his sleeping bag. After interrogating everyone as to who did it, nobody owned up. They went back to sleep and I continued with the watch. 'Thud'. Another rock landed in front of us, and then another on a sleeping bag. We were definitely under attack now. All got up and searched the front of the cornfield, shouts of 'who goes there?', were added as people investigated. It all went quiet and we resumed sleep and watch. Once again after a few minutes, it started again. It was getting funny now as the pelting started to pick up the pace. The guys would let out a laugh if one of the rocks landed on them. I was now under the impression that one of two things was happening. Either one of the other groups had left the sleeping quarters and was giving us a hard time, or some local black kids from a nearby village knew they could cause havoc in this way and had decided to pay a visit. All of a sudden, one of the guys who was standing with me, got a rock to the shin and fell in agony. At this point, we called for backup from the teachers and some more flash-lights. It continued to happen even when they were there with us. They went back to the sleeping quarters to check on numbers and make sure all bags had people in them. Everyone was present and denied any involvement when questioned. We went back with the teachers to continue with the watch, and just as they were about to leave us, it started again. The teachers went into the cornfield and started to confront whoever was out there. At that very point, I took a rock to the temple, which knocked me to the ground. The night watch was abandoned and we were sent back into the sleeping quarters, being questioned by the others there about what had happened. We never did find out who or what was throwing the rocks out there. My temple was sore and bruised for a few days after.

For several days afterward, and after being woken in the middle of the night several days on the trot to go on root marches, we were still planning an escape. All we needed to do was get to a telephone and summon a parent to bring a vehicle to collect us. Things had got worse, as some of the guys had decided to break out at night and go for a wander. Of course, they got caught and we were all subject to punishment, to make sure nobody else had similar ideas. On the last night, I got into my last pair of clean clothes that I had been saving for the journey home. I was going to sleep in these as well, as the rain still hadn't eased off, and all my other clothes had not dried at all. There was a stale, mouldy, earthy smell coming from my rucksack, where they had been rolled up for days. Still, it didn't matter, as soon I would be at home and could stuff them all in the washing machine. Just one more night to go and we were out of here. We were rounded up after dinner and taken to the area where we had been given the talks on local wildlife and first aid procedures. There were no more talks planned though. This was a gift from the staff, who had bought a large gateau for us all to enjoy. Maybe they did for every group? Or maybe it was because they had given us such a hard time? Who knows. It went down well though with hot chocolate. The food had not been awful at the camp, except for the days where you were being 'broken', but we had not had anything sweet in weeks. It revitalized us, which we needed.

That night it was lashing down outside. As I lay there, I could see the torrents pouring down through the chicken wire windows. It didn't matter though. I was contented, sleepy, dry, and warm for a change, and dreaming of the food I was going to lay into when I got back home. This dreaming period suddenly turned into a nightmare though at around 3:00 am. Once again, we were woken by shouting coming from several different staff members. Dustbin lids being bashed. Didn't these guys sleep? Nope. They stayed awake until the early hours, drinking whiskey and beer until they got bored and decided to have some fun. Their fun this time was to give us one last treat before we departed, in the form of shock treatment. Nobody knew what was going on. We had been lulled into a false sense of security with the cake and hot chocolate. Bleary-eyed, and stumbling, we were pushed out the door into the direction of a field not far outside. Then the instructions came at full pelt. 'Get down, keep your head down!', 'Or it will be shot off!', 'Crawl across the field...NOW!'.

As we lined up in fives to start crawling, we were already soaked from the torrential rain, so it didn't matter that we were now going to get caked in mud all over again. The staff were getting stuck in this time, following us as we crawled, pushing you into the ground if they thought your head was too high. Barking orders into your ears. I thought all hell had broken loose. These guys were only doing their job though, and as I look back, doing it well. Their task was to prepare us ready for the military in a few years. That would be hell, and even though what we had been put through over the last fortnight felt terrible, it wasn't going to be a patch on the two years of basic training everyone would be facing in a couple of years or so. It was necessary to be so harsh so that guys survived what was coming, which would help keep them alive when doing their service. I learned an extra lesson that last day, which was 'beware of South African Military men bearing gifts'.

CHAPTER 9 - CHRISTOPHER AND THE BURNING BUSH

I know – it doesn't seem possible. My bleeding parents. You would think to have their dream home and pool designed, and kitting it out with new furniture would have been enough for them. My brother and I painstakingly laid pretty much every brick by hand for the huge driveway. We collected most of them from the surrounding building sites too! Paving 'Ninjas' we were, as we could 'rescue' orphan bricks from the area around, and have it laid in position on the driveway before anybody had noticed it had gone. The grass had grown around the pool area, but out front, it hadn't even had time to take root. We still had a chicken wire fence out the front, and around the right-hand side of the building. There wasn't even a house next door, on either side, or to the rear, and yet we were off. Somewhere. Once again my brother and I had the up-and-coming task of fitting into a new school and making new friends. We had to leave old friends, and potential future business partners behind. This move must have been career-driven. My father was now General Manager of a large commercial bakery business in Krugersdorp. Protea bakery was one of the largest in the Southern Hemisphere, Blue Ribbon bakery in Johannesburg being the largest at the time, where my father had previously been Assistant Manager. I suppose it made sense for us to relocate to Roodepoort, which was next to Krugersdorp so that my father did not have to commute huge distances. The acquisition of our new home must have been a rushed affair though, as we found ourselves living in a townhouse complex in a place called Wilrokrans.

The houses were very close together, joined in fact, with no garden at all. There was a communal pool in a gated area around the back, which my brother and I spent a lot of time in, mainly expelling our lungs of air in the deep end, and sitting on the bottom for as long as we could. There didn't seem to be many other residents that used it. We still had our own bedrooms, mine big enough to house my tropical fish tank, and my hi-fi, which would get me into a lot of trouble. I liked to play my music loud when I got home from school, with the windows open. I distinctly remember getting in trouble when a neighbour who worked nights complained about me playing OMD's 'Tesla Girls' repetitively one afternoon. I still do this today in my car. The complex was over the road from a large park area, with a gazebo building and built-in BBQs. On Friday and Saturday nights, this area was a hive of activity with parties going until late in the night. I could listen to the park music in my bedroom if I had the window open, and I often did. Behind the park was a small river, and then in the distance behind that there was a very long, very high building that was supposed to be a 'Jehovah's Witness' complex. I say 'supposed' as I and others had suspicions about it, and on investigation found it to be potentially a lot more than what it was masquerading as. More about that later. The townhouse complex had a garden and maintenance man called Solomon, who my brother and I knew quite well, and would often talk to. One Sunday Solomon was proud to show off his new car, an Austin Mini in light grey. He was extremely chuffed with his new purchase, and to be honest, it was a good-looking motor in quite good nick. Only one problem though, the starter motor had gone, so it was a bump start every time to get off and running. Hearing from Solomon that money was all that was in his way from getting a new starter motor, I came up with a plan to help that would suit the pair of us. I would grease Solomon's hand with R20.00, and he and my brother would bump me down the slope from the townhouse complex onto the road. Now I didn't have a license as I was just about to turn sixteen, but a quick trip down the road and around the corner, and I would be facing the dirt road track that went down to the Jehovah's Witness complex. I would drive down this, turn around, and come back, getting some quality driving experience in. Solomon then had the deposit for his starter motor. Everyone's a winner. The deal was struck quickly, terms agreed, and I sat in the mini awaiting the push-off. Now, remember, the only driving experience I had up until now was driving a Datsun in the back garden, to and from the pool. This was going to be 'in at the deep end'. Gear changes would be required, and although the road was very quiet on a Sunday, there was the potential to meet other traffic, before reaching 'off-road', and of course the same on the return journey. Adrenalin was pumping hard, I let off the hand brake and pushed the clutch in with the second gear selected. I could see my brother and Solomon pushing hard at the rear. Just before the road outside of the complex, I let out the clutch. The car started and I made off out of the townhouse complex straight onto the road and round the corner to the left. Gear changes were happening smoothly, and I took the dirt road quickly as it came into view around the corner. It was good to be 'legal' again, so I now just enjoyed the dirt road ride. The first five hundred yards or so took me past the commune, and then the dirt road started to go downhill. I could see in the distance where it would start to go up again. Another gear change to get some speed up but it started to choke and then stalled. I tried the key but it wasn't going to start. I tried to push it back up the incline a little, and then jump in to bump start it, but it was insufficient. I was stuck. Looking back, the trees covered the view towards the townhouse complex, so there was no way Solomon or my brother knew what was happening. I don't know how many times I tried pushing that mini back up the incline, and then jumping back in and trying to get it into gear quickly, as it rolled back down, but to put it politely I was shattered. A mini is still very heavy when you are pushing it on your own. Fortunately for me, my perseverance had not gone unnoticed. Part of the 'smoke and mirrors' illusion that was being put on in the gardens around the Jehovah's Witness commune, was a single solitary gardener, in the fields at the front, who would be scratching at the earth with his hoe, pretty much all day. It was always only him, and he was always in the same area, where nothing ever grew or was planted. Just hoed the ground, all the time. Seeing I was having difficulty, he offered to help me push the car up further, and then give me a push down to gather more speed. We only needed one attempt at this and the car fired into action. I drove further on so that I could turn around, and then I thanked him as I whizzed by, setting off back to the townhouse complex. I'd learned my lesson and was extremely careful when having to stop the car at the end of the dirt track, before entering the road. I didn't stop at the entrance to the townhouse complex either, just went straight in where Solomon and my brother were waiting. Solomon was relieved to see me, he thought I had stolen his car and left him with R20.00 until I explained what had gone on. My mini-adventure had come to an end, and despite the troubles, I had enjoyed it. I wouldn't take to another car on the road until I had my provisional license, allowing me to drive alongside a fully licensed driver. Until then I would drive a truck around my father's Bakery grounds, getting so good at it that the security guard there would ask me to teach him!

The move to Roodepoort, had, of course, coincided with a change of school. I was about to turn sixteen, so with a little luck, if my parents could refrain from moving again for a couple of years, this new school would be the last I would have to attend. I decided to make some changes to my outward persona on arrival, to get left alone. I had escaped a school where attendance was daily torture, and there was no way I was going to endure that again. The best attitude, so I thought, was to go in looking like you didn't give a dam, with a face that said 'stay the hell away from me', so this is what I did. My parents had timed things well, with my first day being the first day of the new school year. Most of the students had gone to their new classes for their first registration. The 'newbies', were being taken to their classes afterward. I was taken to mine, introduced to the teacher, and then shown where to sit. I didn't make eye contact with anybody but simply looked towards my seat, flinging my sports bag across the floor, so that it came to an exact stop at the side of the desk, then as cool as you like, strolled up to it and sat down with a thud. It was a complete bad-ass manoeuvre, and I had executed every piece of it to perfection and got the result I wanted. Nobody spoke to me, they just looked away. I slumped in the seat and then started to survey my new classmates, looking particularly for those who looked like they could be a threat. The guy in front of me turned around and said 'Are you English?'. After I replied he said 'thought so', and continued to ask questions about where I had come from. The thing is I stuck out like a sore thumb here. Whereas my last school had been chock full of English immigrants, here it was different. Roodepoort was predominantly a South African/Afrikaans area. The immigrants that there were, were from Zimbabwe mainly, with a scattering of Portuguese. I was out of my depth once again, having no fellow countrymen to side with. To my surprise, the people in the class were quite friendly towards me, but I was careful not to let my guard down. Some of the other guys chatted with me and a few girls were inquisitive too. Looked like the new guy in the class had been accepted. Then the door opened, and In walked a new guy who was introduced to the teacher and then sat down opposite me. I could immediately see he was of the same thought as me. Although weedy-looking and wearing glasses, he came in with the same attitude as I did. They must have all been thinking 'Oh no not another one!'. He underwent similar interrogation to me, but as I had, he also kept his portcullis down, and didn't show an ounce of interest in who was speaking to him. I was relieved at his arrival, as it suddenly took the focus off of me. There was another new guy to find out about. I liked it that he didn't have a clue I didn't belong here either, having only just arrived myself. I introduced myself and found out that his name was Oliver Seitz, and although he had been here several years, he was originally from Austria. It didn't take long before we found out we had a lot in common. Our love for motorbikes, food, music, and women and our dislike for South African schools. I even introduced Oliver to 'Depeche Mode', which he took to straight away. Being Austrian, and with me having German blood, we could appreciate the depressing and finely crafted electronic music they produced back in the mid-eighties. This is pretty much all I listened to at age sixteen, and It would drive my father nuts, having to come into my bedroom and tell me to turn it down. He had no appreciation for it. Buddy Holly, Elvis, and anything 'Country' floated his boat.

A few weeks later, whilst still living in Jerling Court, I invited Oliver over after school to listen to some 'Mode', and set the world to rights. At this point neither of us had motorbikes, and so buses were the only way to get to and from each other's houses, which were quite far apart. This would change in the next month or so, as both of us would get our provisional licenses and take to the road on two wheels. This would open up a whole new world for us, which we would explore late into the evening. This particular day wasn't very good weather wise. It had been raining and there was the threat of more to come, so we took the opportunity to take David out for a walk with my brother. The poor mutt was going stir crazy being locked up all day, with no garden, and so the offer of any walk was met with that enthusiastic tail wagging in its familiar 'helicopter' style, accompanied by a few whimpers and whines of delight. David also had the knack of taking himself for a walk, insisting on holding his lead between his teeth, so that he didn't get lost. Our destination for this walk was down by the river behind the park complex. We hadn't been out half an hour when the heavens opened up like they never had before. We were some way along the riverbank and had a considerable way back to the house. It wasn't worth worrying about getting wet, as we were soaked in seconds. It always amazed me how quickly rain came down in South Africa. Roads turned to torrential rivers, and yet half an hour later could be dry. This day, however, was starting to remind me of the day in the mountains, where I nearly got swept away. It was starting to get dangerous, and so our walk hastened a bit, as the river started to exceed the limits of its bank. David was on the lead and trying to keep up behind us as best he could. Then I felt the lead go limp. As we turned around we could see David being swept away by the torrent of the river, back in the direction we had just come from. He was squealing in terror, and my stomach started to turn as I imagined him drowning. We ran along what was left of the bank, following David's howl as best we could. After a few hundred yards we could hear him nearer to us. Oliver was ahead of me and spotted him stuck in some branches on the side of the river. He was hardly keeping his head above water. Without any worry about his safety, Oliver jumped into the river and began to lift David out, passing him to me. Then we had to get Oliver out before he got swept away. If it wasn't for the branches next to the river bank, who knows where David would have ended up? All I know is that we would not have been able to save him. I owed Oliver a huge debt of gratitude. Soaked through to the skin, he was starting to shiver now. We hurried back home, put the two-bar heater on, and dried David down whilst Oliver had a hot shower and changed into some spare clothes we gave him. David was shivering constantly, but I don't think it was from the cold. I think it was more from being frightened of his near-death experience. His eyes didn't look right at the time for a while, but he pulled through OK, looking extremely grateful. Oliver made a lot of visits over the years, and he always made a point of giving David a fuss when he came. David was always pleased to see him too, obviously remembering who had valiantly saved him from the rapids.

My father had made good friends with his Sales Manager at work. George and his wife Joyce were also from England, both being slightly older than my parents. They soon became good family friends, and we spent a lot of time at each other's houses having meals, BBQs, and fun in the pool. Day's out at the dam, or fishing at the local trout farm. We seemed to do lots together, and it was all great fun. Dad and George got their first Betamax video recorders together and discussed getting Bophuthatswana television when it was due to start, requiring a specialist antenna installation. They seemed inseparable at the weekends, even though they spent all week together at work. They even found themselves amid a riot at work once, having to lock themselves in an office with a gun. George was a middle-aged, balding man with glasses, who liked a drink and was a very heavy smoker. He would do anything for you that he could and taught me and my brother a lot of skills, such as how to fall over and drop the trout you have just caught, so it goes back into the lake at the trout farm (you had to pay for all you caught you see!). Joyce was a lovely lady, grey-haired with glasses, but also having a lot of time for my brother and me. One weekend we were visiting them, as a motorbike had been advertised nearby that may suit me for commuting. I had R150.00 saved up, and this was the price. Myself, Dad, George, and my brother went to see it, taking the truck along in case a deal could be struck. Now I had my heart set on a street-legal scrambler, something like a Yamaha DT50LC or Honda MT50. These are the kinds of bikes I had sat on at the Rand show, and they were both on my wish list. The bike that was advertised, was a road bike. An ageing Suzuki GT50. With my budget limited though, this was all I could afford at the time to get myself on the road. It was in quite good condition, had alloy wheels, with all electrics working. It kick-started easily, and I could not see myself doing better for the money, so we paid up and strapped it into the truck. There was however one small problem with it. The clutch cable was broken so it could not be ridden. It also needed its 'roadworthiness' certificate. Despite being disappointed, we had to leave it at George and Joyce's house that evening, as we had to go back in the car. My father would pick it up in a few days and bring it home. When he did, it sat in the garage awaiting a trip to the mechanics at my father's work, to get the necessary done.

Now we all know from the past that I have a love of motorbikes, so much so that I will do anything to get out on one, even if it means wheeling it through the living room. This bike was more accessible, I did have my provisional license as I had sat the test and passed, and so wasn't going to let a little thing like 'no clutch', or no 'roadworthiness' certificate get in my way either. I had to be careful, and so only made quick trips out under the cover of darkness, when my parents were out. Just to the shops and back to get supplies, you understand. The first time out took some getting used to, having to master gear changes, at low revs, without a clutch. Then there was stopping the thing without stalling it, which required precision selection of the neutral gear, coasting to a stop, and then braking. Fortunately, the center console near the speedometer and rev counter had a large green light for neutral, so you knew if your stopping attempt was going to succeed or not. It took about a month to get the bike fully functional, and road legal, as well as third-party insured, which involved getting a second disc from the post office of all places. When it was delivered back to me, the fun started. I was suddenly free, at any time of the day or night. Free to meet up with other bikers from school, go out on long rides into the wilderness, or into the city. These were some of the best days of my life. Initially, my biking buddy was Oliver, who had talked his mother round into buying him a second-hand bike. He had a Honda MT50, which my old bike had trouble keeping up with. I have memories of us driving down the dual carriageway, with Oliver casually pulling up alongside me, one hand on the throttle, the other on his hip, mouthing through his helmet for me to open mine up and get going. He would then shake his head and throttle past me. I was giving my Suzuki the full beans. The trouble was she was old and tired and would get you somewhere at the speed she wanted to travel. We used to joke that I could get 60km per hour out of her. Oliver would add 'Yes if you were both falling down a mineshaft!'. Oliver was a year older than me, and pretty soon he would be taking his big bike license at eighteen. The teasing would only get worse then, as he would pull alongside me, and rev to drown out the sound from my 50cc. The mouthing would then be

'Why don't you get yourself a big boy's bike?',

'Instead of riding these 'souped-up hair dryers?'.

He loved every minute, whereas I just yearned for the day when I could get on something with a little more grunt. It wasn't long before Oliver decided that school was not for him. Bad grades and a total lack of enthusiasm for school meant that he was going to call it time. You could do this at age sixteen if you had made standard eight, and Oliver had decided that enough was enough. An opportunity to do something more technical came along, and he grabbed it with both hands. He was learning an engineering trade, getting paid, and was as happy as a pig in the mucky stuff. The trouble was that it was starting to rub off on me, and I was having thoughts about doing something similar. My parents, however, were not entertaining these thoughts at all. We occasionally met up in the evening, but the long nights out on bikes soon stopped, as 'some of us have to get up in the morning for work you know?'. I needed to find other bike buddies to hang out with, and these buddies arrived in the form of Steven and Quentin. Both in my class, Steven was tall, blonde, and a bit of a flirt with the ladies. A dab hand at anything mechanical. Hobbies included making his gym equipment, in particular, weights consisting of two concrete-filled paint pots on a metal rod. Also, homemade rockets made of wood, tin foil, and gun powder, helped along with a few hundred volts from the electricity supply. Any martial arts equipment, nun-chucks, ninja stars, knives, swords, and the like floated his boat. He lived with his mother and his down-syndrome sister, who worked at home assembling pipe fittings. Quentin was a short, mousy-haired guy, with an eye condition that earned him the nickname 'squintin' at school. Whereas Steven's mother had access to cash and bought Steven a brand new Yamaha DT50LC, Quentin, unfortunately, had a father who enjoyed making things, from scratch, over a long period. I went round to Quentin's house once after school to see the new 'bike' project his father was working on, which turned out to be some scrap in the corner of the garden at that time. Quentin had a large bedroom at the rear of the garden, joined to his father's workshop. The garden area outside was a dumping ground for anything mechanical that required work to get it running again. The largest thing was the shell of a Fiat car, and when I say 'shell', I mean just that. There were remnants of an engine in the boot and a steering column, and that was it, apart from the grass growing up through the floor inside. This was Quentin's father's big project that would one day be Quentin's first car. Sadly I never got to see the big unveiling of this car but witnessed its transformation over six months. Sprayed bright red and every component of the engine sprayed an equally bright, but different colour, it was a sight to behold I tell you. I did see Quentin's bike transform though, from a frame with a cylinder head and gearbox, missing headlight, and more grass than cables, into a working masterpiece that made more noise than a jet airliner, and yet only managed a top speed of around 30km per hour. For months Steven and I used to go round to his house to see the progress. Mr. Burrell would usually be sitting on the step outside the workshop, dressed in only shorts and a dirty tee shirt. Fag in hand, that hand up against his head as he was deep in thought trying to work out why his current objective was not working. He would greet you, and when you asked how he was, he replied, 'F*ck me this bike is getting to me', or, 'This piece of sh*t is giving me a hard time'.

Leave him there scratching his head long enough, and he would come up with a solution to his problem. He was a top bloke, who always seemed to be home, and yet he wasn't retired. If you had engineering problems of your own, he would drop everything to help you.

I distinctly remember the day Quentin was due at school on his father's creation. Much like the Fiat that lay in the back garden, Quentin's new bike was a work of art, with a few design features of his father's to give it a custom look. Most of us were waiting in the motorbike parking area for Quentin's arrival. You heard him first, and you heard him for quite a while until you saw him. We glanced towards the corner at the bottom of the road, and there appeared Quentin, very slowly, but loudly, with huge plumes of smoke billowing out behind him. Open-faced helmet and goggles, gloves, blazer and tie, bag on the back looking like 'Biggles' returning from a mission. He pulled up next to us and then attempted the 'shutdown' of this contraption his father had conceived. This wasn't easy. This beast refused to die, and in the end had to be stopped by letting the clutch out violently, whilst in gear with the brake on. I think the school trip that morning had been quite an ordeal for Quentin, as he was sweating, out of breath for some reason, and looking extremely relieved he had made it in one piece. He would take on a similar look when he found out it would take 20 minutes of kick-starting to get the beast going again after school. That evening, we would meet up at Biggles house to go out and cruise around town. Take in some video arcades, maybe play some squash at the courts, and catch some food at a cafe in the mall or something. We soon found out that whatever we were planning to do, we had to add lots of contingency time for break-downs, and for the slowness of the journeys due to the beast's maximum speed. Still, we were all together, free, and having a great time.

Now at this point in the book, If I told you my address you would probably be thinking 'That cannot possibly be another new abode?'. Well, it is. Fortunately, it would be the last address I reside at in South Africa. Seven moves in as many years, The Carlton to the Hotel Stephanie, to Plunkett Avenue, to Karee Street, to Mooifontein Road, to Jerling Court, and finally to Ouklip Road. So much for settling down. This house was on the corner of two roads, so had a large, exposed front garden, with a very small one to the rear. Double garage and driveway, with everything else inside as normal. There was a huge expanse of open ground to the right of the house, across the main road, with a large hill in the distance. For me, this house was merely sleeping quarters.

I had a new part-time job that took a lot of my time up, and with being out on my bike pretty much every night, I hardly spent any time at home. There was no pool at this house, as there wasn't room in the rear garden, so there was nothing to entice me into inviting friends around either. The only time I spent any time there was after school, and to do any necessary motorbike maintenance. My new part-time job was at a 'Spar' hypermarket in Wilrokrans. Owned and run by a Greek family and their parents. The Manager was Mr. Zourides, whose Christian name was an unpronounceable title beginning with 'Hippo..', so that's what people called him, and he was quite accepting of it. Hippo ran everything, with his sister and his ageing mother 'Mimi' working in the office. The ageing father worked in the Goods in/out part of the store and warehouse. It was quite a large store, with an in-store bakery, butchery, and fruit and veg department, the rest of the store devoted to everything else you would normally find in a supermarket. I originally got taken on as a Saturday till operator, under the guidance of the weekend till supervisor, but quickly extended to Sundays and evenings during the week. It was a 'clock in', 'clock out' type of setup, and so I quickly built up some extra cash with all the hours I was putting in each month. As this cash was coming in regularly, I started to set my sights on a new motorbike, as the old Suzi was getting me down. After some time I got a promotion to the cigarette counter, where I had to man the Biltong counter as well. A huge cabinet of very expensive, spiced, and air-dried meats hung next to me, with the addition of dried sausage made from beef, and game. Some of this meat would require slicing in the world's most dangerous, open, spinning blade mechanism known to man. No health and safety in those days! Time it wrong or take your eye off the ball, and you would end up with stumps for fingers, and the customer would have your digits mixed in with his meaty snack. Fortunately for me, the only extra I gave a customer was a bit of a fingernail, once or twice. Well, they would have just thought it was a bit of bone or something. I would like to take the opportunity to apologize to all those Biltong customers who got a little something extra in their bag, and also those who had a significant amount of sliced Biltong missing, as I would refrain from clearing it out from the bottom of the slicer after it stopped spinning. This so that I could munch on it once it had gone quiet, which wasn't easy under the watchful eye of Management from the office perched up to my right. It was around this time that I was getting a fortnightly part-work delivered from the UK and put by for me at the Spar. I forget the name exactly, but it was a computing science-based part-work, with the latest regarding home computers, and the computing industry in the UK. I had been receiving this for some time and it had not gone unnoticed by Hippo, as one evening he asked me to stay behind so he could offer me an opportunity. Well, that's how he worded it, but essentially it meant he wanted cheap labour to perform a boring and mundane task. He took me downstairs under the warehouse, somewhere I had never been before. It was in these depths that his father worked, in charge of the goods inwards, and stock ordering parts of the business. In a small office, there was a 'mock-up' of one of the downstairs till counters, complete with the NCR till. I assumed this setup was for training purposes, but there was something different about this setup. In the middle of the belt, to the left of where the cashier stood, was a bar code scanner, red lasers visible through the glass and mirrored surface, with a green and red light to the rear of it, each in a rectangle box. I knew what this was. I had read about these in my magazine. Hippo wanted to know if I could help out by being in charge of the 'go-live' with scanning in the store. This would involve scanning the bar code of every item, from all departments throughout the store on the master till upstairs, adding a description, price, and details of the general sales tax band, and saving it to the stock record. Thousands upon thousands of items, including all of the available packs from the butchery department, and products from the bakery department. After that, I would run one till, 'live', as a scanning till and test of the system. Once Hippo was happy, we would then train staff to use the system, and tell them how to deal with products without bar codes, of which there were a lot back then, and those products that had a barcode but didn't scan. During the testing phase, NCR installers would be upgrading the other tills to include the scanner and interface mechanisms. I had to install the cooling fan mechanism under the counter that kept the system cool throughout the operation. This turned out to be months of work. Working my way down every aisle filling a trolley with one of every different type of item, and then taking them back to the master till to create the scanning stock records. I took it as quite an honour to be offered this role, over and above everyone else who had worked there longer than me. This type of technology didn't exist anywhere else in Johannesburg as far as I knew. It was cutting edge back then, and Hippo had seen the benefits of having it installed, as it would cut down cashier pricing errors, reduce losses from human error, and remove the option for theft by pricing incorrectly for friends or family. I am pleased to say that I added every item in that huge store, ran the testing phase, ironed out the issues, and helped the store 'go live' with scanning., all for a few cents more than the till operators were getting. You would think I would have earned praise from the Management wouldn't you, doing all of this whilst maintaining my high grades at school (that's a joke there by the way...), but I was working for Greeks again, and Greeks do not like losing money of any kind if they can see that money being lost. If Hippo was to see something scanned and was aware the price had changed, he would make the excuse that I had put in the wrong price in the first place. He was supposed to maintain the price increases as he was informed of them, but it was much easier to give me a rollicking and say it was my fault.

One payday all of the part-time school attending staff came in to collect their wages, to find that various deductions had been made from them due to apparent 'cashing up' issues throughout the month. R50.00, and R60.00 deducted for no reason. Funny how we all got deductions, and that we had no way of complaining as we were not allowed to check our takings against what the computer said. This cheesed a lot of us off, especially when it happened more than once. It was funny how the missing amounts were always exactly to the Rand. I put up with this briefly but realized that once again I was being taken for a ride by the owners. You worked hard all month for them, and then they try and swindle you all, just to keep their wage bill down, so they can continue to drive around in their new Mercedes. Another opportunity came my way a little later on. Once again I was going to let myself be exploited, but this time it would be to my benefit, as I would later use the skills I learned to help out with my father's new business when we returned to the UK.

The bakery department was run by two Dutch bakers, and one was leaving. Rather than replace him, Hippo thought the weekend shifts could be covered by me joining Paul in the bakery department. 2:00 am on a Sunday I would turn up at the rear of the store and wait for Paul to turn up. Then into some whites and an apron. I learned how to put various mixes on, shape all different kinds of loaves, French sticks, and rolls, prove bread ready for baking, and bake and turn out. Additional skills in making cakes, morning goods, and doughnuts were also learned. I did this for just over a year before my original supervisor, who had left to work for CNA (Central News Agency), asked me if I would like to join him as a 'Late Sales Supervisor'. I jumped at the chance, as I was getting sick of the treatment I was getting from the Zourides family. There was a transition period where I was helping train my mate Quentin to take over my position in the bakery at weekends, still working behind the cigarette counter Saturday morning, and then working at CNA in the afternoon to learn the ropes. There was a girl in my class at school called Adele, who came into the Spar early one Saturday morning to buy bread and saw me baking. Later that day she came in again to the cigarette counter to find me there and gave me a look of surprise. Imagine how surprised she was when she came into CNA later that day to pick up a record she had ordered, to find me in a shirt and tie behind the record counter in the music department! The next day at school I was asked how many jobs I had. Well, it was to be one very soon as I had given Hippo notice of my intention to leave. He had no issue at the time, but nearer my leaving date, he offered me more money than the rest to stay on, as long as I did not divulge any of this information. I had already signed a part-time contract sometime before, and so declined based on that. It was, however, not going to be a bed of roses working at CNA either. The South African Manager was very difficult to work for. He had no time for English immigrants who struggled with the Afrikaans language, no patience if you needed help, and no sympathy if things went wrong on your shift. It was a good job that I had attracted the attention of an Afrikaans girl who worked on the till during my late shift as Supervisor. My Supervisor knew we had a thing for each other, so did his best to make sure that we were on at the same time for the shift until 10:00 pm. Five whole hours together, and most of it uninterrupted due to the quietness of the shopping mall between five and ten pm. The only thing I didn't like about it was having to wear decent trousers and a shirt and tie. Still, better than stinking like a bakery I suppose. At five o'clock the Manager would shut the main part of the store, using a set of sliding doors. This cut off everything apart from the books, magazines, and newspapers, which we had to sell until the store closed at 10:00 pm. Then it was shut the rest of the store up, and cash up. We both had to count every cent in the till, as well as the old-style paper credit card transactions, and make sure they tallied up with the till reading, minus the float. Everything went in the safe and then we could go home, usually around half ten. Most of the other stores had closed by then, so it was just the music playing through the mall speakers that kept you company on the way out. I worked at this CNA branch up until the time I left to come home to England...sorry for the spoilers!

One good thing about working all hours God made at the Spar, and the extra cash I was getting from the late shift at CNA, meant I was able to splash out on a brand new motorbike. Still riding around on a 50cc due to age restriction, I decided to splash out on my dream motorbike, with a little help from my father setting up the monthly payments for me. My friend Steven's mum had bought him a new Yamaha DT50LC. A liquid-cooled 50cc motorbike, in the street-legal scrambler style, and I wanted one as well. They were quite quick for a 50cc, and other guys who had them at school had swapped the default front sprocket for a 15-tooth one that gave you extra top end at the loss of some initial thrust. Steven and I had gone through many scrap yards, scratching around in the piles of sprockets looking for a 15'er for his bike, and were lucky to find one. He could now leave me for dust on my old Suzuki, but that was soon to be a thing of the past. I remember the day vividly when I had to ride my old Suzuki to the dealership in Krugersdorp after school to pick up my new bike. I had previously gone there with my father to choose my bike. I had chosen the same model as my mate Steven, in the same blue colour as his. It looked best in that particular colour scheme. There was an upgraded version of the bike, with different yellow detailing on the mudguards, and side panels, with a few new modifications to the engine and gearbox. It was also more expensive, so I decided against it and stuck with the same standard model as Steven. Imagine my surprise when I turned up at the dealership to find only the upgraded version of the bike sitting outside the shop. Mine must still be being prepared out the back I thought. When I went in and said I was picking my bike up, the dealer pointed outside to my bike. 'That's the wrong one', I said, to which the dealer replied that was the one my father had purchased. I had no choice but to take it so rode it home and telephoned my father to tell him there had been a mix-up. He told me not to worry about it, and that he must have chosen the wrong one. Too late now, so I've done well out of it. It was only many years later that I realized he didn't choose the wrong one at all. He knew I liked that model when I sat on it in the shop, and he made sure I got the bike I wanted. He didn't admit it back then, but I know now that is what happened. That's my father. Would give or get you anything you wanted. It was a lovely bike, and you cannot imagine how it felt turning up to school on it. Best bike in the parking lot and it was mine.

I know I rattle on about motorbikes a lot in this book, but it is relevant. It was the lifestyle for blokes of my age back then, and some girls too. It was how we got around. Before school in the morning, the roads and dual carriageways were full of school kids, sixteen and over, making their way to school, the boys with their ties flapping behind their helmets, the girls with their skirts blowing. Safety wasn't something that came to mind back then. You only wore a coat and gloves if it was cold, either in the winter or late at night. If any of these girl riders had come off, their legs would have been a mess. There was a girl in my class called Louise, who rode a Yamaha RZ50LC, which was the road bike version of the bike I was about to buy. She was a speed freak and an excellent rider. I saw her several times nearly getting her knee down. Her bare knee I hasten to add. Nerves of steel, firing around on her bike, with little to no protection other than her summer uniform. Bikes were big in South Africa, probably due to the weather, the wide-open expanses of space to explore, and the limited traffic that was on the roads back in the mid-eighties. I had not had my new motorbike long and was exploring the surrounding area a lot more than I used to, simply because it was more pleasurable on my new motorbike. It was smoother, quieter, faster, and much easier to handle than the old Suzuki. I loved every minute of riding it, and couldn't leave it standing for long before I would make some excuse to get out on it again.

A mile or so from my house was a new dual carriageway that had been built through a large hill. It was around half a mile long and took a sharp turn to the right at the exit of the hill. I had used this route several times since it opened as a quick way to get home if I had strayed out towards Johannesburg. On the day in question, it was late afternoon, around 4:00 pm. The sun was still on the horizon, and there was not a lot of traffic using this new carriageway. I was coasting along at around 50 to 60km per hour and just about to take the sharp bend to the left to start the downward coast through the hill cutaway, down towards home. As I turned the corner and started to straighten up my approach, I was suddenly greeted with a huge cloud of reddish-orange dust right in front of me. I slammed the brakes on as I could not see anything, thinking that it was just a whirlwind that had drawn up dust from the hill banks on the side, which had not had a chance to grow any vegetation yet. As I came to a stop and the dust started to clear slightly, I was faced with the awful sight of a bloodied man lying on the road in front of me, his body and limbs twisted and contorted, looking up at me and moaning in agony. About 10 yards behind him were his upturned car, windscreen smashed with a large hole where the man had exited his vehicle. I froze. Cars on the other side, and also those that had arrived behind me stopped, the occupants coming over to aid the man. I could still not move. I suddenly realized that If I had been a second or two ahead of myself, my new bike and I would have been further victims in this carnage. The man had driven up the other side of the carriageway, lost control for whatever reason, crossed the central reservation, and driven into the hillside on my side of the road. It must have been with speed and force to have thrown his unbuckled body from the car. One of the car drivers told me to move as I was right in front of the guy on the floor, so my brain kicked in and I rode off leaving the others to attend the scene. It was an experience that shook me and brought me back to earth with a bump. Motorbikes were dangerous and vulnerable, and I needed to be aware of that, and not ride around without a care in the world. From that day on, every other road user was a potential threat to my safety, and I treated them as such. I don't think my nerve ever came back properly. Even when I started riding again in my thirties, I felt vulnerable and threatened on the roads. I had a few near misses during my motorbike riding days, but nothing where either I or my bike suffered any major damage. My friend and schoolmate Quentin, however, was not so lucky very shortly after my close encounter.

One morning at school Steven and I were called to the office to see our Head of Year. Mrs Ferreira told us that Quentin had an accident on his motorbike. He had survived but was bruised and cut up a bit, recovering at home. We were told that his father said we could go and visit him after school. When we arrived at his house, Quentin was out the back with his father. Assessing the damage to the bike. Quentin was bruised, with a few cuts to the face. This had mainly come about from the fact Quentin used an open-faced helmet with his goggles as the only protection to his face. We asked him what happened and he explained that he was driving down the hill, when the sun, which was low on the horizon, blinded him. As a result, he did not see a parked car ahead of him. He hit the back of this with force, was thrown from the bike, and went right through the rear window, ending up on the back seat of the car. This account sent a shiver down my spine as It was the reverse of what had happened in front of me a few days earlier. The main thing was he had survived, somehow. The wounds would heal, and Mr. Burrell was certain that he could fix the damage to the bike, despite staring at it with a slightly tilted head, whilst singeing his hair with the cigarette that was in the hand that was currently scratching his noggin. Quentin would live to ride another day and once again on his father's creation. Later that year his father would treat him to an upgrade on his eighteenth birthday. A 650cc behemoth that shook so violently when idling, that it was impossible to make out any of the features of the speedometer and rev counter clocks that graced the handlebars. This monster had a single tall cylinder, the piston stroking up and down to such a length that the noise and vibration made Quentin's voice shake uncontrollably when he tried to speak to you whilst perched on it. We could do nothing else but laugh at this, but Quentin had the last laugh as he now had something that meant he would never be at the back of the bike gang again. It must have been as little as six months since I got my new bike when disaster struck for me, and I would once again be riding around on an old motorbike.

I was working the late shift at CNA in the mall and had just locked up for the night. I had to walk out the front of the mall, and around the corner to the back of the goods-in area of the shop. I parked my bike under a lamppost outside of the gates to the goods-in area, which was locked after 6:00 pm. That night as I took the corner, I could not see my bike under the lamppost. I looked all around but there was no sign of it. It had been stolen. My heart sank to the floor, a lump came to my throat as I realized it had been taken from me. I went back inside to use a public telephone to inform my father and ask him to come and pick me up, choking back tears as I did so. I couldn't believe it. As soon as he arrived we went to the police station to report it. They didn't seem positive that it would ever be found. Steven and I spent weeks searching the surrounding area once I had procured a cheap bike from a mate. If we found any bike like it, of either model, we would try my keys in the ignition. We looked for other bikes carrying what looked like new parts from my bike, but nothing. To make matters worse, the dealership and finance company had insisted that we take out insurance with a particular company to secure the finance, which my father agreed to. Around the same time as the theft, this insurance company went bust. That was the end of that. I would be riding around on an old Honda MT50 for the remainder of my time in South Africa.

Even today at age 50, If I could get one of those motorbikes, the same, I would. Just to remember what it was like riding it, and have a little longer doing it. You would think that I would have learned my lesson with my near-miss with the car and Quentin's accident, but it could not have sunk in deep enough. Before you knew it, with us all having turned eighteen, our evenings were taken up with riding to the town bar near the railway station, drinking inside with the locals, and then visiting the roadhouse next door for a toasted sandwich before setting off home. If I thought I had too much to drink and risked being pulled over by the cops, I would push my bike instead, but not every time. Pure stupidity on my part. We became regulars to not only the bar, but the roadhouse next door, so much so that the waiters knew our toasted sandwich preferences, and we even had our own 'table' in the bar. In the late evening, the bar wasn't that full, with only the ageing alcoholic stragglers left, supping late into the night and early morning whilst chatting to the barmaid. The sort of men with shoulder-length, unkempt grey hair, yellow tar-stained fingers, and khaki safari tops and shorts on. The indoor hat wearers, the seasoned whiskey drinkers. Imagine every Australian film you have watched where they show a typical ageing Aussie man propping up the bar in the outback, and you have the right image in mind. As many miles apart from Australia as England was from South Africa, and yet the late-night bar drinkers were so identical, you could swap them over and nobody would bat an eyelid. The only difference would be that an Aborigine man would be welcome to enter and drink in an Aussie outback bar in the eighties. This late at night a black South African man would not be allowed to be in the same town, let alone the same bar as a white man. Every drinking establishment, much like every public toilet, restaurant, bus, school, hotel, and hospital, was off-limits to the black South African. That is unless they were part of the service industry that kept them running during the day. You could tell where the black South African man was not welcome, as there were constant reminders in the form of signs and placards. Written in both English and Afrikaans, these signs made it clear by stating 'Whites only!', or 'No Blacks!'. The bar we were in was no exception. Sad to think that my friends and I were welcomed into a shebeen. There were no signs saying 'No Whites!' there. Back then I was indoctrinated like every teenager my age, so I never questioned how the country was run, or considered just how much the lives of Black South Africans were suppressed by the then government. I sadly just went along with it. With none of my current gang being lovers of the Shebeen brews, we stuck to downing our horrific brews at this watering hole. Our drink of choice was called a 'depth charge'. A shot glass of 'Crème de Menthe', placed inside a pint glass full of the strongest lager available on tap. You waited until the oily green liquid had dissipated into the lager, and then removed the shot glass before drinking it. God only knows why one of us suggested drinking this concoction regularly. All I remember is that it wasn't me. After a pint of it, you soon forgot your worries, not that you had any, and ordered more, or a whiskey and lemonade which was a favourite of mine. The bar did not offer any kind of food. Not even nuts or crisps, so as soon as the munchies kicked in (which was very quickly), we would head next door to the roadhouse. This closed around midnight, so we had to get out of the bar before that to secure some food.

Late at night, you could sit out 'al fresco' style, and order a burger, hot dog, or toasted sandwich, as the temperature would still be very desirable. It wasn't a good idea to wash anything you had down with a huge milkshake, not after what we had put down our gullets before. We all lived in different directions, so the trip back home, as short as it was, was still a lonely one, with very little traffic on the roads, and everybody pretty much tucked away in their houses. Maybe just the glint from the drive-in movie theatre screen as I passed by, but with hardly any cars parked up mid-week. I have to admit to my parents that on the occasion where I felt OK to ride my motorbike back, I rode slowly, and felt OK to do so. Any time I didn't feel up to it, I pushed it all the way home, fearing that I could be stopped by the cops. I was never stopped whilst riding my bike on those nights, but I did get stopped whilst pushing it. Figure that out? I explained why I was pushing it rather than riding it and was allowed to continue on my way after some scrutinizing of my 'book of life'. The traffic police in South Africa mainly rode motorbikes themselves. Remember the American series 'Chips' with Eric Estrada? That was the South African traffic cops back then, right down to the open-faced helmets, shades, thigh-high black biker boots, and khaki uniforms with white tee-shirts underneath. It was like the South African government had to find a look for the force, saw 'Chips' on television, and said 'That's how we will kit our guys out'. If they were not pulling you over for minor traffic offences, or checking the roadworthiness of your vehicle, you would usually come across them parked at the side of the road. Sitting there with a speed monitor device, and a pair of gas strips across the road. If you didn't spot them in time, you risked driving over the strips too quickly. They would radio ahead to another bike cop further down the road to wave you in. I never got caught this way, but that is probably because any 50cc motorbike struggled to get anywhere near the speed limit, let alone exceed it. Oliver and Quentin had much larger motorbikes though and had to be a lot more careful.

It was in the summer of '85 that I started to hang out with some other guys from school, also bikers. Jarvis, Gary, Wayne, and Gary's older brother Steve, who was currently doing his national service, soon became new mates. These guys were a bit more hardcore than Quentin and Steven and I was about to start mixing in a different scene, where drinking was the order of the day, no matter what time of day it was. Also chilling, chasing women, clubbing, and indulging in the odd 'smoke' or two. These guys always seemed to be up to something, especially when Steve had either had an authorized break from barracks or gone AWOL for a while. I was surprised to get invited to some of the jaunts, but my parents didn't seem to mind me disappearing without knowing where or how far I was going. The first of these 'jaunts' was to a house right out in the middle of the sticks. I couldn't tell you where but we all went on our motorbikes, with Steve going pillion on Wayne's XT500. Another guy who was lucky enough to have turned eighteen already, enjoying the riding experience of a more powerful bike than the rest of us. This two-night getaway was sold to me as a lager and 'Zohl' funfest with the added excitement of a soundproof recording studio, complete with a full drum kit. Wayne's brother's place needed 'looking after' whilst he was away, and the fool had trusted that we were the appropriate bunch to do it. We would eat, drink, and smoke ourselves into oblivion, aiming to produce some serious music of quality alongside. Well, we certainly fulfilled the first part. Two days and nights passed and I could not tell you where they went. From my vague recollections, I can remember being told that I was an excellent drummer by several stoned onlookers, who had wasted themselves to the point where they could no longer stand. Quite an achievement as I had never seen a set of drums let alone played any. This is probably how so many drummers, in so many rock bands across the world, achieve their status of greatness, getting drunk and high before every performance. The muscles relax, and the drumsticks become one with their hands, allowing them to beat out in fury any combination of riffs that synchronize with the accompanying music perfectly. Occasionally Wayne's body would find an ounce of adrenalin left in his bloodstream, to wake his failing eyelids, allowing him to stand up and adorn his bass guitar. Spliff hanging from the side of his mouth, he would try to get his mind, arms, and fingers working in some sort of unison, to produce dulcet bass tones to accompany the racket I was producing from the snare, toms, and cymbals. If that wasn't bad enough, an ageing drum machine with bright orange and red switches, pulsed out sequenced lights as it added smooth 'Bossa Nova' into the mix. Gary and Jarvis sat propped up in corners, mouths open, heads back, drooling, the electric guitars and microphone lying in their laps, their sound absent from the masterpiece that the rest of us were creating. To us then, it sounded awesome. In reality, it wasn't. Eventually, all of us would expire to the ground, so out of it that none of us could find the door to this soundproofed room. The soundproofed tiles made every wall look the same, and there was no hint of a seam anywhere to suggest that was where a door might be. We had partied and rocked hard that weekend, being given a glimpse into Wayne's World (well Wayne's brother's world actually).

All that had to be done on Sunday morning was clean up the sick, hoover up the remnants of grass that had escaped our fingers and not made it into the 'rizzlers' that evening. Filling the bin with the numerous empty lager cans, whiskey bottles, and remains of the food we had tried to prepare. It had been a great weekend, even if most of it was a blur. So great that it wasn't long before the next exciting party jaunt was being planned. This next one would involve some extensive travelling, clubbing, bodyboarding, and another close encounter with death! I'd been spending a lot of time with Jarvis, Gary, and Wayne despite Gary and Wayne leaving school to work in factories. They had enough of school and wanted to earn some money to spend on women. Who can blame them? One weekend word came out via Jarvis that they were all planning to go down to Durban for the weekend. Steve would drive us down in his bakkie, which could fit three up front, and the rest of us in the rear under the canopy. The plan was to crash at Gary and Steve's grandparent's caravan that they had on an old people's campsite just off one of the beaches. I was up for this and so armed myself with 24 long-toms for the journey as suggested. These would be split with Steve as he was doing all the hard work in getting us there and back. We set off around 7.00 pm one evening, with Steve, Gary, and Wayne riding up front and myself and Jarvis in the rear laid upon a mattress with everyone's sleeping bags and the stash of beer for the weekend. There were at least four trays of lager bouncing around in the back with us for the journey.

Over six hours it took to get there as we got lost near some cornfields and could not locate the campsite for the life of us. Finally, at around some time after 1:00 am, we arrived and it was heads down in various places until the next morning. Not before a nightcap though... lagers for most of us, and a good start on his bottle of Whiskey for Steve. Some of us kipped on the floor in Grandma and Grandpa's awning, and some in the back of the bakkie. The next morning came quickly. Very quick, and the lads were eager to stroll the minute or so from the campsite to the quiet beach. It was around 7:00 am when we hit the sand. The sun was shining and there was not a cloud in the sky. Everyone had their can of breakfast, so there were smiles all around as we enjoyed the warm air and the walk along the beach. I still have a photo of this morning to this day, as I took my camera. Sadly no more of the excursion though. During the walk we planned the trip to the main beach in Durban, the itinerary for the day was as follows. Some major beach time, including bodyboarding, with some serious food intake and drinking, to set us up for the evening visit to some local nightclubs. Then back to the campsite for some brief shut-eye before doing it all again on Sunday. As a liquid breakfast had been all that had been consumed early that morning, the first thing on our minds was proper food when we got to the beach.

Fortunately, Durban Beach was full of food stalls, selling everything to accommodate our needs. My needs, much the same as everyone else, were burgers and chips with a serious amount of tomato sauce. It was a busy Saturday at the beach and it was difficult for us to find a spot free where we could place the mattress from the bakkie. More people than you could count were enjoying the morning sun, either sunbathing, splashing in the waves, or bodyboarding. As soon as half an hour had passed, after consuming a very heavy breakfast of fried food, it was time to buy a bodyboard from the shack on the beach. They were as cheap as chips, so no worries in leaving it in Durban afterward, rather than accommodating it in the already very cramped bakkie on the trip home. I was looking forward to this immensely. Durban had waves and a half, big waves that could consume you and spit you out if they caught you right. I had experienced these waves on several occasions whilst holidaying with my family. Durban was home to the 'Gunston 500' surfing championships, where the best surfers from all over the world came to try and tame the huge swells that the Indian Ocean produced. They were dangerous. Very dangerous with the added threat of many warm-water sharks, including Great Whites. The beach area had shark nets way out, so providing you didn't stray passed them, or a shark didn't manage to get under or around them, you had a good chance of being OK. Hardcore surfers who wanted to catch the really big waves, strayed way out past the protective nets, taking their lives into their own hands while facing two major threats. The first being eaten, and the second being overcome by some of the biggest waves you will ever see. Our bodyboard antics would take us out quite far, far enough so that you could catch the big waves just as they were forming. If you caught them just right you would be able to lean into them sufficiently, so that you rode the crest as it grew, gaining some immense speed before the wave began to break, encasing you in a flurry of foam. If you still managed to keep the balance just right, you would sit atop the wave, looking down from around 12 to 15 feet in the air at the other beach-goers as they were engulfed by the wave. You just hoped they ducked enough to avoid your board as you went speeding overhead. There was no way of stopping or manoeuvring out of the way, you just had to go with the flow. Until you were suddenly propelled onto the shale on the beach, which brought you to an abrupt stop. Sometimes so abrupt that you came off the board and carried on skimming belly down onto the beach. The adrenalin rush was huge, so much so that all you could think of was getting right back out there to catch another one. As easy as this sounds, it wasn't. Not only did you have to get yourself through all the large breakers, out to the calmer waters to wait for the next big one, but you also had a large bodyboard to get out there too.

Sometimes you would make it and the board would catch the wave, taking you back ten feet. The trick was to go under the waves as they approached, diving down with the board, riding under the wave, and then resurfacing on the other side. Look ahead of you and you could already see the next one coming, so you paddled like mad to make as much progress as you could. Soon things would start to get quieter as you left the main congregation of bathers enjoying the breaking waves. The sea would also get calmer and quieter. Eerily quiet. So quiet that you felt extremely vulnerable, and apart from your eyes scanning the horizon for any sign of the beginning of a forming wave, it was also scanning the depths beneath you for any large moving shadows, and the surface of the water for any sign of a tail, or dorsal fin. You had heard the stories of those who had been caught whilst surfing. Some escaped with horrific scars to their boards and themselves, some not being so lucky to survive.

In the evenings you could take a boat trip out to the net to watch men getting any sharks that had got snagged in the nets free. Those that were alive were set free, and any that didn't make it were brought ashore to be sold to deep-sea fishermen for bait. I can remember on one occasion getting spooked as I lay out there, with just a few other boarders for company, but at a distance. Thinking I saw something in the water, I paddled and kicked violently towards the beach, head down as fast as I could. Occasionally looking up to see how far away the people were in the surf. As far out as we were, they looked like pinpricks in the distance. You could hardly hear the screams of enjoyment that were coming from them. They were unaware of your panic, and your hasty retreat from the deeper, calmer waters. Despite the apprehension we body-boarded for hours, stopping on the odd occasion to dry off in the sun and relax on the mattress listening to the radio. This was an equally good place to be, as there was the constant distraction of scantily clad, bronze-skinned young ladies to gaze over. These were the same young ladies that we would be hunting down later in the bars and nightclubs. I use the word 'hunting' as ladies on nights out in Durban gathered in groups like Gazelle. As the primal lions we were, we would aid each other in separating them from the pack, picking them off one by one. Now I never had the 'gift of the gab' so to speak, and little confidence around women, so if any of the pride was going to go hungry, it was going to be me. Before the nightclub jaunt started though, it was into the bar off the beach. We found a booth and started to get a few down before the night was to begin. 'A few' meant many Whiskeys and lemonades, to help hydrate a bit. This was a welcome drink in the humidity of the evening.

Around ten o'clock it was time to head for a club. I cannot remember what the name of it was, or whereabouts it was, all I can say is that we waited in the queue until we got beckoned in by the bouncers. We were all frisked before entering, and I was surprised to see that Gary was caught carrying a pocket knife whose blade was considered too long. This was confiscated at the door. Once inside, it was like another world. The thumping music was so loud that you could not hear a word anyone was saying, flashing, strobing and spinning lights accompanied the dance music blasting out at eardrum bursting decibel levels. A plethora of beautiful young women and a bar as long as the horizon. I was in heaven. At age 18 then, this was my Mecca. Where I had to come to worship the skill of the DJ in pumping out never-ending, hypnotic dance music, whilst I supped on endless alcoholic concoctions, laced with whatever Steve had dropped in to help us all enjoy the night. My eyes became laser-guided, scanning the room like the 'Terminator' for young women who ticked all the boxes. The several that had caught my eye, were being subjected to my constant gaze, waiting for their friends to inform them they were being watched. The others were drinking or dancing, drinking and dancing, or just drinking. I was off on my hunt, but having little to no success, when suddenly I got a tap on the shoulder. A guy and his girlfriend stood behind me, and he leaned into my ear and shouted 'Kiss my girlfriend'. I look at his eyes, and can immediately see he is smashed, his girlfriend not so. She was hot. I leaned back and shouted at the guy 'I can't kiss your girlfriend mate, that wouldn't be right?'. He replied waving his glass in the air in front of me 'It's her birthday, you've got to give her a kiss!'. I looked at her and she nodded in agreement, saying it was OK, she wanted a kiss as it was her birthday. I quickly went through the consequences of such an action, it might be a ruse to get me to kiss her so he can punch me and get me thrown out. They could be swingers and might be eyeing me out for a potential hookup later. They might be nutters and want to kill me later? She was hot though... I was relieved when I finished snogging his girlfriend, wished her Happy birthday, got a thank you from her, and a handshake and a pat on the back from him. The evening was getting off to a good start, and I now had an ego the size of the moon and was suddenly brimming with confidence. I should have stopped there... Many drinks had gone down since we entered the club and coupled with the spice added by Steve, things were starting to get blurry. The facial definition was starting to go. That's what Tequila does to me. Now all I had to go on, was to spot a good-looking pair of legs in a dress, and long blonde hair. It wasn't very long until I found a match. To my surprise, despite wobbling on my feet like I was treading an earthquake, and missing several items of furniture that I was trying to hold onto whilst circumnavigating the dance floor, I caught the eye of an attractive woman some ten yards away. Eye contact was made several times accompanied by smiles in both directions. I spent some time surveying the young lady, not quite believing that she was alone and that out of everybody there, she was making eyes at me. One last long sip of my drink and it was time to make a move. I started to make my way towards her, under her constant gaze and ever-increasing smile, when suddenly I got grabbed by the arm from behind. To my surprise it was Gary. 'Where are you going?', he asked. I replied that I had 'pulled' and I would catch up with him and the others later, showing him by way of a discreet nod the young lady who was waiting for me some five yards away. He grabbed me harder and pulled me in the opposite direction. Confused, and somewhat angry I asked him what he was doing. 'No mate, you gotta come back', he said trying to conceal the laughter that was desperate to come out of him. Then he proceeded to burst my bubble. My beautiful bubble. 'That's the club transvestite mate!'. 'He's here all the time?'. 'Thank God I caught you in time!'. I gazed back at her... I mean him.. squinting hard to try and see what I had missed. By now I had been dragged back to the group, where Gary took the first opportunity to fill everyone in on my narrow escape. This would be the source of much merriment the next day, as well as for weeks to come. The only thing that I had going for me was that they had all seen me get stopped by the couple, and then snogging his girlfriend. So out of all of us, I had seen the most action that evening!

I looked at Steve's eyes and he was completely messed up. He had put away a serious amount of drink, and God knows what else. Pupils did not look right and he could hardly keep his eyes open. He was our designated driver too. The bakkie was parked down a side street waiting to take us back to the campsite. At the time I didn't realize the seriousness of letting Steve get behind the wheel. It was around 2.00 am when we decided to depart. Everyone was shattered as it had been a long day, and all we could think about was getting some shut-eye. During the evening it had been raining, and although it had stopped, the roads were wet. Wayne and Gary were eager to grab the back of the bakkie so they could sleep on the mattress on the way back. That left me upfront with Steve, which turned out to be a good thing, as I believe I was the most 'compos mentis' of all of us. The roads in Durban were quiet, with no other vehicles around, and this made it easy for Steve to navigate his way around the 'block' type 'New York' style design of the streets. One corner proved too much at the speed he was going though, and after negotiating it he lost control, spinning the bakkie and its contents, (us), around a full 360 degrees, coming to an abrupt stop as he woke to slam the brakes on. This had woken the two sleeping in the rear so that they now had their faces up against the glass partition exclaiming to Steve 'What the hell just happened?'. This brief interruption had woken Steve a little, but he was still struggling to stay awake. Me on the other hand... I was now wide awake and realizing the danger we may be in on the journey home. I watched Steve like a hawk every mile until we got back. Whenever I saw his eyelids dropping, or his head starting to droop, or felt the vehicle veering towards the wrong side of the road, I would make some sort of loud noise to wake him from his slumber, especially when we were navigating windy roads with a drop either side. I honestly could not tell you how he knew where he was going, how he managed to drive, how we got back alive. It was a close call, and we still had a five or six-hour journey back to Roodepoort on Sunday night. I was praying he would have such a hangover that he didn't want to touch a drop on Sunday.

You will remember I wrote about the Jehovah's Witness complex, and how Steven, Quentin, and I were extremely suspicious about it. It looked out of place and warranted some time investigating. Something didn't seem right about it. That lone gardener hoeing the soil out the front, the complete absence of any other people around. At first, our reconnaissance trip took us away from the complex, but still well in sight of it, and on the same land. Nobody seemed to mind if you crossed the river, came through the poorly kept fence, and walked across the hills on the land. I say didn't mind, but once we were buzzed by a low-flying carrier aircraft. So low we had to hit the ground. Not sure if it was intentional on their part, or whether they were just practising low-flying manoeuvres across the hills, we took cover on lower land. Here we found some 'Danger keep out', and 'Military shooting range' signs up against the fence. The signs were old and rusting so it did not look like this was an active range. We went through and could see the old remnants of target practice sessions. The area had a strange chemical type smell to it. Smelt sort of toxic in the air, and so we did not stay there long. We pondered the question of whether this was all military ground, and if the aircraft came from a nearby base lower down the hill. Maybe the complex was future barracks for recruits? Or a forward operating base for a deeper base out of sight and reach? We decided that the best course of action was to go on night manoeuvres up in the hills at the back of the complex. Looking down from there we may be able to spot something. We would meet later, ride most of the way, and then hit foot so as not to be spotted. Steven knew exactly how to approach the exercise and was coordinating everything, supplying the boot polish for our faces and the binoculars. Steven was military ready, his father had been a designer of one of the South African Air Forces helicopters, (I forget which), and so Steven was very proud of his military background. It showed as he was ready for every covert occasion, carrying hunting knives, air pistols, and whatever was needed to make a fire or a meal.

That night, after meeting far back at the top of the hill overlooking the complex, we ditched our motorbikes and headed on foot to the perimeter fence at the edge of the hill. Military precision was required here, whilst we leopard crawled through the bush up to the fence. If either Quentin or I made even a hint of noise, we would be subject to Sargent Van Graans wrath, which could be violent and abusive at times. It was best to do what you were told and keep on the right side of him, as the guy had a temper with a fuse wire the length of an ant's bum. There was only one altercation along the way, and fortunately, it was Quentin who was first on the receiving end of Stevens's psycho-style treatment, after cutting himself on something sharp on the ground and screaming out in agony. I usually found myself as the mediator between these two when they didn't see eye to eye. I could usually diffuse the situation quickly, reminding them that we were all buddies, and should be looking out for each other, rather than trying to strangle each other with the collar of our shirts scrunched up into our fists. Sometimes diffusing the situation that quickly was a warning sign of how unstable Steven was. He could switch from a foaming mouth to a smile far too quickly for my liking. Very 'Jeckel & Hyde', and in the blink of an eye. Shortly after this incident, we arrived at the fence, where Steven took out the binoculars from his rucksack and started to survey the complex below. We must have been no more than two hundred yards up at the top of the hill. It was a sheer drop down after the fence. Below you could see a small dirt courtyard about 15 to 20 yards away from the base of the hill. Steven was already muttering to himself with the binoculars scanning the area. I don't think he could believe what he was seeing. We could see it without the aid of binoculars. The rear of the complex was adorned with tall thin hanger doors, eight to ten of them, that looked like they worked on roller mechanisms. It seemed a very strange setup indeed for a religious complex. The doors were too thin to accommodate any aircraft, and even if they did, you would not be able to get that aircraft out of the door, and round in the courtyard to any exit at the sides of the building. There was no room for vertical take-off of any kind. Even helicopters were out of the question. I think we all concluded that this was some sort of manufacturing facility. Whatever they were making in there, could come out of those doors on trolleys and be loaded up and shipped out. This probably happened under cover of darkness, so we settled in to see if tonight would be our lucky night. This was no 'Jehovah's Witness' complex. Taking turns to keep watch with the binoculars, we must have stayed there a good few hours before getting bored. Not a sign of anything. Could be we caught them on the wrong night, or could be that unknown to us, we were being monitored, and all activity had been stopped. We will never know. By the way,... brown boot polish ain't half hard to get off your face.

A few days later at school, Steven approached Quentin and me and suggested that we camp out for the night on the hill next to the complex. He had already found a spot near a huge cave that would be ideal for spying on the complex and the nearby airfield that we were convinced existed not far away. We would camp out at the weekend, kipping out under the stars in sleeping bags. We would explore the cave, have a cook-out and some beers, and then see what happens in the local vicinity. Plans were made, provisions acquired and suitable weaponry obtained. An air rifle belonging to Quentin, and several large hunting knives from Steven. I brought the sausages. It was a short motorbike ride over rough terrain before we arrived at the campsite. You could see for miles as the view was amazing. We were near a cliff edge that spanned out over a huge area. A vast expanse of nothing but African land. We set our three sleeping bags up in a row facing towards the complex. Behind us a fireplace ready to cook dinner on, surrounded by rocks we had collected to prevent a bush fire. This was important as the grass and bush were dry. It hadn't rained in ages, and any stray flame would burn the surrounding area uncontrollably. This happened a lot. You would wander across a field, or piece of waste ground completely burnt down to the ground. A black, grassy coating is the only thing remaining. Usually started by a discarded cigarette stub belonging to a trekking black South African making his way home from work. The first item on our agenda after making up camp was to explore the large cave a few hundred yards from us. It was a man-made cave. You could tell from the huge entrance in the hill, with deposits from the excavations scattered out front. What had they been excavating for here? Precious stone maybe? Could have even been for gold on a small scale? There was something of interest within the stone of this cave, and with some luck, we might find evidence of it inside. Armed with torches, and the air rifle should we need it, we ventured deeper and deeper in. Very quickly it became apparent that we were not alone. The current owners of the cave were starting to awake as the sun was setting, and our presence and noise were causing them to start to flee the cave in large amounts. Bats, quite literally hundreds of them, mainly hanging from the ceiling and walls which were encrusted with droppings. The floor, which we hadn't noticed, was a mess too. A mixture of white, green, and grey slurry coated it, with the odd dead bat thrown in. Over our heads flew dozens of them making their way out of the cave into the twilight. A hundred or so yards into the cave it opened up into a huge chasm. Our torches scanned the ceiling to reveal more bats than you could imagine. The size of large mice hung no further than a few centimetres apart. Some were startled by the torches shining into their faces and stretched and then departed. It must have taken ages to excavate this huge cavern. There was no sign of any drill marks, and with the mess, smell, and constant bombardment from above, we didn't hang around long to find evidence of what prize was within this cave that made prospectors take on the mammoth task of carving it out of solid rock. Back at camp and after filling ourselves with provisions, Steven had started to explore. Quentin had been playing with his large hunting knife and stupidly had been working the blade against a stone to make sparks. At the point Steven returned from his travels, Quentin was showing me the sparks generated in the semi-darkness. All hell broke loose as Steven pounded over and grabbed Quentin by the throat, taking the knife from him, and threatening him with it at very close quarters to his neck. All the time spouting profanities, and almost spitting blood. He was angry, and angrier than I had ever seen him before. It was a frightening side of him neither of us had witnessed before. This knife was more precious to him than we had bargained, and he was extremely displeased at the abuse his prized blade was getting from Quentin. It was obvious to me that I had to step in very quickly and try and calm the situation down, and very tactfully and gracefully. Once again I had to remind Steven that we were all buddies, on the same team, and that it was stupid of Quentin to play with his knife in this way, risking damaging the blade beyond repair. It took some talking from me to defuse the bomb, and fortunately, Steven headed off into the night to cool off, all the time muttering how he would have knifed Quentin had he damaged his knife. Quentin was visibly shaken, and we laid on our sides on the sleeping bags, facing each other, quietly discussing how Steven had gone psycho, and how lucky we were to come out of the situation unscathed. An apology was going to be the order of the day when Steven got back. Unbeknown to us, Steven had gone away to resharpen the blade of his knife back to his former glory. Not more than half an hour must have passed, and Quentin and I had relaxed somewhat and were just chatting and joking. All of a sudden we were brought back to earth when we heard a firm thud between us. We could not have been half a meter apart, and yet there between us, inches from our arms and hands was Steven's knife, the blade buried a third of the way into the ground at a forty-five-degree angle. After the astonishment had passed we looked at each other in horror. We then glanced at our rear, expecting to see Steven standing right behind us. Instead, our gaze had to continue further, around 25 feet further, and elevated on higher ground. There stood Steven, or shall we say 'Steven Segal', still in a completed knife-throwing pose, with an increasing grin adorning his face. I think our two hearts stopped briefly when we realized what he had attempted, and fortunately for us, had successfully executed. He walked towards us, still grinning, neither of us daring to point out his stupidity this time. It was a message being sent to the pair of us. Fortunately, Jekyll had now turned into Hyde, and Steven was accepting of the apologies from Quentin. The monster side of him was not there, but there was still a look in his eye that made us treat him with kid gloves for the rest of the excursion.

At school discussions between boys usually turned to motorbikes. Almost everyone had one, and at every opportunity, you discussed what you had done with them, and more importantly, what you had done to them. Steven was always researching alternative fuels for his Yamaha and had changed various parts for scrapyard replacements to try to increase top speed. He had also tried adding mothballs to his fuel tank to aid the 'anti-knocking' properties of the engine, to make it run smoother. Indeed a lot of experiments were done, but there were never any consequences. It was on this particular day at school that we learned from friends of his, that a German classmate had been in an accident. Marcus had tried to make his machine more efficient by 'de-coking' the exhaust. A risky procedure, fraught with danger. We found out just how dangerous when he finally returned to school, with a red blistered face, and a couple of missing eyebrows. He was very lucky. He explained the procedure he undertook and what went wrong. You have to first remove your exhaust from your bike, and remove the baffle. Block the manifold connection end with a rag, and then pour a small amount of methylated spirit down the baffle end. You would then hold at arm's length and then drop a lit latch down the exhaust pipe. After a loud, deep bass-like, woosh, the 'carbon' contents of the exhaust would be expelled violently. Do this a couple of times and you will have cleaned the exhaust fairly well, and your bike should run a lot better. The thing to remember was that you must make sure that the match you put down the exhaust had gone out before attempting to pour more meth down. Unfortunately for Marcus, this was not the case, and his addition of meth went up in smoke and flames right next to his face. A valuable lesson to us all, and so we were destined not to make the same mistake if attempting this cleaning ritual.

Now my prized brand-new motorbike had been stolen, and I found myself with a crappy old Honda MT50 I had purchased from Gary, which had no acceleration, no speed, and no street credibility. It was running awfully due to neglect, and so the sensible thing to do seemed to be starting with a 'de-coke' of the exhaust. It was an afternoon after school when I decided to do this, and I managed to rope my brother Christopher into helping. I explained to him what had happened to Marcus at school, and how we would make sure no accident happened that afternoon. Chris was going to hold the exhaust upright whilst I poured the fluid down, and then eventually the match. Everything was prepared, the exhaust removed, de-baffled, and clogged at one end with some old tea towels. The only thing missing was the methylated spirit. There was none in the garage, but there was a bottle of white spirit. Would be OK wouldn't it? It had 'spirit' in the title so it must be almost the same right? The first operation went like a charm, performing the cleaning operation with a deep whoosh. Then carefully I checked the exhaust for the lit match. Nothing, and so I proceeded to pour further spirit into the exhaust. To my surprise, fire flew up quickly towards the bottle, startling me and Chris so much that liquid fuel coated our hands. In a quick reaction, I threw the bottle far away to our left, and it landed in one of the large bushes against the garden wall. This promptly went up in flames. My hand was on fire and I was desperately trying to put it out. Chris was screaming as he had an entire arm on fire. I jumped on him and we hit the ground, where I tried to roll us both around to extinguish the flames. As we were rolling around I took in the surroundings. By now the bush was burning violently, and there were two large burning circles on the lawn where the spirit had spilled. The exhaust was also still on fire as well as the ground around it. Chris was still screaming as flames still lapped at his arm. It was like a biblical apocalyptic scene. Reality set in as you realized something very bad had happened. We stopped rolling and flames had disappeared from Christopher's arm. After some reassurance he was OK, we set about getting various receptacles from the kitchen with water to put the flames out in the garden. The grass and bushes were dry. Very dry due to the lack of rain, and they had gone up in a shot. Once all flames had been doused, we looked on at the mess of the garden. I would have to perform some repair work but first had to tend to Chris. His arm, although not burnt in any manner, was painful. I put him standing by the fridge with his arm in the icebox. He was in pain and he wanted to tell our parents that I tried to sacrifice him at the first opportunity! This was going to take some bribery for him to keep it quiet. The offer of money and the fact that I would clean his school shoes and make his sandwiches for the next week or so seemed to do the trick. The deal was done and I set about cleaning up the garden. A few spadefuls of topsoil covered the lawn patches and some artistic cover-up of the burnt bush, with surrounding bush cover, sorted that out. It was a stupid thing to attempt, and then to get it so wrong, knowing what could go wrong, was unforgivable. I would hereby like to apologize to my brother for originally asking for his involvement, risking harming him, and then actually going through with it and harming him. I learned my lesson though, as I had got quite a shock and was a good few Rand lighter in the pocket. Chris had some good sandwiches for lunch the next few weeks, and for the first time, he could see his face in his shiny black school shoes.

We lived in a fairly sleepy suburb of Johannesburg. I say 'sleepy' as life seemed to go at a slower pace in Roodepoort than it had in Kempton Park, well for me at least. Maybe it was because there were not as many English immigrants, and so Roodepoort was spared the 'yobbery' and culture clashes that occurred in an up-and-coming suburb like Kempton. You certainly didn't expect something big to occur in Roodepoort, over and above the city or closer to surrounding suburbs. It was about an hour or so after school when the doorbell went. An excited Steven stood there in his motorcycle gear, informing me of something big that was going down. I was urged to quickly get changed, get on my motorbike, and follow him to our favourite 'scrambling' track. This was about a quarter of a mile from Steven's house, where a working quarry processed large rocks into smaller chippings for transport by bulk carrier lorries. To where and for what reason is unknown. To the back of the quarry, section lay endless waste ground with hidden enclosed areas where motorbike enthusiasts had made race tracks. You could ride for several miles without seeing a soul. On this particular afternoon, Steven had fancied taking his motorbike off-road for a scramble, as we often did after school. The dry and dusty ground was perfect in the winter for doing 'doughnuts' and producing huge billowing clouds of light-coloured dust behind your bike. I have several photos of Steven and myself performing this action, as well as a few staged 'accident aftermaths'. One of us would throw a handful of dust into the air and take a quick picture, whilst the other lay in a mangled mess with his bike on the floor, pretending that something had gone wrong after completing a jump. No such fun for Steven this afternoon though. As soon as he approached the entrance to the quarry, he was greeted by the sight of armed army personnel, who quickly encouraged him at gunpoint, to abandon his current course and remove himself from the vicinity. With Steven being Steven, he stopped and asked why he could not proceed, only to be told forcefully to remove himself. I got my gear together, and we rode to the closest possible lookout point so that I could also witness what was going on. The area had been sealed off, and we were certainly not going to be scrambling there today, or possibly for some time to come. We racked our brains for some explanation, but as I said sleepy old Roodepoort had not seen any action before, certainly not during my stay or Steven's lifetime. The only thing we could think of was that something had been discovered, but what was it? And why had we not seen it on our numerous travels through the area? It was about a week or so later when an excited Steven once again graced my doorstep late one afternoon. This time he had information and lots of it. Firstly, news that he had gained access to the area, which was now clear of the military. Secondly, he had found evidence of the excavation of large car-sized areas of ground to a depth of a meter and a half to two meters. Almost like a mass of very large graves belonging to giants had been dug up. To explain these excavations, he showed me a current cutting from the local newspapers, which disclosed the reason for the military presence and secrecy. The 'largest', I will repeat the 'largest' arms cache in South African history had been found buried in a plethora of locations in the area of the quarry. Stashes of AK-47 rifles, land mines, grenades, grenade launchers, and even a few RPG7 rocket launchers were among the listed finds. According to the media, all belonged to terrorist organizations that intended to use them at some point against South Africans. Now to this day, I do not know who this organization would be. During this particular era, the only countries I can think of that might want to assault or attack South Africa would be Angola maybe? They were many miles away though and held off at the South African border. No way they could haul that amount of gear over the border and down here. The 'ANC'? Or another Afrikaans group called the 'AVB' maybe? Then my thoughts went back to the cable car baskets going over the mountains from Mozambique. That would provide a suitable mechanism for getting arms into South Africa, but were the Mozambicans a threat back then? Whoever it was, they had achieved their objective and kept it hidden for some considerable time. Fortunately, though, it looked like the government must have been tipped off, and seized it all before it could be put to some horrific use. That afternoon I went with Steven so he could show me all the burial places he had located. I was shocked by how many there were, and how big they were. It was also shocking to think that some of them we had ridden straight over pretty much every week. One faulty land mine and I might not have been here to write this book! There is also the fact that the 'owners' would have been watching their stash very closely, and should Steven or I have been a threat to their buried treasure, we could easily have been taken care of. A frightening thought, and a reminder that South Africa during the mid-1980s could be a very dangerous place.

Motorbiking was our favourite after-school pursuit. It didn't matter where we were going or whether there was any real need to go there, we just enjoyed the journey. Sometimes though we wanted to get out of town to enjoy some other pursuits. Two of our favourites were playing squash and going ice skating. We were lucky to have an ice-skating rink just outside of town at a complex called 'Horizon'. A large shopping mall with various outlet stores, café, restaurants and the like, but also a fantastic huge ice-rink. Now you would think that I would be avoiding ice rinks like the plague after what had happened with Elsabe, but you have to remember that I was an apprentice on ice back then. A few years of roller skating in the backyard and many visits to the rink with my brother made me a lot more confident about the shiny stuff. So much so that I could skate around unaided and had even learned to stop without requiring static obstacles. My brother who is slightly younger than me, was equally good on the ice, that is until he slipped up, went flying in the air, and landed on his head, knocking himself out. This happened when I was on the other side of the rink, and the first I saw of it was my brother being handed horizontally over the side barrier to the waiting staff. He was spark-out, nobody home at 'hotel noggin'. Just the two yellow canaries circling above his head in a circular motion. Fortunately, after a few minutes, he came round. Dazed and confused and unwilling to partake in any further skating. I'd like to say that I stayed by his side to make sure he was OK, but the call of the ice, and the cute girls skating on it, was too much for me. I had to show off my skills, even though they were a very small set, and try to impress any eyes focused on me. My brother was alright, I had sorted him out with a drink and he was sitting down watching events, with apparently a very bad 'headache'. On occasions when I went to the rink with buddies, my efforts to impress were futile. Quentin was a seasoned skater and could attempt most things. Some of them whilst doing his signature robot, or electric boo-gal-loo breakdancing steps. I can still see him spinning around on the ice, a hand underneath him, only to end up lying on his side with his hand behind his head, one leg bent at the knee over the other. A classic breakdancing manoeuvrer of his that was impressive to watch on dry land let alone on the ice. He was a born showman and oozed confidence allowing him to approach any girl on the ice. Being able to speak fluent Afrikaans meant his target audience was twice as large as mine. No problem chatting up girls in either language whilst showing off what he could do. I was still struggling with Afrikaans at school and any conversation attempt with an Afrikaans girl usually involved some sign language, pictures, and saying the required word in English, but louder and slower in case that miraculously helped them understand. I had been in South Africa for around five years but had never got the hang of the Afrikaans language. It wasn't easy to learn at all. Having to write Afrikaans essays for exams was an absolute nightmare, and I am still surprised today that I managed to pass sufficiently to move up each year at school. Most of my essay attempts were filled with English words enclosed in apostrophes, to indicate to the examiner that I knew not what to put there in the language they required. These hybrid documents must have made very interesting reading, and comical too as I did see my Afrikaans teacher laughing and reading some of my work with another teacher once. Their amusement and glances in my direction were met with a stare of disapproval from me.

Another pursuit, that was void of ice, girls, and language barriers, was squash. We loved squash and used to play it at every opportunity, sometimes late into the evening. We were not restricted to the Horizon Center for this as there were plenty of bookable squash courts around. As this was more suited to two or four people, I usually played against Quentin. He had an Afrikaans mate who sometimes doubled up with Steven if we needed it. In the early days, we got through a few rackets, as they smashed against walls where we had got to close before swinging. You never lost a ball though, and we had favourites that suited our play with a particular coloured yellow dot on them. Attire was the normal shorts, tee shirt, and trainers. The only other thing present on the court was Quentin's 'Boom-box'. A classic, silver, 80's twin cassette player, with signal level meter, two massive round speakers, and a large handle so that you could hold it on your shoulder whilst strutting down the road. These are highly sought after nowadays, and fetch huge prices, and were equally hard to find back then. This pumped out mixes that the both of us had produced on our home stereo systems, or tapes that Quentin had obtained from his older brother, who was working as a Manager of 'Nello's' nightclub in Durban. As soon as Quentin took delivery of another set of tapes from his brother, he would cut me a copy. It was listening to these tapes that got us both interested in deejaying. Quentin would sometimes do a set at the local Afrikaans school dance nights, due to social networking connections, playing some of the good tracks from his brother's tapes. I explored the record shops to find originals of the recordings so I could do my mixing, and later on used these whilst running a mobile disco with a mate back in England a year or so later. It was the perfect music to accompany the fast pace of the sport of squash and helped to keep your energy levels up to handle the hour or so we would book the courts for.

Off-road motorcycling fun - The quarry near where the arms cache was found

Hidden gem - the motocross track in Roodepoort

Me trying to capture Steven mid-flight on my Honda MT-50

Another attempt of mine to photo an action shot of Steven on his new Yamaha DT50-LC

CHAPTER 10 - ESCAPE FROM SPORTS DAY

It was whilst living in our last house in Roodepoort, that we were told my sister from England was coming to visit. She would be coming with her husband Gary and baby daughter Lauren for a few weeks. During this time, we were going to travel to the Cape by road, staying in a timeshare that my parents had managed to borrow between George and Knysna. It was going to be a long trek of some 993 kilometres (617 miles), going through parts of the country that not even my brother and I had seen before, let alone my sister and her husband! It was going to be an adventure and my father, like always, had put a good plan in place to get us all there comfortably and safely over a day. Cape Town was on the roster for visiting and was a further 427 kilometres away. The vehicle of choice chosen by my father was his employer's Volkswagen camper van. This would be ideal, seating all 7 of us easily, and allowing us all to be together for the entire journey, or so we thought...

It was a long drive to our first rest stop in the evening, so we set off early. The camper was packed and checked, the roof rack filled with suitcases and hold-alls. I was happy, I had sufficient music laid down on cassette that I had been preparing for the last month or so, my Walkman by my side, and my bright orange

Walkman earphones as well as spare batteries. Everything was covered. We set off through Johannesburg to the highway that was going to take us out and beyond. Soon we would be travelling on roads straight as an arrow. Mountains in the distance on the horizon. Each time we met the horizon we would pass through the mountains only to be greeted with a clone of the sight before. A long stretch of straight road with mountains on the horizon. It was like 'Ground-hog Day', over and over again. Before we met this sort of terrain, we would have to navigate the highway out of Johannesburg and the small villages that appeared after. This didn't take as long as I was expecting, maybe an hour or so before we started to see fewer and fewer signs of life. I was deep in music by now, the others all excited were chatting away. The next thing I remember is the camper van coming to a halt on the side of the road. My immediate thought was somebody was already desperate for the loo, feeling sick, or baby Lauren had deposited something in her nappy that required immediate attention. Taking my headphones off I soon realized that it was more serious. The van had broken down and was refusing to start. We all exited the van and helped Dad investigate by checking out the engine at the rear. It was obvious that something was wrong as the engine was hot and smoking. It probably would have been alright if it had stayed 'hot and smoking', but it didn't. A pop sound and then the sight of flames greeted us all, licking the engine casing. The sudden influx of air from opening the engine bay lid must have been the missing catalyst that was required to ignite the fuel, which was making its way out of the engine from somewhere. Panic set in, especially in the two women present, and everyone tried to find a liquid to help put the fire out. We didn't have an abundance of water on board, but fortunately, the men had come prepared, and my brother-in-law handed my father a four-pack of lager. This particular brand in a white can was one of my favourites, and nobody was as sad as me seeing it go to waste. We could have put the fire out with a blanket or something. Further panic set in as we realized there was one member of the family still exposed to danger and the fact that she was, had completely slipped all of our minds. Baby Lauren, oblivious to it all, was still in her travel cot in the back of the van. She was hurriedly collected and we all sat down on the side of the road. My father had a plan to resolve the issue and quickly set off for the nearest telephone (no mobile telephony in those days!). He contacted the garage back at work. Work being Protea Bakery in Krugersdorp where he was General Manager. The plan was that two guys from the maintenance department would drive my father's company car and my mother's car over to us. We would alight these two vehicles and continue on our way. The maintenance guys would wait for a tow truck for the camper van and take it back to base. It was surprising how quickly the guys got to us. I don't remember having to wait much longer than an hour. We split into two groups with a designated driver in each and set off on our way. I couldn't tell you where we stopped that night. Somewhere past Bloemfontein, Reddersburg, or Edenburg ring bells, but it could have been further if the light was still with us. All I do remember is that there was not much around for miles. On the side of the road, in the middle of nowhere (nowhere being Reddersburg, Edinburgh, or beyond), was a small roadside motel. That was pretty much it. I think we saw a wandering black man with a donkey and cart on the approach, but apart from that, I think it was pretty much just us and the owners of the establishment. It got dark quickly once we had been assigned rooms. Time for some quick food and then you had to get your head down for an early start in the morning.

We didn't have breakfast before we left, another stop would be made once we found civilization again. I wasn't a fan of this approach. I was a growing teenager and could put away food like nobody's business. Leaving an establishment that was offering breakfast to set out on the road not knowing where or when we would get to eat went against every grain of my being. I had learned my lesson when being invited to Dean's for dinner and being served up his homemade speciality of cold baked beans in a roll! After that incident, I was always going to be prepared when it came to food. 'Fail to prepare... prepare to fail...', was my new motto back then and still is today. My father's motto at the time was a 'Boer maak a plan', and fortunately he always 'made a plan', executed it, and delivered, including breakfast this particular morning.

Later on, that evening, we arrived at the villa. The villa that my brother and I knew nothing about. It was to be our first trip to it and our last. It was on a small coastal complex containing many Austrian-style apartments. Each had a dark brown roof and lighter coloured exterior with dark wood panelling, the garden fenced off with a gate and surround of dark wood. Against the side of the wall was a two-man canoe. Not for use in the small pool that graced the garden, but for the saltwater lake a few hundred yards further down the road. This lake contained an estuary that let water in from the Indian Ocean. It was the wrong time of the day to arrive at such an exciting-looking place. It was dark and all my brother and I wanted to do was go out and explore. Instead, it was get settled and get your head down until the morning. When morning arrived you could appreciate the surroundings. The villa was nestled in amongst trees providing some shade from the sun and privacy from Neighbors. There were not many Neighbors though as these dwellings were well spaced apart. I cannot remember seeing many people around at all. It was very quiet and peaceful. Before being allowed to go down to see the lake, breakfast had to be sorted. Dad, as always took care of feeding everybody. I quick trip to the local shop had been performed before bed to get fresh Grenadilla and Guava juice, bread for toast, eggs and bacon, and sausages. I wasn't too keen on Grenadilla juice but my mother liked it. A light brown-orange kind of liquid with large pips in it that still contained a coating of the flesh from the fruit. It reminded me of frog spawn too much. I was more of a fan of Guava juice. This thick, sweet, pinky-red juice was delicious ice cold and I could put away pints of the stuff with no problem.

Breakfast out of the way, it was time to explore the surrounding area. This would start with a trek down to the lake. Just my father, my brother, my brother-in-law and me to start with. We had brought fishing rods with us and that was one of the first things on our agenda in an attempt to catch some fish for a BBQ that evening. We were the only people on the side of the lake, apart from a single motorboat parked on the shore. A man was sitting inside with his feet up on the side. Now and then he cast into the lake, sat for a minute or two, and then reeled in a small flatfish. Re-baited his hook, cast back in, and within two minutes was going through the procedure again. Watching this we got excited. The fish were giving themselves up, or so it looked. Dad remembered that the local shop sold fish, so we made a quick trip to get some squid. This was a favourite of the mackerel my father had fished for, back home off the coast of Looe in Cornwall. Surely African sea fish would be no different. I think an hour had passed when we thought something must be wrong. The fish were not biting, well at least not for us! The man further down the lakeside, still sitting in his boat, was reeling them in one after the other. He was being choosy about the size now and throwing smaller ones not suitable for eating back into the lake to live another day. The consensus was that we should take a wander up and see what this fellah was using for bait. The fish were fussy in these parts, and we needed to find out what delicacy was being presented to them that they just could not resist. We watched for a while and could see that the bloke had a bucket of something he was putting on his line. Small shrimp-like-looking creatures. They were alive and before putting each one on his hook he pinched off something. Curiosity got the better of my father and so he established contact and started questioning. It turned out these were sand shrimp. About one and a half to two inches long and retrieved from the sandy shoreline using a special pump that you could purchase at the nearby shops. This large bicycle pump was open at one end with a handle at the other. The open end was about two inches in diameter. You pushed this end firmly into the ground and extracted the handle out of the unit to fill the pump tube with the contents of sand and whatever else. You lifted the pump out of the sand and then pushed the handle back in to extract the contents it had collected. Most of the contents were sand, but amongst them were these little sand shrimp gems. Underground beneath the sand was their home. It was moist, dark, and full of nutrients for them. Just how they liked it. The man explained that before you pushed them over the hook, you had to pinch off their tiny claws as these could give quite a nip. The shrimp were then curled up the hook and you were done. This was enough info for us. We had to get back to the shops fast, get one of these contraptions, and then get fishing! It was afternoon before we had purchased said implement, started foraging for shrimp (very successfully I hasten to add), and cast our first lines into the lake with our new and improved bait. It did not disappoint. Pretty much every cast resulted in a bite, some of which we successfully brought in. Now by this time, my father had returned to the villa and the remaining three of us didn't have any receptacle to put our catch in, so it was a short jog back to the villa with the fish still on the line. Not being experienced fishermen, it was left to my father to remove them from the hooks and place them in the sink full of water for filleting. We would then race back to get another line in. Usually when you got back to the lake, whoever was left there was ready to jog back themselves. This happened repeatedly. It was starting to get dark, but every few minutes somebody shouted, 'I've got another one!', and a dark figure would run off into the distance to get it removed. This went on for some time and I think it was my father who called a halt to the day's catching once the sink was filled with more than enough fish. We would be eating well tonight and perhaps try for some bigger fish the next day.

My evenings were mainly spent listening to music. This was very much the past time for 17-18 year-olds. I never went anywhere without my cassette player and a good selection of tapes. I was very much into Depeche Mode, OMD, Howard Jones, and ABC, but listened to anything available in the mid-eighties, and that wasn't a lot in South Africa. You cannot imagine my joy when I saw that this villa was equipped with state-of-the-art stackable hi-fi in the living room. Perched upon a sideboard at the back of the room, I could sit there for hours and listen to my cassettes or the radio. There was even a record player on top which would come in very handy on my birthday when my sister would buy me the latest 'Dead or Alive' album. The place even had a fantastic set of headphones as well, so you can imagine I was in heaven being able to listen to my tunes on such a quality piece of machinery. One evening it was announced that my parents, sister, and brother-in-law would be going out for a meal, without my brother and I. We weren't very happy about this as it was supposed to be a family holiday. I can remember kicking up quite a fuss about it at the time, but it very quickly became apparent why it was important for my brother and I (but mainly me), to stay behind. That reason was baby Lauren. Baby Lauren was staying behind too. I particularly wasn't happy when I found out that my duties would include changing and feeding her at the appropriate time i.e. when she woke up around 8.00 pm. Now, as you can imagine a young teenager like me cannot think of anything worse than looking after a crying baby, unless that thing is changing a crying baby, but here I was being thrust into the realm of responsibility for another human life. Given my history of looking after my brother, they should have thought twice about this decision. Unfortunately, they were fine with it, as all good new parents know a night out with endless booze and good food fully trumps looking after your own flesh and blood creation, even if she has only graced the world for mere months. This was going to be an experience for me, one that would set me up for what was to come later in life when my own children would soil their undergarments with unmentionable and indescribable contents. Expecting me to remove those contents, clean them thoroughly, and then demand that I provide them with suitable liquid refreshment so that they could do the whole thing again in a few hours or so. That once I had got them back to sleep (which incidentally took a few hours or so). The only thing that was going to make the whole experience bearable was the fact I would finally be able to unplug the headphones from the hi-fi and finally hear my music through the speakers, which would be set to a suitable level so as not to wake baby Lauren prematurely. I was crossing my fingers at the time. Maybe, just maybe, they would return from their night out before she woke up and I wouldn't have to get involved at all. On the other hand, my sister and brother-in-law were probably thinking the opposite. Maybe, just maybe if they could stay out late enough, they would get back and I would have taken care of things. I'm sorry to say that their plan worked out instead of mine. I cannot remember much of my dealings with my niece that evening. A lot of soldiers who have endured war, block out memories that are too horrific to revisit. Now whilst I am not comparing my ordeal to anything like a soldier of war, on this occasion the memory blockage of our experiences brought us into the same circle within the Venn diagram. I do have flashbacks occasionally. The odd black and white image of my niece laying on her change mat, The Cult blaring out 'Here comes the rain..', as baby Lauren decides to relieve herself of further fluids now that the contents of her nappy have been revealed to the audience of one. The doctors say this is all to be expected when suffering long-term 'PTPD' (Post Traumatic Poo Disorder). I had no help. My brother was sound asleep well before all this happened, oblivious to the suffering that I was enduring downstairs. I learned a valuable lesson that night, a lesson that stayed with me through all the years of going through the same with my children. This a lesson I passed on to others, and still do to young fathers starting today. Before setting out on any 'nappy' adventure, even if you are 95% certain that all is 'clear', do yourself a favour and put a scented nappy sack over your nose and mouth, using the carry handles as ear attachments. With this, you will only have to endure the visual aspects of the spectacle, and should it all become too much to take, anything that decides to exit your stomach through your mouth is caught with ease in a handy disposable receptacle. This leaving you free to complete the job in hand with your dignity intact.

Whilst in the vicinity of the Cape we made many excursions, taking in beaches on both the Atlantic and Indian ocean sides. This whilst dining on the very best barbecued fish steaks and langoustines, also visiting animal parks with alligator or crocodile farms. I forget which breed was native to this part of South Africa but what I do remember was their biggest specimen. At the entrance to the park, there was an old swimming pool, now home to filthy water, leaves, insects, and a scaly reptile filling it from end to end. It had no room to manoeuvre its entire body filling the pool. I can't remember exactly how big it was, but it was the biggest I had seen both on and off-screen. I questioned the fact at that time that it was real. It seemed too huge and never moved a muscle whilst we were viewing it. It also seemed extremely cruel to keep it in the sunken pool without giving it room to move about. The park had much smaller specimens on show being displayed by a keeper, also showing us the nasty scars on his bare legs where some of them had taken a dis-likening to his handling. Despite the cuts of war with these small reptiles he still tried to convince members of the public to join him in their enclosure. This coupled with Ostriches and other strange creatures made for a good day out, but it was far from my favourite.

One of the most memorable outings was to the 'Cango Caves'. This was of great interest to me as I had learned in school back in England how South African caves had been the location for some great prehistoric finds. In addition, it gave me the chance to view the world from underneath, and in musical, multi-coloured glory like nothing I had seen before. Once again my schooling came in handy as I recognized the references to stalactites and stalagmites and other rock formations. Our tour took us deep into the caves stopping now and then for a presentation or light show until our tour guide stated that we had reached the end. However, for those that were not claustrophobic, and small enough, the adventure could continue at their own risk. The next section of the caves was open to the brave who didn't mind getting dirty or wet, had the stamina to climb, and had a slim enough figure that they could negotiate the narrow passages between rock formations. My brother-in-law and I were well up for this and volunteered immediately. The first section that had to be passed through was called the 'devil's letterbox'. Not something you would pass through horizontally, but instead vertically. Just wide enough a rectangle to allow a body through with your arms outstretched above your head. Over six feet in height to the exit as I remember. My brother-in-law below me had to bear the brunt of my trainers on his shoulders as he followed behind me. It was a tight squeeze even for my nine-stone body, but we made it through and were able to view some further sights the caves had to offer that only a privileged and slight-framed few could visit.

Some excursions were only made by the men and boys of the family, and one such outing was to a secluded beach nearby where we planned to do some swimming. As it turned out this particular beach was the last place we should have attempted this. Oblivious to the fact that the waters contained no shark nets, there were no flags indicating safety to swim, and there was nobody else in the water on the entire beach, we still entered the water up to a depth of seven or eight feet and cooled down in the waters of the Indian ocean. A very stupid thing to do as it turns out. Swim completed and with no loss of life, we trekked around the beach being drawn to items lying in the sand at the head of the beach. Many large jellyfish lay flat on the sand, their tentacles protruding around them, and we could see other larger sea-dwelling creatures alongside a fisherman further up the beach. On arrival we soon found these to be stingrays that the fisherman had landed. When questioned about sharks he advised he had already caught one and that it lay behind us about 100 yards towards the top of the beach. When asked where he caught it, his reply was unwelcome. Pretty much where we had been swimming was the beginning of the reef drop-off, and he had brought in a five-footer, with sufficient a set of jaws to do severe damage from that area earlier. Most of us were counting our lucky stars that we had escaped unscathed. My father, however, was more interested in investigating the shark and showing it to my brother-in-law, as he would probably not get further opportunities to view a specimen this close. Now I am not aware of what the laws were on fishing or sharks in this particular area of South Africa during 1985/86, but the fact is that this shark had been hunted by a fisherman and left to die on the beach. There was no way that it could have survived being motionless and out of water for the period we had known it was there, let alone any longer. Or was there?

It didn't take long before my father suggested we take some of the shark for bait to use elsewhere. None of us questioned this decision and went along with it. My father drew out his bright orange-handled diving knife and began to cut flesh from the shark's back, having extreme difficulty piercing the sharkskin. Then another idea sprang into his head, and I warn you this is quite barbaric so skip this next bit if you feel you will be offended. My father thought it would be great if we could send my brother-in-law home to England with a set of shark jaws. To us this shark was dead. It had shown no signs of life and was going to be eaten anyway by bigger sharks when the tide came in. To cut a long story short, my father cut into the shark with his knife, cutting the jaws away. The plan was to boil the jaws to remove the remaining flesh leaving the bone and teeth intact. It was hard going, but my father being a strong man was getting the job done. A seasoned fisherman himself he was used to cutting up all sorts of large fish, conga eels, and the like whilst on wreck fishing trips. The rest of us sat around on our knees, fairly close to the action. A bit too close as it turned out. Whilst negotiating a particularly hard piece of flesh around the jaw, the whole body of the shark came alive, lashing violently from side to side. The head raised as it did this, and it looked like my father was going to be at the end of an attempted bite. All of us, my father included, dived backward out of the way, our hearts racing. Now I would have been happy to leave things there but my father wanted to finish what he had started, assuring us that he had hit a nerve and it had caused the reaction. This proved to be the case as the shark showed no further signs of movement. We had the jaws, in a plastic bag. As much as I am ashamed to say it, a mutilated shark lay on the beach where once it lay whole. All this for a trophy. We didn't know it then but the shark would have its revenge on us. Despite being cleaned and boiled those jaws stunk out the cars on the journey home to the Transvaal, making everyone sick to their stomachs through the two days of travelling. The stench was unbearable and seemed to pass through any structure we wrapped it in with ease. When we got back to Roodepoort it was decided that the best course of action would be to bury it for a while, letting natures insects feed on the remaining flesh. We would dig it up a few days later and continue to clean it up. The only trouble was that David the dachshund was attracted to the smell, and whilst unattended did some cleaning up of his own. Not just the flesh but the jawbone, teeth, and all. There would be no jaws for my brother-in-law to show to anyone or to adorn the bottom of his home-made fish tank.

Somehow, and I am not sure how it happened, I had been fortunate enough to scrape through the various years of school and make it to my final Matric year – Standard 10. The day I went to school to collect my Standard 9 results was a nervous one. My friend Quentin had not made the cut and would be staying behind another year, I, on the other hand, would scrape through by the skin of my teeth. Standard 10 brought with it many changes. I would find we would all get slightly more respect from the teaching staff. More opportunities to display your growth into young adulthood. Tied in with this there would be greater expectations about homework, more intense classroom sessions, and a lot more exams. I hated exams. Well nobody liked them, but most of my peers were focused on achieving the best results throughout the year to obtain the qualifications they required for University. This was more the outlook of the young women in Standard 10. Most guys were thinking of nothing else but the compulsory military service that awaited them next year, should they matriculate. A failure would mean dodging the bullet (so to speak), for another year. During our final year all young men in Standard 10, much as they did in Standard 9, would fill out a government questionnaire, detailing their availability as well as which arm of the military they had an interest in, and why. Mid-year we would all receive letters in the post, stating which arm of the military we had been selected for, Army, Navy, or Air Force, as well as details of what part of Africa we would be shunted to in early January the following year. This could be anywhere in South Africa and would be for two years, with little to no time given for returning home to see family. After that, you could return home, and look for work or attend University, having to perform a month's camp duty, usually on the borders, every year until you were thirty-five. Many young men decided to prepare themselves for basic training so it would not come as such a shock. After school, they would adorn heavy rucksacks and go out for a few hours jog over the wasteland and up hills. This seemed sensible to me even though it looked like it was killing them in the heat of the afternoons. I decided it wasn't for me though, primarily as I worked part-time most days after school. I can remember the day vividly when I got home to find that brown, official-looking envelope in the outside postbox. I didn't get any post of the official kind, and this letter was addressed to me and required me to open and read it. I got inside the house and didn't even change out of my school clothes. I sat on my bed and opened it, wondering if my wish to join the Air Force would be granted much as it had for my cousin David many years earlier. In filling out my questionnaire this year I had adopted the approach of asking for what I didn't want. Last year I had asked for the air force and got the army, based in a camp a hundred or so miles away. This year I tried a different tactic, asking to be put right in the thick of the action, as near to the border as possible, also throwing in that I would like to be part of a transport corp. riding motorbikes through the veld. This reverse psychology would result in me getting something close to home, probably in the navy or air force, and as far away from 'Bootie gaan border toe' territory as possible. Or so I thought. Turns out that whoever read my questionnaire thought 'If that is what he wants.... that is what we will give him...'. I imagined some office-based military official looking at my form for a few seconds and then thumping down a great, red-inked rubber stamp on it 'APPROVED'. My fate was sealed. I was going far. Very far. So far away that it would take over a day's train journey to get there. A place in South West Africa very close to the border with Angola. 'Grootfontein'. I had never heard of this place and got quite a shock when I looked it up on a map. After the expulsion of various expletives, I decided it was time to see where my mates were being sent. Maybe they too had been chosen to visit this remote place and I would have some familiar company at camp. Not bleeding likely. Steven got sent less than 30 kilometres down the road to a physical education camp. Probably not surprising with his father's military connections. Quentin didn't care where they were sending him as he had another extra year to perform at school and would have to send new forms in the following year anyway. These were the only two guys I was concerned about at the time. The following day I was subject to much ridicule by my classmates and those other young men in my year. Word quickly got around that I had been dished out a lousy placement, and guys lined up to read my call-up papers, usually bursting into fits of laughter afterward. A lot of scaremongering ensued with comments like 'You're going to die dude...', or 'They are going to break you...'. There were not many similar or worse off than me that day. Even some guys had pulled off the impossible and landed in either the navy or air force. There was no use worrying about it, I had to accept it and prepare for it, as it was my duty like every other young man to prepare to serve the country in which I resided. That evening, when they returned home from work, I showed my parents. My father didn't show as much shock as my mother, but that was to be expected. She was adamant that I would not be going there, which I thought was a little naive at the time. Things were left like that for the time being and I prepared myself for the army vehicle to collect me on the 5th of January 1987, where I would make haste to the train station. After that, there would be a long, hot, and uncomfortable journey of some 1255km, taking approximately 16 hours. Then who knows... I only had the stories of my older cousins to go on, plus what I had seen in films. Whatever it was It wasn't going to be easy or pleasant.

It was during the summer that the Princess High School was to attend an annual inter-school sports day at an outdoor arena around halfway between Roodepoort and Johannesburg. Not being the athletic type, I found myself and my usual partners in crime confined to what can only be referred to as 'cheerleading' duties in the stands whilst watching the day's events. This while monitored by the head cheerleaders and prefects in my year. An extremely degrading activity, laborious, repetitive, and uncomfortable in the warm African spring sun. A ritual that I had the pleasure to take part in over many schooling years in South Africa. The only respite this year would be that as Matric students, Steven and I would be at the top of the stand, out of sight and mind, with Quentin a few rows below. I think it was Steven who suggested a few weeks earlier that we prepare for this event a little differently. He was not keen on having to endure the event for the entire day and suggested that we plan an escape which would ultimately rely on us convincing our headteachers to allow us to make our own way there via motorbike. Marcus was also well up for this and helped with the plan-making as well as the movement to propose our transport to and from the event. This is put forward as a means to quickly attend part-time work commitments after school. I can remember the classroom session where this was proposed, and very stupidly accepted by Mrs. Ferreira, our year head and English teacher. I was gobsmacked. I couldn't believe they were going to allow us to do this and with our track record in previous years? Anyway, with that sorted it all came down to planning the execution of the escape plan, as well as where we were going to go afterward. This was the hard bit which would involve a change of clothes, a picnic, and some very skilfully scheduled requests for toilet breaks.

On the day the majority of the school alighted coaches and made their way to the sports ground. For us lucky individuals it was a quick whiz up Ontdekkers road on two wheels. On arrival, Steven, Quentin, Marcus and I parked our bikes up against the wire fence near the toilet facilities. The fence was the usual eight to ten feet high but in its aged state provided enough flexibility to lift at the bottom to crawl under. This area was well out of sight and to the far left of the stadium which would provide the opportunity to escape the day's festivities later on. I say later on but in all honesty, we were not going to last more than an hour. We had only sat down for about ten minutes before Steven started to get itchy feet. Roll-call was going to be made initially by those prefects in charge at the front of the seating area. There were about 50 – 60 students in this particular section, with adjacent sections having a similar count with others in charge. Steven soon gave the nod that he was going to get things in motion, around half an hour after roll-call. We were ticked off on the list, and as long as they did not perform periodic updates of this list we would be OK. Quentin was a few rows in front of us and watched anxiously as Steven made his way to the front to ask permission to visit the facilities. Ridiculous having to ask permission at age 18 but that was how it was back then. Those in charge had no reason to doubt that Steven wasn't going to return. All he had on was his school uniform. His rucksack with clothes and food as well as his bike helmet and gloves were stashed near his bike, as were mine and Quentin's. I suppose because it was a hot day and the three in charge at the front had so many to keep an eye on, they failed to notice the absence of Steven. They were too busy orchestrating the singing and cheerleading in time with the various events. All this whilst Steven had executed his escape and made off at speed to the meeting point at the nearby park. I was going to be next. My toilet request went without a hitch. Timing it between track events I received no questioning at all, not even though the person who was sitting next to me at the beginning of proceedings had not returned. I had a quick look around and with my heart racing, started to climb under the wire fence. Helmet on, rucksack on, one kick-start of the bike and away. Not looking back and concentrating on getting as far from the ground as possible, in as short a time. The 50cc two-stroke motorbikes we rode made a lot of noise that would give the game away, mainly due to the absence of baffles in the exhausts. Five minutes down Ontdekkers Road and then I exited to the right and entered the park. Steven was there as expected and had already made himself completely at home. His bike was parked up and he was sprawled out on his side, now in jeans and a tee shirt tucking into his sandwiches with a huge grin that said 'We pulled it off!'. I joined him and we waited for the third member of our party. It took a while for Quentin to turn up. He was at a disadvantage with his slow bike, which in the past had taken some thirty to forty kicks to get it started. He must have been sweating waiting for it to kick into action. Around half an hour later we heard the distinctive roar of Quentin's bike. Unfortunately for him, you could hear it five or so minutes before it came into view. A tired, shaken, and sweating Quentin pulled up, undoing the strap of his open-faced helmet he explained his ordeal to us. Stuck on the wire fence, he panicked and ripped his school clothes a little. His bike refused to start and, in the end, he had to bump start it, which also took longer than he had wanted. We chuckled at his misfortunes as we invited him to sit down and join us at the picnic. We had done it. Three escape victims were all accounted for. It had been hard for some but there were no casualties. The day was ours now. We could go anywhere and do anything, and the farther away from the sports ground the better. Our choice? Jo-burg of course. A bar, some food, some pool maybe? Record shops in Hillbrow and then back home to relax for the rest of the day. All would go well apart from the fact we would be down a few Rand at the end of it. A few more Rand than we would have hoped for.

In the Carlton Center shopping mall underneath the hotel, there were a few areas that even at that time were undesirable. One of these was a bar with some pool tables where we decided to shoot a few games. The tables had previously been occupied by some black men in their late twenties to early thirties. We had watched them completing their games and none of them looked any good and they were laughing and joking amongst themselves as they missed shots. It was a few games in when one of them asked if they could join the table now and suggested that I and Quentin play against two of them. The game went well for both of us, finishing on the black easily. The other guys suggested that we made things a little more interesting by each putting in a Rand, the winners taking the pot. Based on their previous performances we agreed to it immediately. It looked like it was going to be easy money. It was as once again we ended up sinking the black. The other guys wanted a chance to win their money back so upped the pot to two Rand each. Quentin looked at me and whispered that we should go for it as we could take these guys simply. We did so, once again making and potting the black easily. It was a close call this time but we pipped them at the post. This was enough for me and Quentin. We were a few Rands up and eager to get out and enjoy our winnings. The other guys were in begging mode. One more game to give them a chance to win some money back. We declined, but still, they pleaded, saying that they would put five Rand in each, a total pot of twenty Rand. Quentin looked at me whispering we would be fools not to take this offer. We would clean up and then get out of there. Maybe hit Juicy Lucy's for lunch. I agreed and the balls were set up on the table. Twenty

Rand in five Rand notes sat on the side of the table under the watchful eye of Steven. We won the toss and so Quentin broke off. A shot from one of the other guys missed and so my turn for a shot which I missed. What happened next was weird. It was like time stood still as we both stood in awe and watched what happened next. The other guy took a shot and potted. Then another, and another, increasing in speed as he continued to clear the table in front of us. Only the black left he didn't even look towards the ball or the pocket as he sank it with ease. Quentin and I looked at each other in disbelief. The guys were now giving each other a traditional black African handshake, laughing and grinning ear to ear. And there endeth our first lesson in pool hustling. There was no love lost though as we shook hands with the victors, smiling back and shaking a finger and our heads at them. We had lost some money and had our pride dented but had also learned a valuable life lesson. A few Rand down but that wasn't going to spoil our day or stop us from getting Lunch at 'Juicy Lucy's', which may surprise you was a vegetarian sandwich and salad bar, and not a strip joint...

Things were a little unsettled in South Africa around my matriculation year. There was unrest in the townships, and nobody knew more about this than my father. As Manager of a large bakery in Krugersdorp, he was finding things difficult to handle, as truck after Mercedes truck arrived back, burnt out, and in most cases missing all of the takings from the internal safe. It was becoming a common sight to me when I visited the bakery. Trucks sitting near the maintenance area, the whole cab burnt out. Drivers of these were lucky to escape with their lives. It was hard to figure out why people in the townships would risk harming men of the same colour, just to hurt the white man and his businesses, but they did. Drivers were told to get out or be torched along with the vehicles.

Aside from the troubles brewing in the townships, there were often threats of the white areas being stormed by township dwellers. White schools were particularly targeted, and we lived on a knife edge at this time wondering if we would be victims of a mass invasion of some kind. South Africans had the right to hold firearms licenses at age 16 or over. Your 'book of life' held several pages on which firearms could be registered. My older cousins were well-tooled up for any eventuality, but my parents had forbidden me to hold a firearm. Guys in my year with like-minded parents took to carrying any sort of weapon they could lay their hands on. Hidden in their rucksacks lay anything that could be used for self-defence. Steven's weapons of choice were ninja stars and nun-chucks. He was extremely talented in whipping these two pieces of cylindrical hardwood, joined with a chain, around his torso. Over his head and under his arms, swapping from hand to hand with ease and without injury. Many an hour was spent watching old Bruce Lee films and a similar amount of time practising his art. Some were even better prepared for any invasion, and none other than Simon. A recent new member of the school, our year, and our class, Simon was an excited military enthusiast and an even bigger fan of James Bond films. It will come as no surprise to you then that one day in assembly, during this heightened tension period, Simon decided to show me his weapon of choice. Out of his blazer pocket, without batting an eyelid, he drew out his Walter PPK. I was stunned. I had never seen anyone carrying at school. Simon had no problem informing me just what he was going to do with it should trouble surface in any shape or form. He had come in that day fully prepared for war, and the 100 or so rounds of ruck-sack ammunition that he carried for his side-arm proved that without a doubt. It was a little unsettling, to say the least. Simon wasn't from a very stable home, and there was a look in his eyes that suggested he might be a little unstable himself. Fortunately, there were no invasions of the school that year, and probably just as well, as I believe Simon would have been on the front line giving it his all. I saw that firearm drawn out in self-defence only once, and it was on a late night out with the lads. It was on this one evening we decided to do something different. Steven, Quentin, and I would ride our motorbikes to Simon's house. Pick him up and then we were off out to a local bar not far from the park. It was well within walking distance from Simon's house so we could leave the bikes there and pick them up later on. Now the three of us had got to know Simon quite well by now and had picked up on the fact he liked all things military. He was one of the young South African guys for whom military service could not come quickly enough. He, unlike the rest of us, was ready to adorn his camouflage and be put through the torture of basic training, so he could get out on the front line as soon as possible. It was the call of the guns. Bigger, better, and with a never-ending supply of ammunition that attracted him. On arrival at his house, he invited us all to his room whilst he finished getting ready. We were not quite ready for the sight that waited for us. His bedroom was a military action station, or to put it more correctly, a military 'action-man' action station. The rest of us had put our eagle-eyed six million-dollar men, and our scuba, air-force, and desert warfare action men away many years ago, never to surface again. For Simon however, the need to remove oneself from the activity of interacting with toy action figures at age eighteen had not kicked in. Instead, his entire bedroom was adorned with them, involving themselves in a variety of military escapades, none more apparent than the one going on over his bedroom curtains. Here the bedroom had become a military training ground, complete with suitably sized roping, netting, and equipment. Several of the 'action-men' were undergoing their basic training, scaling the heights of his dark green curtains, each achieving different heights, the ceiling the end goal. His lampshade had not escaped the militarisation either. Aircraft and helicopter models utilized this to achieve flight within the war zone. To our surprise, more military personnel and vehicles from the armoured corp were initiating manoeuvrers from under the bed and built-in wardrobes. I believe that the only demilitarized zone was the actual top of the bed, but who knows what lurked beneath the sheets. To our surprise, Simon was quite proud of his handy work. Handy work that would be kept a secret between the three of us, never to be mentioned, as this guy carried a gun. A short while later Simon was called by his mother for some food and disappeared for a few minutes. Just long enough for the three of us to look at each other with faces of disbelief. I think we all realized at that moment that we were in the company of a bit of a crackpot. I think Quentin and I were the most nervous as we realized we were going to be in the company of two slightly unstable individuals that evening. So after Simon's quick bite, it was time to head off to the bar. What could go wrong eh? Well, initially nothing.

We went to the bar and had a good few drinks. Beer and whiskey and some fantastic drunken chats with the old regulars. Men dressed like gold prospectors. Covered in dust as they had just finished prospecting for the day, their mouths parched to such a state that only a glass of ice-cold amber nectar could bring them back from the brink. Men who had seen everything and done everything. Tales as old as time told to the four of us. Nobody was more interested than Steven. He asked many questions of the old-timers, and with some difficulty due to the amount of alcohol he had consumed. Still, the company was in the same state, so everybody could understand each other… in a way… It was getting on for the small hours when we attempted to drag Steven away from his new friends. The rest of us had more than a skinful, and fresh air and food were desperately needed. When we did convince him it was time to go, we stepped outside into the cool night air. It was refreshing. Like you had never breathed in fresh air before. The hot, stuffy, and alcohol-infected air of the bar had made us dozy, and this venture into the outside world woke us with a jolt.

It was a short walk across the park to areas that would contain potential eateries, so we strolled across, towards the play area of the park. In our sight were the swings, roundabout, and slides. In our inebriated state, these items looked inviting and there would be no doubt that some or all of us would partake in some playground antics when we reached it. Everything was quiet. Most of the town was asleep, the only noise in this particular area was coming from us. Suddenly, out of nowhere, we heard the roar of a car engine as the pedal went to the metal. The car entered the park straight from the road and tore through the middle of it, hand-brake turning 29 to 30 yards in front of us, the left passenger side door flinging open as it came to a halt. It was obvious we were under some sort of attack, so all four of us hit the deck with fear. That open door meant that someone may be going to take a potshot at us before speeding off. I am pretty sure that this would have been the case if it wasn't for 'Walter' making an unexpected appearance. Before I could blink Simon had drawn out his trusty side-arm (which none of us knew he had on him!), had taken aim, and was about to return fire to any hint of enemy hostility. Seeing this, the driver and rear occupants of the car closed the passenger door promptly. It didn't depart straight away. The door closed and it sat there for a further 15 to 20 seconds before speeding off out of the park and up the road. We didn't get off the ground straight away either. Hearts were racing fast, and we wondered what it was all about and whether we had escaped something nasty. That night I was extremely thankful that a fourth\ member of the gang had joined us, and that he showed his metal just when we needed him to. All thoughts of food had gone out of the window. All we wanted to do now was get to our respective homes, and quickly without further incident.

Soon, it was time for the school prom. Well not quite a 'prom', but the South African equivalent. Around October time when exams were coming to a close, it was customary for the 'Standard Nine' year group to arrange, organize, and present the 'Standard 10' Matric farewell dinner and dance! This year it was our turn. Well, I say 'our' but I mean Steven, Simon, and I. Quentin, unfortunately, would be on the organizing committee as he hadn't made the grade last year. Still, we had someone on the inside so we could get some good info on what was being organized. It was an event that everybody talked about. Excitement was in the air, especially for the young ladies of the year who waited eagerly for a young man to ask them to accompany him. There were hairstyles and dresses for the ladies to talk about, and suits and 'after-show' parties for the young men. Now I had someone in mind for my partner, and I wasn't going to leave it until the last minute, as ladies were being snapped up quickly.

My intended partner was a partner in crime in my class. Jeanine Minnar. I spent a lot of time alongside Jeanine, especially in science class, where we often got into trouble for messing about. Jeanine had coloured dark and blonde hair, in a big bold eighties hairstyle. Very cute with a lovely smile and rosy red cheeks. This was the woman I wanted on my arm for the up-and-coming evening, even though this young lady used to stab me in the leg with a compass. Quite often this causing me to shriek out during Mr. Derek's lessons on the periodic table of the elements. Aside from the fact she got a buzz from inflicting pain with sharp instruments, pens, fists, or fingers, I had a soft spot for her, and I think the feeling was mutual as on some occasions she would switch from a devil-eyed temptress to a calm, affectionate and tactile beauty. I think as a girlfriend she would have been an absolute handful, but I would have gladly put up with that. On cold winter mornings, whilst lined up outside classrooms, it would be me from whom she chose to seek warmth. There was nothing better than having Jeanine inside your blazer, her arms wrapped around you and her head against your chest as she warmed her cheeks. I won't say I was surprised when she accepted to be my date for the evening. To me, it was pretty much a given. We had been flirting all year, and this just seemed to be the perfect ending to it.

With a few weeks to go until the big evening, I was calm and happy. Everything was sorted, and I wasn't still running around like a mad thing trying to sort out a date as some guys still were.

That is until Jeanine took me aside one day and told me that her ex-boyfriend, from the same year but in a different class, had convinced her to go with him instead. To say I was livid would be an understatement. I couldn't believe what I was hearing but took the knock and thought about what I was going to do. What I was going to do was nothing. Steven had already resided himself to the fact that he was turning up alone, as he had not managed to locate a date. I would turn up in the same manner. Solidarity amongst brothers! We didn't need women to have a good time. We would turn up, have dinner, see what activities they had planned then scarper down to the bush to get some drink down our necks. Unfortunately, our head of year, Mrs. Ferreira had a different plan up her sleeve which would change things slightly. Mrs Ferreira was quite a good teacher. Strict but fair and differed from other teachers in that she explained things well in class. Throughout the year she had pretty much followed a routine from which she did not stray. We knew what she expected from us, and always delivered, otherwise, you would be in serious trouble. One day, however, was very different. She sat on her desk facing us, looking a little more relaxed than normal. We all wondered what was going on as this relaxed approach to teaching was not her style at all. I forget how she first approached her chosen topic for discussion that day, but once she started to reveal her thoughts to us, we began to wonder why it was being brought up and delivered in this particular manner. The discussion, and I say discussion because it was in both directions, with students all allowed to ask questions at any point, was a prediction about coming changes in Southern Africa. Although it was not evident at all in 1986, it was like Mrs. Ferreira had prior notice of an up-and-coming event that would change the country forever. An event she felt she had to tell us about so we could prepare. There was mention of there being a change very soon that would see an end to the segregation of whites and blacks. A new South Africa where all colours and races were equal. A time when you could not expect to get a job in the city just because you were white. Instead, a coloured or black man with the same qualifications could be chosen over you. She was trying to drill into us the fact that the day was coming when this would be normality, as much as we could not see it now. We needed to make sure we were prepared, by achieving the highest qualifications possible. Competition, in huge numbers, was around the corner, waiting and preparing to compete for jobs, houses, goods, and services. It was a very strange vision to receive, and I do look back now wondering where she got her inside information on what was coming, so early before it did. Perhaps her husband was involved with the government in some way? Perhaps she was involved with a political party in some manner and was advised to spread the word. Maybe she had a premonition or a dream? Whatever the source of the information was, it was going to turn out to be 'right on the money'. It made you see her in a different light, albeit a slightly suspicious one.

At age eighteen I had not had much call for a suit. There had been family weddings but all that had called for was a shirt and tie. With the Matric Farewell looming I had mentioned to my parents that I needed something to wear and that suits were what everybody was talking about. So one Saturday I was whisked off by my mother to town to get me kitted out for the big event. I had no experience in this arena, so it was a good thing that my mother took charge at this point, locating a suitable vendor to supply my garment for the evening, and more importantly, bringing her chequebook. The man in the shop was quite knowledgeable about what young men should wear to their Matric Farewell and suggested a variety of light-coloured grey suits for evening wear, which I tried on. One particular one looked good to me, and I gave my mother the seal of approval with a head nod. At this point, I thought that was it and I could get changed and we could go home. Naive to the fact that I had to be measured thoroughly as the suit would need to be tailored for a perfect fit to my unusually skinny and lanky torso. Whilst measuring my inside leg with his tape measure the shop assistant looked up at me and asked 'What side do you dress sir?'. I gave him a puzzled look back as I scrambled my brain for details of what the correct answer to this question would be. Did he mean what side of my room do I get dressed on in the morning? Well, my bed was up against the wall on the left, so I got out of bed on the right, so I guess I dress on the right? But how was this relevant? Did I have to put this suit on in a particular orientation in my room? I looked towards my mother with the same puzzled look as I had given the gentleman in the shop. Then back at him, and again towards my mother who was going to begin to explain things to me through the smile and grin, she was now wearing, before the gentleman shook his head at her and they both said 'Never mind'. Nothing more was said in the shop, but I asked my mother for an explanation on the way home as to what this secret 'dressing side' question was all about. I have been for many suit fittings over the years and have never been asked this question again, so it perplexes me to this day why this information is of importance. As far as I am concerned making any adjustment to suit trousers to accommodate a preference in dangle direction, is extremely restrictive, and could prove unnecessarily uncomfortable, if one wishes to alternate between left, right, and middle of the road.

With a new pair of shoes sorted, and a thin red fabric tie and handkerchief, that was me done and ready for the big event. The only thing left to do was to help sort out my mate Steven. Coming from a single-parent family, things were tight, and he needed help. My father's retired suit collection came to the rescue, in the form of a beige three-piece that fitted Steven as well as it was going to. A little breathing room was available in most areas, as well as a little length in others, but Steven didn't seem to mind and was thrilled with how he looked in it. We were all set. Hopefully, we were going to knock the ladies bandy with our 'get up'. They had never seen us look this handsome. I was hoping that a certain someone would regret jilting me at the last moment once she saw me in my new grey two-piece with all the accessories.

Pretty much resigned to the fact that we were going to be a small club of loners at this Matric Farewell, Steven, Simon, and I made plans for a quick exit from the evening's proceedings. We would not be attending any of the popular people's after-party events. Instead, we would be drowning our sorrows and putting the world to rights over a few bottles of whiskey in one of the nearby parks. Steven was riding his motorbike to the event so would give me a lift down to the park afterward. If things had worked out as planned, and I would have had the hand of Ms. Minnar for the evening, I would have been hoping to pick her up in my father's car. That is if I had passed my test a week or so earlier. Things didn't work out on both counts.

The officers at the test centre had made it extremely difficult for me to pass through to the stage where I would be taken out onto the road. Having gotten through the question and answer session in the office, I was taken into the test centre car park. This contained a variety of driving obstacles, but none so daunting as the columns of death. Huge metal poles suspended from over-hanging apparatus lay in two long rows, with a car gap in the middle. The officer moved the poles into what he deemed to be a suitable distance apart and snaked them as he desired on that day. The aim was that you would approach in reverse from the left-hand side, and then the right, reversing through the heavy metal poles, zig-zagging as required so as not to damage your car, or in this case your father's new Toyota Corolla. I had been left little to no room to manoeuvre through these poles, and the officer showed his amusement with a grin, knowing too well he had set an impossible task. The poles ended up being my nemesis, and there were no further tests required. Still, I wasn't going to let it spoil things. We would have a great night anyway.

It was one break time before the farewell that I was collared by Mrs. Ferreira, who asked if she could have a word with me. This was never a good sign. If this lady wanted a word with you, it meant there was trouble brewing of some kind. She picked a strange place for our little chat, perhaps because it was close to the staff room, and she could get her break-time fag in quickly afterward. Or perhaps because it was a busy, bustling admin area, away from the view of most of my peers. Mrs. Ferreira stood me at the bottom of the stairs leading up to the hall gallery and placed herself two steps up as she guided my shoulders to face her. It was immediately apparent to me that she needed to assert a level of authority during this discussion. Her ascent a few steps up gave her just sufficient height advantage for me to feel intimidated. She was a small woman of around five feet tall and I was closing in on six feet, so for her, this was the only suitable location to get her message across loud and clear. I had never been this close to Mrs. Ferreira. Despite her large, shaded glasses, I could see her dark brown eyes and smell her perfume. I wondered what on earth was coming my way. She proceeded to tell me that she had a request to ask of me and that she had chosen me as I displayed a level of maturity greater than that of my peers. She was adamant she could not ask anyone else. During the conversation, it was revealed that one girl in the entire year did not have a date for the Matric farewell. Esme Jackson was in most of my year classes. Although a little on the larger side, she was a nice blonde-haired girl, with not a bad bone in her body. Popular with her female classmates but ridiculed by the majority of the males who were quite nasty in the way they referred to her. Mrs. Ferreira looked me in the eye and pleaded with me to take her, as it was unacceptable that there was one girl left without a date. I was the only one she could turn to out of the remaining young men to escort Esme to the ball. This was not easy to take. I have to admit at the time I was more worried about the unwanted attention this would bring to me should I accept. My brain hurried to find excuses but there weren't any valid ones. I even at one point considered bringing on the charm and saying to her 'But Mrs. Ferreira, I was hoping that you would accompany me?'. That statement may have landed me in hot water, or maybe not. We will never know. Part of me thinks that she might have risen to that challenge to embarrass me in some way. Anyway, after pausing for a few minutes and debating the other possibilities with Mrs. Ferreira, I decided to do the right thing. I was man enough to take all the ridicule that was going to come my way. Maybe I could teach my fellow year members a thing or two about how to treat a young lady. We decided that Mrs. Ferreira would break the news to Esme, who quickly sided with me a few hours later to discuss things.

The excitement on her face was immediate confirmation to me that I had done the right thing. It seemed silly for there to be members of the two sexes going alone when you could have a date for the evening. I can remember telling Steven about my change in plans, and the laughter and ridicule that followed. He didn't understand it at all and made the usual nasty remarks about my new date for the evening. There then followed a barrage of ridicule from pretty much every male in my year, and some from below, as to why I would ask Esme to the farewell. They came in groups to get confirmation that what they had heard on the grapevine was true. Each time I explained how Mrs. Ferreira had explained the situation to me, how shallow they all were, and how nobody should go to the evening alone. After a while, they grew tired of ridiculing me. They were not embarrassing me, it was like water off of a duck's back. It was actually becoming exciting again. I had to ask Esme what colour dress she was wearing to get an appropriate corsage, and there was the fact that I would have a young lady on my arm during the couple's photos. Also, was going to be nice to have company over dinner and a dancing partner. It wasn't going to be bad at all.

It was going to be an emotional evening for me. In the lead-up to the farewell, my parents had disclosed the desire to take me and my brother home to England. This was now going to happen a week or so after the farewell. With exams nearly finished, and my participation in them going to be cut short, this would be the last time I would see my friends and classmates. On the evening of the farewell, my father dropped me off at the school. There I met Esme and some others in the car park where I gave her the corsage for her dress. She looked lovely in her light blue dress. I had never seen her wear make-up as it was banned in school, so Esme stood before me an entirely different young woman to what I had seen previously. I was proud to have her on my arm. We entered the building joining a queue of couples waiting to have the photographer take their picture. An area had been set up against a white backdrop with a bench decorated with flower arrangements. It's sad, but I never got to see the picture. After the official photograph was done, we joined another queue at the entrance to the hall. Here a member of Standard Nine stood in his tuxedo, announcing the arrival and entrance of each couple. It was quite nerve-racking as the hall was fairly dark, so you could not see who was in there and where. 'Mr. Carl Williams & Ms. Esme Jackson', the announcer stated loudly when it came to our turn. My stomach was doing butterflies. Music was playing in the background, and as your eyes adjusted you could see the line of tables containing teachers and their partners up against the hall wall. Other tables were placed around the other outside walls to accommodate us for our dinner. We sat down opposite each other as name badges had been assigned to seats, and waited for other guests to come in. Soon we were joined by classmates, including Ms. Minnaar and her ex-boyfriend. The young man that had convinced her not to go to the farewell with an 'Englishman', but instead to grace his arm. As much as I was disappointed in her jilting me, she looked stunning in her dress, her newly styled shoulder-length hair dazzling with a few drops of silver glitter. Still, I didn't let this phase me, I had my date for the evening, and she deserved my full attention. Dinner was a quick affair, and as I remember quite palatable considering that it was being put together by a bunch of seventeen-year-olds, with a few volunteer parents for guidance. The usual after-dinner speeches by the head and heads of the year, and then onto the most embarrassing bit. The couples dance. Something I was unprepared for, in every manner. It would seem that the majority of the couples had been attending lessons so they did not mess up on the night. Fortunately for me, Esme was unprepared as well. So, after a few embarrassing starts and treading on her foot, we found a rhythm of sorts and managed to keep the gaze of the teachers off of our efforts. It also helped to steer your dancing effort towards the other side of the room from them, where we spent most of our time. Very soon, thankfully, it was time to dispense with the formalities, as the disco started. On stage with an extremely small setup, was one of the parents, spinning the 'wheels of steel', and doing a good job considering the lack of technology he had to aid him. Popular music from the year was played but one song stood out for me, and it is the only one I remember from the evening. Bananarama's 'Venus'. This track relaxed everyone, and serious dancing ensued. Ladies in a line on one side and their partners in a line opposite. This was a first for me as I had never bothered with the regular school disco evenings. It was the first time I had seen 'shapes' thrown by my classmates, both male and female. It was also the same for them, as this was the first time I had been forced to put on a display. There were a lot of eyes on me from the opposite side, and it was difficult to tell from the smiles whether they thought I was doing alright, or whether they were laughing at whatever it was I was trying to put together. Still, nothing was said afterward so I am assuming what I improvised passed the inspection of the female onlookers.

I had perfect company that evening from Esme, and I said goodbye to her with a kiss on her cheek. She was aware I would not be back at school due to my departure back to England. I was also adamant I was going to say goodbye to Jeanine before departing for the evening and made sure I could. She looked at me and said 'Oh, I'm not going to see you again...'. I nodded and wished her well for the future, gave her the same peck on the cheek, and then took the red rose from my lapel and gave it to her as a parting gift. She held it in both hands and drew it towards her nose to smell. Then smiled and looked at me, her eyes sparkling as she did so. I think if things had been different, and I had stayed, I may have been able to win her affection because despite being an 'Englishman', I was far more romantic than my South African counterpart. Other goodbyes were said to those who were aware I was leaving, and then Steven and I departed with me riding pillion. Simon was going to join us later with Quentin, who had to help clear up before he could leave. Steven had been down to the retreat before the farewell to stash our booze, fags, and snacks. Amazingly these were exactly where he had left them, being undiscovered by passers-by who would have made off with the loot had they found it. A bottle of Bell's whiskey, several four-packs of lager, and some Chesterfield smokes finished off the evening nicely and allowed Steven and the others to try and convince me to stay. I was looking forward to coming home though and tried to explain to them how they would feel if they lived away from South Africa, where they were born, and yearned to go back.

Mum, Dad and baby Lauren at the timeshare in Knysna

*Mum, my sister Dawn and baby Lauren
inside the timeshare at Knysna*

The only photo I took of Sun City - sadly blemished by inferior camera film

CHAPTER 11 - 'MANDELA DAY' THOUGHTS

The day was approaching fast. On the 26th of October my mother, my brother, and I would be flying home, my father left behind for a month or so to tidy things up regarding the house and furniture. With nowhere to go, we would be staying temporarily with my sister, her husband, and their young daughter in Cheltenham, Gloucestershire. An old stamping ground of both my parents, who met there whilst working in various restaurant establishments as a chef and waitress. In the days leading up to our departure, I grew very nervous. I had to fly out on my South African passport, where my brother and my mother could fly out on their British passports. I have no idea why things had to be different for me, but I put it down to the authorities being difficult, knowing that I was most probably staying in England never to return. My parents had briefed me several times on what to say at the various border checks on both sides. I was having a short holiday before going into the army in early January. January 5th, 1987, if I remember correctly. That was the date I was to assemble with other recruits at a nearby train station, to start my extremely long trip into the north of South West Africa.

My mind wandered to what would happen on the 5th if I didn't turn up. I pictured army personnel coming to the house to arrest me only to find the entire family gone. Maybe they would try and come and arrest me in the days leading up to my departure having got wind of our intentions? So many things were going through my mind, and it was quite stressful. I just could not wait to get through the various passport desks and get on that plane. That would only be half the problem though. At Heathrow, I would have to go through separate passport control from that of my brother and mother, and there would be a similar tense time knowing whether I would get back into my home country on a South African passport. In the weeks leading up to our departure, I was pretty much grounded. My parents were worried about me going out and getting into some sort of trouble that would cause their plans to be cancelled. This was very difficult for me, as I was unable to enjoy the last days in South Africa with my friends. At the time I knew the importance of them protecting me in this way, so I did not rebel against the decision. I wanted to get home without a hitch and dreamed of kissing the ground once I got out of Heathrow Airport.

Another sad part of our departure was that my grandparents who lived in Pretoria had decided to stay in South Africa. As old as they were, they wanted to enjoy the remainder of their lives there. They had a good life, and good friends, and at the time were still safe. This meant that I would probably never see them again. This was in the days well before any video messaging services, so letters would be our only link. I don't remember them coming to the airport to say goodbye. Maybe it was too painful. My father, however, was there to see us off, and at the time I had no idea how much I was going to miss him over the next month or so.

There was a tense moment for me as I queued in the line at customs at the then 'Jan Smuts' Airport. I remembered how to answer any questions that came my way from the South African official and must have done OK, as my South African passport was stamped with my exit Visa and I was allowed to progress. My brother and mother waited patiently for me having gotten through their checks a lot quicker. Delays were minimal and we got to board the plane on time. Our journey back home would be much different, and much quicker than the original one that carried us to South Africa. This time we would be flying on a British Airways 747, taking a much quicker route up to Nairobi for refuelling and then onto Heathrow. Compared to the 19-hour journey on South African Airways it would only take just over 13. This was because British Airways were allowed to fly over African states. Quite an impressive time saving considering it's all uphill. I didn't sleep too well on the plane and awoke in the morning tired and uncomfortable. Not quite with it, and certainly not ready to have to jump into action. Breakfast was doing its rounds, and I decided to have some coffee and something to eat to help bring me back to life. Opening the window screen revealed a horizon-based sun. Not yet at full brightness but just beginning to illuminate clouds and bring a orange glow to some of them. Hazy darkness still filled most of the sky though. I glanced out the window at the view whilst taking a sip of my coffee that had been delivered by the attendant along with my breakfast. Within a second or so the plane started to dive downwards, hitting some turbulence or an air pocket, taking me completely by surprise. In my half-awake state, I was unable to react in the necessary time to save my coffee, and subsequently my shirt from that coffee. Fortunately, I was not scolded too badly, and no permanent damage was done to my exposed areas of skin, but it did help with the waking process, despite not being in the usual manner. The rest of the morning part of the flight went without a hitch, and it was not long before we were on approach to London. Nerves set in again as I faced the thought of having to go through customs alone on my South African passport, hoping that my home country would accept me. 'Just on holiday for a month before I go back to South Africa', I stated once asked. Some eye contact from the customs official, and then my passport was handed back to me. It looked like it was a done deal. Just the cases to pick up and then that final walk through customs to freedom.

It all went smoothly and at last, I started to relax realizing my ordeal was over. My sister and her husband were picking us up from the airport, and it was a relief to see them waiting for us as we exited. There were still going to be a few hurdles for me to get over now that I was home, but for now, I just embraced the cold, crisp air that surrounded me. The traffic noise, hustle and bustle, and the grey sky and rain confirmed that I was indeed back in England.

It took a week to get used to being back in England, so my mother was easy on me for that length of time. Pretty soon though I was being pushed to get into town to visit the job centre. I hated school and was welcoming getting out into the big brave world (or Cheltenham), so that I could start to earn money. The Job Centre was a daunting place. In those days it was walls of cards in various categories. If you liked the look of one, you took it to an assistant who vetted you for suitability. If successful, they would phone the employer to try and arrange an interview for you. My first few cards of interest got me interviews at a local greeting card shop and the General Hospital. I was persuaded out of the card job, even though I had significant retail experience in this area, purely because I was a young man and the rest of the staff, including the Manager, were female. 'I wouldn't fit in', she said. My how times have changed. I would love to see them attempt that nowadays. The Hospital job was as a cook in the canteen which appealed to me. It looked like I had it in the bag seeing as how the interview went. In the end, I was asked if I had time to stay for some medical tests, including a chest x-ray. I made my excuses and got out of there. Hospitals were not my favourite places and still aren't. I could have handled serving up breakfasts to doctors and nurses, but there was no way they were going to prod, poke, and picture me for me to do it. Onto the next, which turned out to be a winner. A local supermarket chain wanted a shop floor supervisor on the twilight shift. This would mean I started around two or three pm and would be finished by ten or eleven pm, with weekends free. Sounded great as I could have a lie in each morning and even get the last pint in on the way home before the pubs shut. This ended up being the job I would get, working with a great bunch of people. The only downside to the job was that back then England was not embracing new technology as quickly as the Spar Hypermarket was back in South Africa. Everything had to be priced up by handgun, which meant it took the staff involved a hell of a lot longer to do. What was good though was the wage packet. After-tax, I was taking home nearly £75 a week initially. I felt like I was rich. What was I going to do with all this money? Well, whilst the local bus transport was OK, I needed a motorbike to get around better, especially If I was working late into the evening. A local Honda dealer would sort me out with a great Honda XL125 scrambler on finance. This would be just the ticket and come in handy when the supermarket asked me to provide cover for holiday staff in a neighbouring Tewkesbury store. Being a 'telly addict', I would miss all the evening programs that the BBC and ITV had to offer. Granada Rentals would sort me out with another finance deal on a portable TV and VHS video recorder. Now I could schedule all my recordings and watch them in bed when I got home. Everything was coming together nicely, and I was starting to settle.

With everything that was going on, it was easy to forget that one member of the family was still not present. My father was still tying up loose ends back in South Africa. Working hard to save up enough money for his flight back home. Our only contact with him was the few minutes we had to speak to him from the local telephone box. Must have been once a week when we had the chance to speak briefly and ask him when he was going to get home. Hopefully, it would be before Christmas, which was drawing ever near. As it turned out he did come home before Christmas, surprising us all with his secret arrival. Commission due from his job came unexpectedly, and he was able to secure his flight home. It was great to be together again as a family. There were still lots of things to do and sort out, but now my father was here, everything would fall into place. It wasn't long after Christmas that he found us somewhere to live in Cheltenham, not far from where I worked. Much like his first car when we got to South Africa, he soon acquired a 'Morris Marina' on his return, this time in white instead of green. It was like a reset had been performed. Seven or so years ago we all started off our lives in South Africa, with little or nothing. Now it was happening again, and much like back then, I eagerly awaited the arrival of my tea chest with what little belongings I had.

It was several years later when things started to get worse in South Africa. Those we had left behind were in constant touch, informing us frequently of unrest, gun crime, and an increase in burglaries in the white areas, often resulting in the deaths of the dwelling owners. Most of these usually occurred in remote areas such as farmland, but instances were starting to be reported in the cities and suburbs. Nobody knew at the time that this situation was only going to get worse, but with my grandmothers failing health, my grandfather decided to return home. It would be a further few years when my aunt, her husband, and my cousin David and his children would return also.

The 'New' South Africa also beckoned. A man I had hardly heard of whilst in the country, a man who was allegedly jailed for terrorist activities against his country, was going to be released. I did not know any of the history, it had been kept from me and my friends at school. The country's government was being sanctioned from all across the realm, and under increasing pressure to end 'apartheid'. Their only way to resolve the situation was to give equal rights to the black citizens of South Africa, and more importantly, give them the right to vote in the next General Election. I remember the day Mandela was released. The TV footage of the rejoicing going on in South Africa's streets as the majority of the population knew their day had finally come. This was the beginning of their freedom. No more bowing down to the white man. They were going to have the same rights to dwell, eat, sleep, and travel across South Africa, without restriction and abuse. The outcome of the election was inevitable. There was only one person the black South Africans were going to vote for. The only man they trusted, was Nelson Mandela. I remember the inauguration well. There was not a person in the world that didn't know about it. The day that Mrs. Ferreira spoke of had come. Every citizen of South Africa was equal from that day. Knowing how the country had been during my stay, it was extremely strange to me to see the white government officials of the time, standing alongside Mandela and his entourage. Welcoming him, and congratulating him, even speaking highly of him during their speeches. The same people who had put him away, so that he could not be of influence to the majority of the country, were now standing beside him. We all thought this would be great for South Africa. An end to black oppression, perhaps an end to hostilities and crime that were stemming from that oppression. Peace and harmony throughout the country. In reality, the freedom of movement within the country for its non-white citizens meant that unscrupulous individuals and gangs from neighbouring African countries would be tempted by the opportunities for rich pickings from the country. The capital Johannesburg would be what they set their initial sights on, and over the years they would destroy the beautiful capital, making it an area that could no longer be enjoyed, but had to be avoided completely. Car-jackings would be rife. Gun crime is prevalent throughout. Businesses ransacked and over-taken. People are murdered daily. The once-thriving 'New York' style city would become a den of iniquity, with nothing to offer any law-abiding citizen of the country. A far cry from the safe city that once welcomed me to my new home, and where I spent a lot of time enjoying the hustle and bustle and nightlife. The 'New' South Africa had not turned out to be what everyone had expected.

My parents, despite how the capital had turned out, decided to go on holiday with some friends some years later. Braving the flight in and out of Johannesburg airport (the name Jan Smuts had been dropped for one more in keeping with the multi-cultural society now..), and made their way South to a safer environment. Their holiday was without incident, and extremely enjoyable. There have been many others who have not been so fortunate on their holiday. Ultimately, it would turn out to be the last time my parents would venture to 'deepest', 'darkest' Africa.

Myself? I do not have any desire to go back. Primarily from fear of being kept there if I returned! Yes, it would be great to see how other areas of the country had turned out, especially Durban and the Cape of which I have fond memories. It would also be great to see a different side of the country. The 'correct' side, where I would see all people of different creeds and colours interacting, knowing that they are the same... just 'South Africans'. Proud of their country, their heritage, their history, and their future. I was a South African once, but no longer. However, there will always be a bit of South Africa within me, and it's a 'bit' that I hold dear.

It's been raining outside today. It has been raining every day for what seems like ages, and as I gaze out the window looking at the bleak grey sky, I can't help but remember,

'It's sunny in South Africa today...'.

THE END

Printed in Great Britain
by Amazon